1

FIFTH EDITION

GRAMMAR *in* CONTEXT

SANDRA N. ELBAUM

The cover photo shows the Leonard P. Zakim Bunker Hill Bridge over the Charles River in Boston, Massachusetts.

HEINLE
CENGAGE Learning·

Australia • Brazil • Japan • Korea • Mexico • Singapore • Spain • United Kingdom • United States

Grammar in Context 1, Student Book
Fifth Edition
Sandra N. Elbaum

Publisher: Sherrise Roehr

Acquisitions Editor: Tom Jefferies

Associate Development Editor:
  Sarah Sandoski

Director of Global Marketing: Ian Martin

Director of US Marketing: Jim McDonough

Product Marketing Manager: Katie Kelley

Marketing Manager: Caitlin Driscoll

Content Project Manager: Andrea Bobotas

Senior Print Buyer: Susan Spencer

Project Manager: Chrystie Hopkins

Production Services: Nesbitt Graphics, Inc.

Interior Design and Cover Design:
  Muse Group, Inc.

Library of Congress Control Number: 2009936997
International Student Edition
ISBN 13: 978-1-4240-8247-6
ISBN 10: 1-4240-8247-1

Heinle
20 Channel Center Street
Boston, Massachusetts 02210
USA

Cengage Learning is a leading provider of customized learning solutions with office locations around the globe, including Singapore, the United Kingdom, Australia, Mexico, Brazil, and Japan Locate our local office at international.cengage.com/region

Cengage Learning products are represented in Canada by Nelson Education, Ltd.

Visit Heinle online at **elt.heinle.com**

Visit our corporate website at **www.cengage.com**

Printed in the United States of America.
1 2 3 4 5 6 7 8 9 10 — 13 12 11 10 09

Contents

Lesson 3

Grammar Context

Lesson 4

Grammar Context

Lesson 5

Grammar Context

Lesson 6

Grammar Context

Lesson 7

Lesson 8

Lesson 9

Lesson 10

Acknowledgments

Many thanks to Dennis Hogan, Sherrise Roehr, and Tom Jefferies from Heinle Cengage for their ongoing support of the *Grammar in Context* series. I would especially like to thank my development editor, Sarah Sandoski, for her patience, sensitivity, keen eye to detail, and invaluable suggestions.

And many thanks to my students at Truman College, who have increased my understanding of my own language and taught me to see life from another point of view. By sharing their observations, questions, and life stories, they have enriched my life enormously.

This new edition is dedicated to the millions of displaced people in the world. The U.S. is the new home to many refugees, who survived unspeakable hardships in Burundi, Rwanda, Sudan, Burma, Bhutan, and other countries. Their resiliency in starting a new life and learning a new language is a tribute to the human spirit.—*Sandra N. Elbaum*

Heinle would like to thank the following people for their contributions:

Elizabeth A. Adler-Coleman
Sunrise Mountain High
    School
Las Vegas, NV

Judith A. G. Benka
Normandale Community
    College
Bloomington, MN

Carol Brutza
Gateway Community
    College
New Haven, CT

Lyn Buchheit
Community College of
    Philadelphia
Philadelphia, PA

Charlotte M. Calobrisi
Northern Virginia
    Community College
Annandale, VA

Gabriela Cambiasso
Harold Washinton College
Chicago, IL

Jeanette Clement
Duquesne University
Pittsburgh, PA

Allis Cole
Shoreline Community
    College
Shoreline, WA

Fanshen DiGiovanni
Glendale Community
    College
Glendale, CA

Rhonda J. Farley
Cosumnes River College
Sacramento, CA

Jennifer Farnell
University of Connecticut
    American Language
    Program
Stamford, CT

Gail Fernandez
Bergen Community College
Paramus, NJ

Abigail-Marie Fiattarone
Mesa Community College
Mesa, AZ

John Gamber
American River College
Sacramento, CA

Marcia Gethin-Jones
University of Connecticut
    American Language
    Program
Storrs, CT

Kimlee Buttacavoli Grant
The Leona Group, LLC
Phoenix, AZ

Shelly Hedstrom
Palm Beach Community
    College
Lake Worth, FL

Linda Holden
College of Lake County
Grayslake, IL

Sandra Kawamura
Sacramento City College
Sacramento, CA

Bill Keniston
Normandale Community
    College
Bloomington, MN

Michael Larsen
American River College
Sacramento, CA

Bea C. Lawn
Gavilan College
Gilroy, CA

Rob Lee
Pasadena City College
Pasadena, CA

Oranit Limmaneeprasert
American River College
Sacramento, CA

Linda Louie
Highline Community
    College
Des Moines, WA

Melanie A. Majeski
Naugatuck Valley
    Community College
Waterbury, CT

Maria Marin
De Anza College
Cupertino, CA

Michael I. Massey
Hillsborough Community
    College-Ybor City Campus
Tampa, FL

Marlo McClurg-Mackinnon
Consumnes River College
Sacramento, CA

Michelle Naumann
Elgin Community College
Elgin, IL

Debbie Ockey
Fresno, CA

Lesa Perry
University of Nebraska at
    Omaha
Omaha, NE

Herbert Pierson
St. John's University
New York City, NY

Dina Poggi
De Anza College
Cupertino, CA

Steven Rashba
University of Bridgeport
Bridgeport, CT

Mark Rau
American River College
Sacramento, CA

Maria Spelleri
State College of Florida
    Manatee-Sarasota
Venice, FL

Eva Teagarden
Yuba College
Marysville, CA

Nico Wiersema
Texas A&M International
    University
Laredo, TX

Susan Wilson
San Jose City College
San Jose, CA

A word from the author

My parents immigrated to the U.S. from Poland and learned English as a second language. Born in the U.S., I often had the task as a child to explain the intricacies of the English language. It is no wonder that I became an English language teacher.

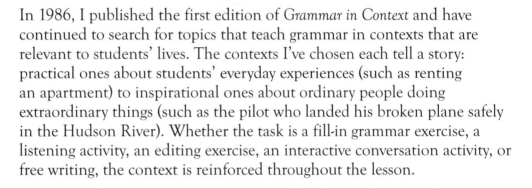

When I started teaching over forty years ago, grammar textbooks used a series of unrelated sentences with no context. I knew instinctively that there was something wrong with this technique. It ignored the fact that language is a tool for communication, and it missed an opportunity to spark the student's curiosity. As I gained teaching experience, I noticed that when I used interesting stories that illustrated the grammar students became more motivated, understood the grammar better, and used it more effectively.

In 1986, I published the first edition of *Grammar in Context* and have continued to search for topics that teach grammar in contexts that are relevant to students' lives. The contexts I've chosen each tell a story: practical ones about students' everyday experiences (such as renting an apartment) to inspirational ones about ordinary people doing extraordinary things (such as the pilot who landed his broken plane safely in the Hudson River). Whether the task is a fill-in grammar exercise, a listening activity, an editing exercise, an interactive conversation activity, or free writing, the context is reinforced throughout the lesson.

I hope you enjoy the new edition of *Grammar in Context!*

Sandra N. Elbaum

In memory of
Herman and Ethel Elbaum

Welcome to *Grammar in Context,*
Fifth Edition

Grammar in Context presents grammar in interesting contexts that are relevant to students' lives and then recycles the language and context throughout every activity. Learners gain knowledge and skills in both the grammar structures and topic areas.

The new fifth edition of *Grammar in Context* engages learners with updated readings, clear and accessible grammar explanations, and a new full-color design.

New To This Edition!

Full-color design makes grammar more visually contextualized and even easier to study and teach from.

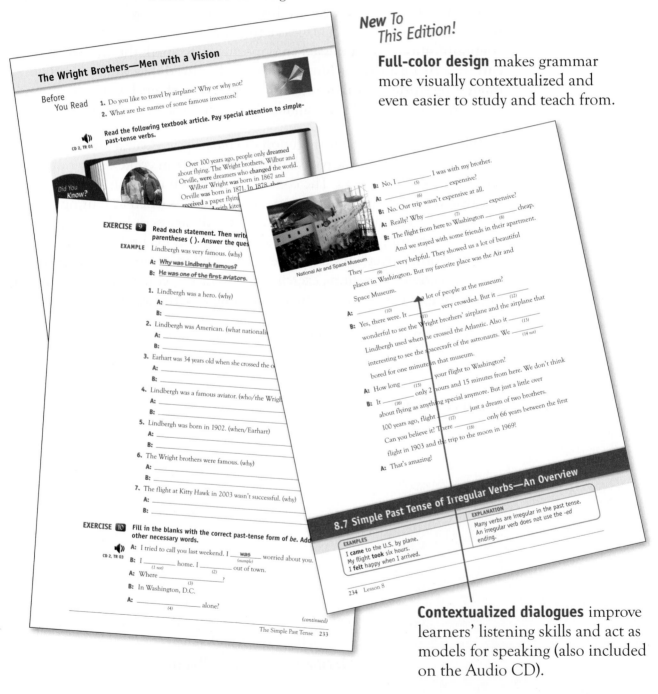

Contextualized dialogues improve learners' listening skills and act as models for speaking (also included on the Audio CD).

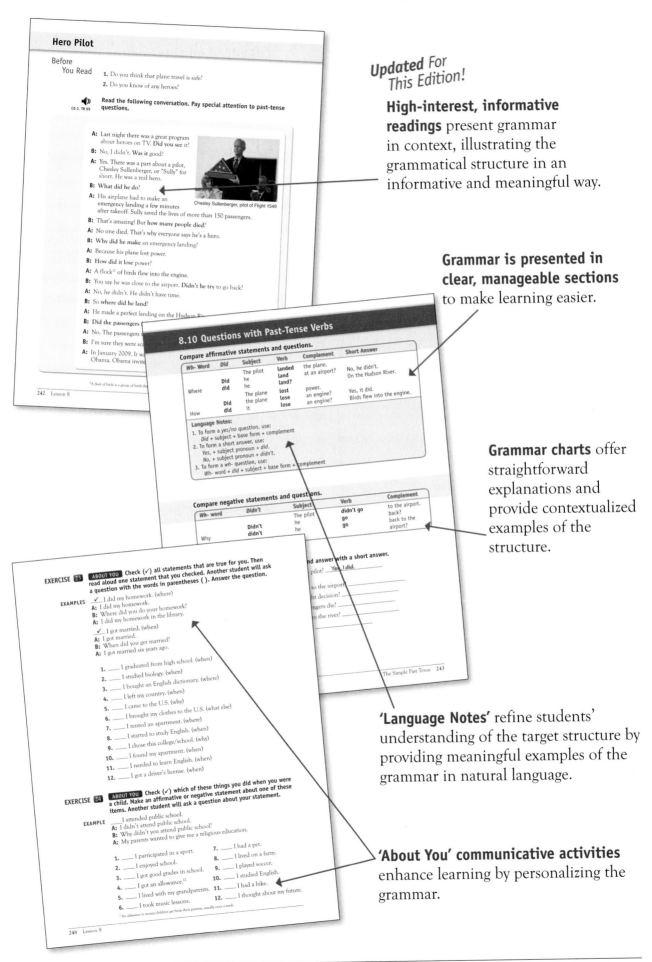

Hero Pilot

Before You Read
1. Do you think that plane travel is safe?
2. Do you know of any heroes?

🔊 CD 2, TR 05 Read the following conversation. Pay special attention to past-tense questions.

A: Last night there was a great program about heroes on TV. **Did you see** it?
B: No, I didn't. **Was it** good?
A: Yes. There was a part about a pilot, Chesley Sullenberger, or "Sully" for short. He was a real hero.
B: **What did he do**?
A: His airplane had to make an emergency landing a few minutes after takeoff. Sully saved the lives of more than 150 passengers.

Chesley Sullenberger, pilot of Flight 1549

B: That's amazing! But **how many people died**?
A: No one died. That's why everyone says he's a hero.
B: **Why did he make** an emergency landing?
A: Because his plane lost power.
B: **How did it lose** power?
A: A flock[11] of birds flew into the engine.
B: You say he was close to the airport. **Didn't he try** to go back?
A: No, he didn't. He didn't have time.
B: So **where did he land**?
A: He made a perfect landing on the Hudson R
B: **Did the passengers**
A: No. The passengers
B: I'm sure they were sca
A: In January 2009. It w
Obama. Obama invite

242 Lesson 8

[11]*A flock of birds is a group of birds th*

Updated For This Edition!

High-interest, informative readings present grammar in context, illustrating the grammatical structure in an informative and meaningful way.

Grammar is presented in clear, manageable sections to make learning easier.

8.10 Questions with Past-Tense Verbs

Compare affirmative statements and questions.

Wh- Word	Did	Subject	Verb	Complement	Short Answer
	Did did	The pilot he he	landed land land?	the plane. at an airport?	No, he didn't. On the Hudson River.
Where					
	Did did	The plane the plane it	lost lose lose	power. an engine? an engine?	Yes, it did. Birds flew into the engine.
How					

Language Notes:
1. To form a *yes/no* question, use:
   Did + subject + base form + complement
2. To form a short answer, use:
   Yes, + subject pronoun + *did*.
   No, + subject pronoun + *didn't*.
3. To form a *wh-* question, use:
   Wh- word + *did* + subject + base form + complement

Compare negative statements and questions.

Wh- word	Didn't	Subject	Verb	Complement
	Didn't didn't	The pilot he he	didn't go go go	to the airport. back? back to the airport?
Why				

Grammar charts offer straightforward explanations and provide contextualized examples of the structure.

nd answer with a short answer.
pilot? _Yes, I did._
to the airport
ht decision? _____
ngers die? _____
to the river? _____

The Simple Past Tense 243

'Language Notes' refine students' understanding of the target structure by providing meaningful examples of the grammar in natural language.

EXERCISE 23 ABOUT YOU Check (✓) all statements that are true for you. Then read aloud one statement that you checked. Another student will ask a question with the words in parentheses ( ). Answer the question.

EXAMPLES ✓ I did my homework. (where)
A: I did my homework.
B: Where did you do your homework?
A: I did my homework in the library.

✓ I got married. (when)
A: I got married.
B: When did you get married?
A: I got married six years ago.

1. ____ I graduated from high school. (when)
2. ____ I studied biology. (when)
3. ____ I bought an English dictionary. (where)
4. ____ I left my country. (when)
5. ____ I came to the U.S. (why)
6. ____ I brought my clothes to the U.S. (what else)
7. ____ I rented an apartment. (where)
8. ____ I started to study English. (when)
9. ____ I chose this college/school. (why)
10. ____ I found my apartment. (when)
11. ____ I needed to learn English. (when)
12. ____ I got a driver's license. (when)

EXERCISE 24 ABOUT YOU Check (✓) which of these things you did when you were a child. Make an affirmative or negative statement about one of these items. Another student will ask a question about your statement.

EXAMPLE ____ I attended public school.
A: I didn't attend public school.
B: Why didn't you attend public school?
A: My parents wanted to give me a religious education.

1. ____ I participated in a sport.
2. ____ I enjoyed school.
3. ____ I got good grades in school.
4. ____ I got an allowance.[12]
5. ____ I lived with my grandparents.
6. ____ I took music lessons.
7. ____ I had a pet.
8. ____ I lived on a farm.
9. ____ I played soccer.
10. ____ I studied English.
11. ____ I had a bike.
12. ____ I thought about my future.

[12]*An allowance is money children get from their parents, usually once a week.*

248 Lesson 8

'About You' communicative activities enhance learning by personalizing the grammar.

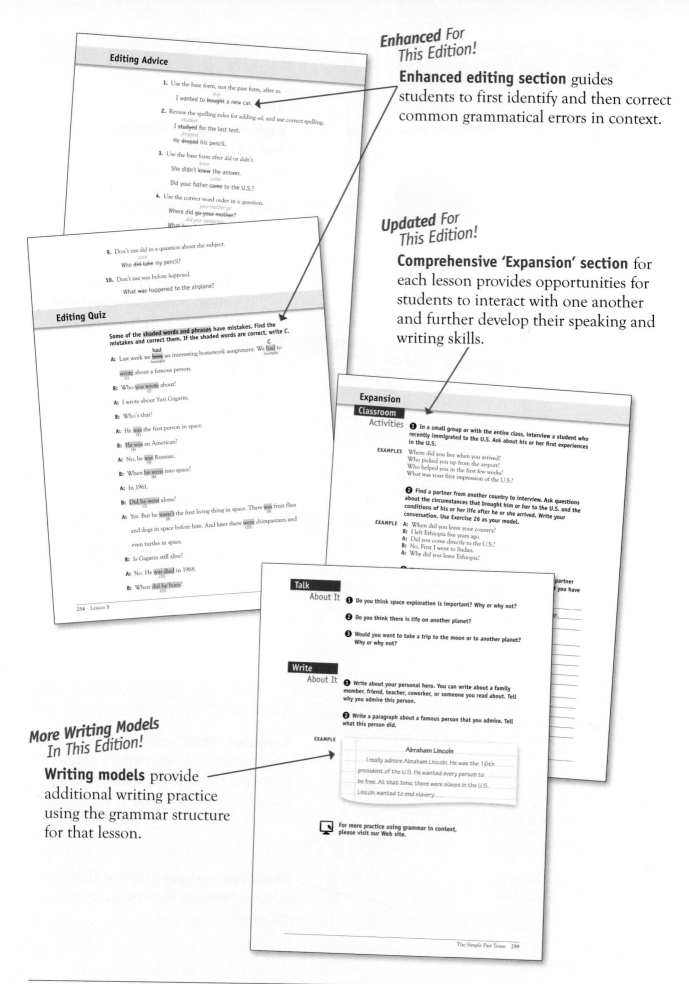

Editing Advice

1. Use the base form, not the past form, after *to*.
   buy
   I wanted to ~~bought~~ a new car.

2. Review the spelling rules for adding *-ed*, and use correct spelling.
   studied
   I ~~studyed~~ for the last test.
   dropped
   He ~~droped~~ his pencil.

3. Use the base form after *did* or *didn't*.
   know
   She didn't ~~knew~~ the answer.
   come
   Did your father ~~came~~ to the U.S.?

4. Use the correct word order in a question.
   your mother go
   Where did ~~go your mother~~?
   did your sister buy
   What h...

9. Don't use *did* in a question about the subject.
   took
   Who ~~did take~~ my pencil?

10. Don't use *was* before *happened*.
    What ~~was~~ happened to the airplane?

Editing Quiz

Some of the **shaded words and phrases** have mistakes. Find the mistakes and correct them. If the shaded words are correct, write *C*.

A: Last week we ~~have~~ *had* an interesting homework assignment. We had to *(example)* *C (example)*

~~wrote~~ about a famous person.
(1)

B: Who you wrote about?
(2)

A: I wrote about Yuri Gagarin.

B: Who's that?

A: He was the first person in space.
(3)

B: He was an American?
(4)

A: No, he was Russian.
(5)

B: When he went into space?
(6)

A: In 1961.

B: Did he went alone?
(7)

A: Yes. But he wasn't the first living thing in space. There was fruit flies
(8) *(9)*
and dogs in space before him. And later there were chimpanzees and
(10)
even turtles in space.

B: Is Gagarin still alive?

A: No. He was died in 1968.
(11)

B: When did he born?
(12)

254 Lesson 8

Expansion

Classroom Activities

❶ In a small group or with the entire class, interview a student who recently immigrated to the U.S. Ask about his or her first experiences in the U.S.

EXAMPLES Where did you live when you arrived?
Who picked you up from the airport?
Who helped you in the first few weeks?
What was your first impression of the U.S.?

❷ Find a partner from another country to interview. Ask questions about the circumstances that brought him or her to the U.S. and the conditions of his or her life after he or she arrived. Write your conversation. Use Exercise 26 as your model.

EXAMPLE **A:** When did you leave your country?
B: I left Ethiopia five years ago.
A: Did you come directly to the U.S.?
B: No. First I went to Sudan.
A: Why did you leave Ethiopia?

Talk About It

❶ Do you think space exploration is important? Why or why not?

❷ Do you think there is life on another planet?

❸ Would you want to take a trip to the moon or to another planet? Why or why not?

Write About It

❶ Write about your personal hero. You can write about a family member, friend, teacher, coworker, or someone you read about. Tell why you admire this person.

❷ Write a paragraph about a famous person that you admire. Tell what this person did.

EXAMPLE

> **Abraham Lincoln**
>
> I really admire Abraham Lincoln. He was the 16th president of the U.S. He wanted every person to be free. At that time, there were slaves in the U.S. Lincoln wanted to end slavery . . .

For more practice using grammar in context, please visit our Web site.

The Simple Past Tense 259

Enhanced *For This Edition!*

Enhanced editing section guides students to first identify and then correct common grammatical errors in context.

Updated *For This Edition!*

Comprehensive 'Expansion' section for each lesson provides opportunities for students to interact with one another and further develop their speaking and writing skills.

More Writing Models In This Edition!

Writing models provide additional writing practice using the grammar structure for that lesson.

Additional resources for each level

FOR THE STUDENT:

New To This Edition!

- Online Workbook features additional exercises that learners can access in the classroom, language lab, or at home.

- Audio CD includes all readings and dialogues from the student book.

- Student Web site features additional practice: http://elt.heinle.com/grammarincontext

FOR THE TEACHER:

New To This Edition!

- Online Lesson Planner is perfect for busy instructors, allowing them to create and customize lesson plans for their classes, then save and share them in a range of formats.

Updated For This Edition!

- Assessment CD-ROM with ExamView® lets teachers create and customize tests and quizzes easily and includes many new contextualized test items.

- Teacher's Edition offers comprehensive teaching notes including suggestions for more streamlined classroom options.

- Instructor Web site includes a printable Student Book answer key.

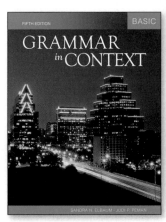 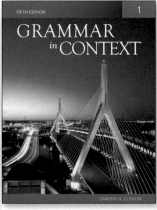 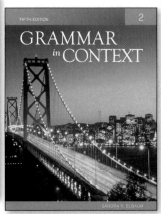 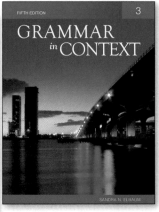

Grammar
The Present Tense of the Verb *Be*

Prepositions of Place

This, That, These, Those

Context
College Life

Community College Life in the United States

Circle *T* for true or *F* for false and discuss your answers.

1. Most of the students in my class are immigrants.   T   F

2. My school is in a convenient[1] location.   T   F

CD 1, TR 01

Read the following magazine article. Pay special attention to *is* and *are*.

> **A community college (or two-year college) is a good place to begin your education in the U.S.** The tuition **is** usually cheaper than at a university. Because a community college **is** often smaller than a university, foreign students **are** often more comfortable. They **are** closer to their professors and get more attention.
>
> Truman College **is** a typical community college. It **is** one of seven City Colleges of Chicago. It **is** a two-year college on the north side of Chicago. It **is** near public transportation—buses and trains—so it **is** convenient for everyone. For students with a car, parking **is** free. Credit classes **are** $75 per credit hour for Chicago residents. Adult education classes **are** free.
>
> Truman College **is** an international school. Many of the students **are** from other countries and **are** in ESL courses. Some of the students **are** immigrants. Some of the students **are** international students. International students **are** in the U.S. only to study. Tuition for international students **is** much higher.
>
>
>
> Many of the students have jobs, so evening and weekend classes **are** convenient for these students. Some students have small children, so Truman has a child-care center.
>
> The semester **is** 16 weeks long. A summer semester **is** 8 weeks long. Students **are** free to choose their own classes.

Did You Know?

The average age of a community college student is 29.

[1]Something that is *convenient* is easy for you. A convenient location is near your house or near public transportation. Convenient classes are at a time that is good for you.

Read the following student composition. Pay special attention to *is, am,* and *are.*

About Me

My name **is** Rolando Lopez. I **am** from Guatemala. I **am** a student at Truman College. My major **is** engineering. I **am** married, and I work during the day. My engineering classes **are** at night, and my English class **is** on Saturdays. The college **is** a good place for me to start my education in the U.S. because the tuition **is** low and the attention to students **is** very high. My plan **is** to take 60 credit hours here and then go to a four-year college, such as the University of Illinois. I like it here because the teachers **are** friendly and helpful, and the students from other countries **are** interesting. I **am** unhappy about one thing: Chicago **is** cold in the winter.

1.1 Present-Tense Forms of *Be*

EXAMPLES			EXPLANATION
Subject	**Form of *Be***	**Complement**	
I	**am**	a college student.	Use *am* with *I*.
My teacher He My college It My wife She	**is**	an American. friendly. a City College. in Chicago. a student. busy.	Use *is* with *he, she, it,* and singular subjects (*teacher, college, wife*).
We You The students They	**are**	students. the teacher. from all over the world. immigrants.	Use *are* with *we, you, they,* and plural subjects.

EXERCISE **1** **Fill in the blanks with *is, are,* or *am*.**

EXAMPLE My name ____is____ Rolando Lopez.

1. I _____ from Guatemala.

2. My wife _____ from Mexico.

3. My wife and I _____ students.

4. The University of Illinois _____ a four-year college.

5. My classmates _____ from many different countries.

6. We _____ immigrants.

7. The professors at my college _____ friendly and helpful.

8. My major _____ engineering.

9. The semester _____ 16 weeks long.

1.2 Uses of *Be*

EXAMPLES	EXPLANATION
The college is **good**. Evening classes are **convenient** for me. The tuition is **low**. The teachers are very **friendly**.	Use a form of *be* with a description of the subject.
Truman College is **a community college**. The University of Illinois is **a four-year college**.	Use a form of *be* with a classification or definition of the subject.
Truman College is **in Chicago**. Chicago is **in Illinois**. The college is **near public transportation**.	Use a form of *be* with the location of the subject.
I am **from Guatemala**. My wife is **from Mexico**.	Use a form of *be* with the place of origin of the subject.
I am **24 years old**. My teacher is **about 40 years old**.	Use a form of *be* with the age of the subject.
It is **cold** in Chicago in the winter. It is **warm** in Guatemala all year.	Use *is* with weather. The subject is *it*.
It is **6 o'clock** now. It is **late**.	Use *is* with time. The subject is *it*.

EXERCISE **2** **Fill in the blanks to make true statements. Answers will vary.**

EXAMPLE Chicago is __in Illinois__.
             (location)

1. Chicago is a _____. Illinois is a state.
                    (classification)

2. My college is _____.
(location)

3. The teacher is about _____ years old.
(age)

4. The teacher is from _____.
(place of origin)

5. It is _____ now.
(time)

6. It is _____ today.
(weather)

7. This college is _____.
(description)

1.3 Word Order with *Be*

EXAMPLES			EXPLANATION
Subject	***Be***	**Complement**	• The subject is first. The subject tells whom or what we are talking about.
I	am	from Guatemala.	• The verb (*am, is, are*) is second.
Guatemala	is	in Central America.	• The complement is third. The complement finishes, or completes, the sentence with a location, classification, description, etc.
It	is	a small country.	
Spanish	is	my native language.	
You	are	from Vietnam.	
It	is	in Asia.	

EXERCISE 3   **Put the words in the correct order to make a statement. Use a capital letter at the beginning and a period at the end.**

EXAMPLE   a two-year college/my college/is   <u>My college is a two-year college.</u>

1. am/I/a student _____

2. my parents/in Guatemala/are _____

3. high/is/tuition at a four-year college _____

4. is/convenient for me/my college _____

5. my teacher/is/40 years old _____

6. is/from New York/my teacher _____

7. eight weeks long/the summer semester/is _____

8. Rolando/married/is _____

9. cold/it/is/in the winter _____

1.4 The Subject

EXAMPLES	EXPLANATION
I am from Guatemala. **You** are an American citizen. **It** is warm in Guatemala. **We** are happy in the United States.	The subject pronouns are: *I, you, he, she, it, we, they.*
Chicago is very big. **It** is in Illinois. **My wife** is a student. **She** is from Mexico. **My teacher** is American. **He** is a native speaker of English. **My parents** are in Guatemala. **They** are happy. **My wife and I** are in the United States. **We** are in Chicago.	• Subject pronouns (*it, she, he, they*) can take the place of nouns (*Chicago, wife, teacher, parents*). • A noun can be singular (*my father*) or plural (*my parents*). A plural noun usually ends in *s*. • When the subject is "another person and I," put the other person before *I*. Use *we* to substitute for "another person and I." **Note:** In conversation you sometimes hear "me and another person" in the subject position. This is common but incorrect.
My classmates are from many countries. **They** are immigrants. **English and math** are my favorite subjects. **They** are useful subjects.	We use *they* for plural people and things.
The U.S. is a big country. **It** is in North America.	The *United States* (*the U.S.*) is a singular noun. Use *the* before United States or U.S.
You are a good teacher. **You** are good students.	*You* can be a singular or plural subject.
It is cold in Chicago in the winter. **It** is 6 o'clock now.	Use *it* to talk about time and weather.

EXERCISE 4 **Fill in the blanks with the correct pronoun.**

EXAMPLE   Nicaragua and Guatemala are countries. ____They____ are in Central America.

1. My wife and I are students. _____ are students at Truman College.

2. Guatemala is a small country. _____ is south of Mexico.

3. _____ is warm in Guatemala all year.

4. Some students are international students. _____ are from China, Japan, and Spain.

5. _____ am a busy person.

6. English is a hard language. _____ is necessary in the U.S.

7. Adult classes at my college are free. _____ are for ESL students.

8. My book is new. _____ is *Grammar in Context.*

9. My parents are in Guatemala. _____ are old.

10. My teacher is a nice woman. _____ is from Boston.

11. My classmates and I are interested in American life. _____ are new in this country.

Journal Entry (by Maya Levina)

Before You Read

Circle *T* for true or *F* for false and discuss your answers.

1. All the students in my class are from the same country.　T　F

2. Most of the students in my class are the same age.　T　F

CD 1, TR 02

Read the following journal entry. Pay special attention to contractions with *am, is,* and *are.*

College is so different here. Students in my class are all ages. **I'm** 22—**that's** a normal age for college students back home. But some students here **are** in their 50s or 60s. One man in my class is 74. **He's** from Korea. This is very strange for me, but **it's** interesting too. Some students are married. Most students have jobs, so **we're** all very busy.

The students are from all over the world. One **student's** from Puerto Rico. Her native language is Spanish, but Puerto Rico **isn't** a foreign country and it **isn't** a state of the U.S. **It's** a special territory. **It's** a small island near the U.S.

The classrooms are different here too. **They're** big and comfortable. But the desks are so small. Another strange thing is this: The desks are in a circle, not in rows.

In my country, **education's** free. But here **it's** so expensive. At my college, the **tuition's** $125 per credit hour. And books are expensive too.

The teacher's young and informal. **He's** about my age. His **name's** Rich Weiss, and **he's** very friendly. **We're** always welcome in his office after class. But English is so hard. **It's** not hard to read English, but **it's** hard to understand American speech.

I'm in Minneapolis. **It's** in the northern part of the U.S. **It's** January now. **It's** very cold here in the winter. But the summers are warm and sunny.

I'm happy to be in the U.S.

1.5 Contractions with *Be*

EXAMPLES		EXPLANATION
I am You are She is He is It is We are They are	**I'm** in Minneapolis. **You're** a student of English. **She's** a young teacher. **He's** 74 years old. **It's** cold in winter. **We're** so busy. **They're** big.	We can make a **contraction** with a subject pronoun and *am, is,* and *are.* We take out the first letter of *am, is,* and *are* and put an apostrophe (') in its place. We usually use contractions when we speak. We sometimes use contractions in informal writing.
My cla<u>ss</u> is big. Beli<u>z</u>e is in Central America. Engli<u>sh</u> is the language of the U.S. Ri<u>ch</u> is my English teacher. Colle<u>ge</u> is different here.		We don't make a contraction with *is* if the noun ends in these sounds: *s, z, sh, ch,* or soft *g.*
Books are expensive. **The classrooms are** big.		We don't make a contraction with a plural noun and *are.*

EXERCISE 5 Fill in the blanks with the correct form of *be* (*am, is,* or *are*). Make a contraction whenever possible. Not every sentence can have a contraction.

EXAMPLE   The United States ____is____ a big country. It __'s____ between Canada and Mexico.

1. Puerto Rico _____ an island. Puerto Ricans _____ American citizens.

2. English _____ the main language of the U.S. Spanish and

    English _____ the languages of Puerto Rico.

3. My classmates and I _____ immigrants. We _____ in the U.S.

4. Maya _____ in Minneapolis. She _____ at a city college there.

5. Minneapolis _____ a big city. It _____ in the northern part of the U.S.

6. The teacher _____ informal. He _____ friendly.

7. The students _____ from all over the world. They _____ nice people.

8. The classroom _____ on the first floor. It _____ big.

EXERCISE **6**   **Fill in the blanks. Make a contraction whenever possible. Not every sentence can have a contraction.**

🔊

CD 1, TR 03   I **'m** _____ a student of English at Truman College. _____'m
(example)   (1)

happy in the U.S. My teacher _____ American. His
(2)

name _____ Charles Madison. Charles _____ an
(3)   (4)

experienced teacher. _____ patient with foreign students.
(5)

My class _____ big. _____ interesting. All the students
(6)   (7)

_____ immigrants, but we _____ from many different
(8)   (9)

countries. Five students _____ from Asia. One woman _____
(10)   (11)

from Poland. _____ from Warsaw, the capital of Poland. Many
(12)

students _____ from Mexico.
(13)

We _____ ready to learn English, but English _____ a
(14)   (15)

difficult language. I sometimes tell Charles, "You _____ a very kind
(16)

teacher." Charles says, "_____ all good students, and I _____
(17)   (18)

happy to teach you English."

1.6 *Be* with Descriptions

EXAMPLES				EXPLANATION
Subject	*Be*	**(Very)**	**Adjective**	After a form of *be*, we can use a word that describes the subject. Descriptive words are **adjectives**. *Very* can come before an adjective.
My teacher	is		**young.**	
The desks	are	very	**small.**	
The weather	is		**cold** in winter.	
The school is **big.** The classrooms are **big.**				Descriptive adjectives have no plural form. *Wrong:* The classrooms are *bigs*.
Some of my classmates are **married.** My class is **interesting.** I'm **interested** in American life.				Some words that end with *–ed* and *–ing* are adjectives: *married, divorced, worried, tired, interested, interesting, bored, boring.*
It's **cold.** I'm **thirsty.** We're **afraid.**				We use a form of *be* with physical or mental conditions: *hungry, thirsty, cold, hot, tired, happy,* etc.

EXERCISE 7 Complete each statement with a subject and the correct form of *be*. Write a contraction wherever possible. Make a true statement. Use both singular and plural subjects.

EXAMPLES _____ My teachers are _____ intelligent.

_____ The library's _____ quiet.

1. _____ expensive.
2. _____ cheap.
3. _____ new.
4. _____ big.
5. _____ friendly.
6. _____ difficult.
7. _____ interesting.
8. _____ married.

EXERCISE 8 Write a form of *be* and an adjective to describe each of the following nouns. You may work with a partner.

EXAMPLES This classroom __is clean._____

New York City __is interesting._____

1. The teacher _____
2. This city _____
3. This college _____
4. Today's weather _____
5. American students _____
6. The school library _____
7. The students in this class _____
8. The tuition at this school _____
9. The school cafeteria _____
10. I _____

1.7 *Be* with Definitions

EXAMPLES					EXPLANATION
Singular Subject	*Be*	*A/An*	**Singular Noun**		We use a noun after a form of *be* to classify or define the subject.
I	**am**	a	student.		Use *a* or *an* before the definition of a singular noun. Use *a* before a consonant sound. Use *an* before a vowel sound. (The vowels are *a, e, i, o, u*.)
You	**are**	a	teacher.		
Puerto Rico	**is**	an	island.		
Plural Subject	*Be*		**Plural Noun**		Don't use *a* or *an* before the definition of a plural noun.
You and I	**are**		students.		*Wrong*: You and I are *a* students.
They	**are**		Americans.		
Subject	*Be*	*(A)*	**Adjective**	**Noun**	We can include an adjective as part of the definition.
Chicago	is	a	**big**	city.	
We	are		**good**	students.	

EXERCISE 9 **Fill in the blanks to change from a singular subject to a plural subject.**

EXAMPLE   Math is a subject.

Math and __*biology are subjects*.__ _____

1. I am a student.

   _____ and I _____

2. Chicago is a city.

   Chicago and _____

3. Wednesday is a school day.

   Wednesday and _____

4. Rick is an English teacher.

   Rick and _____

5. Spanish is a language.

   Spanish and _____

6. Puerto Rico is an island.

   Puerto Rico and _____

EXERCISE 10 Add an adjective to each statement. Be careful to use *a* before a consonant sound and *an* before a vowel sound.

EXAMPLE Maya is a student.

Maya is a new student.

1. January is a month.
2. Puerto Rico is an island.
3. *Grammar in Context* is a book.
4. I'm a student.
5. Minneapolis and Chicago are cities.
6. History is a subject.

EXERCISE 11 Fill in the blanks with the correct form of *be*. Add *a* or *an* for singular nouns only. Don't use an article with plural nouns.

EXAMPLES The U.S. ____is a____ big country.

The U.S. and Canada ____are____ big countries.

1. The University of Illinois _____ state university.
2. It _____ old university.
3. Chicago _____ interesting city.
4. Chicago and New York _____ big cities.
5. You _____ English teacher.
6. Some students _____ immigrants.

EXERCISE 12 Fill in the blanks to talk about this city. Make true statements. Remember to add *a* or *an* for a singular noun. You may work with a partner.

EXAMPLES _____*Chez Paul is an*_____ expensive restaurant in this city.

_____*January and February are*_____ cold months in this city.

1. _____ popular tourist attraction.
2. _____ big stores.
3. _____ beautiful months.
4. _____ beautiful park.
5. _____ inexpensive restaurant.
6. _____ busy streets.
7. _____ good college.

EXERCISE 13 Fill in the blanks to make true statements about the U.S.

EXAMPLES _____ Hip-hop music is _____ popular.

_____ Athletes are _____ rich.

1. _____ the biggest city.
2. _____ the most common language(s).
3. _____ a popular sport.
4. _____ a common last name.
5. _____ a beautiful place.

1.8 Prepositions of Place

We use prepositions to show location and origin.

PREPOSITION	EXAMPLES	
On	The book is **on** the table. The cafeteria is **on** the first floor.	
At (a general area)	I am **at** school. My brother is **at** home. They are **at** work.	
In (a complete or partial enclosure)	The students are **in** the classroom. The wastebasket is **in** the corner.	
In front of	The blackboard is **in front of** the students.	
In back of/Behind	The teacher is **in back of** the desk. The blackboard is **behind** the teacher.	
Between	The empty desk is **between** the two students.	
Over/Above	The exit sign is **over** the door. The clock is **above** the exit sign.	

(continued)

PREPOSITION	EXAMPLES
Below/Under	The green textbook is **below** the desk. The red dictionary is **under** the textbook.
By/Near/Close to	The pencil sharpener is **by** the window. The pencil sharpener is **near** the window. The pencil sharpener is **close to** the window.
Next to	The light switch is **next to** the door.
Far from	Los Angeles is **far from** New York.
Across from	Room 202 is **across from** Room 203.
In (a city)	The White House is **in** Washington, D.C.
On (a street)	The White House is **on** Pennsylvania Avenue.
At (an address)	The White House is **at** 1600 Pennsylvania Avenue.
From	Rolando is **from** Central America. He is **from** Guatemala.

EXERCISE **14** **ABOUT YOU** Use a form of *be* and a preposition to tell the location of these things or people in your classroom or school.

EXAMPLE   My dictionary

My dictionary is in my book bag.

1. My classroom
2. I
3. The library
4. The cafeteria
5. The parking lot
6. The teacher
7. We
8. My books

1.9 Negative Statements with *Be*

EXAMPLES	EXPLANATION
I am **not** married. Maya is **not** at home. We are **not** Americans.	We put *not* after a form of *be* to make a negative statement.
English **isn't** my native language. The students **aren't** in the cafeteria now.	We can make contractions for the negative.

Language Note: There is only one contraction for *I am not*. There are two negative contractions for all the other combinations. Study the negative contractions:

I am not	I'm not	—
you are not	you're not	you aren't
he is not	he's not	he isn't
she is not	she's not	she isn't
it is not	it's not	it isn't
we are not	we're not	we aren't
they are not	they're not	they aren't
Tom is not	Tom's not	Tom isn't

EXERCISE 15 **Fill in the blanks with a pronoun and a negative verb. Practice using both negative forms, if possible.**

EXAMPLE The classroom is clean and big.

_____ It isn't _____ dirty. _____ It's not _____ small.

1. We're in the classroom.

_____ in the library. _____ in the cafeteria.

2. Today's a weekday.

_____ Saturday. _____ Sunday.

3. I'm a student.

_____ a teacher.

4. The students are busy.

_____ lazy. _____ tired.

5. You're on time.

_____ early. _____ late.

6. My classmates and I are in an English class.

_____ in the cafeteria. _____ in the library.

EXERCISE 16 **ABOUT YOU** Fill in the blanks with a form of *be* to make a true affirmative statement or negative statement.

EXAMPLES I **'m** busy on Saturdays.

My English class ___**isn't**___ in the morning.

1. My class _____ small.
2. The students _____ all the same age.
3. The students _____ from many countries.
4. Books in the U.S. _____ expensive.
5. The teacher _____ from my native country.
6. The seats in this class _____ in a circle.
7. I _____ a full-time student.
8. My classes _____ easy.
9. We _____ in the computer room now.

EXERCISE 17 Put a check under "true" or "false" to give your opinion. Discuss your ideas.

	True	False
1. English is easy for me.		
2. English is easy for children.		
3. American teachers are very strict.[2]		
4. This school is in a nice area.		
5. This course is expensive.		
6. Most Americans are friendly.		
7. A college education is important.		
8. Algebra is an important subject.		

EXERCISE 18 **ABOUT YOU** If you are from another country, tell your classmates about life there. Fill in the blanks with a form of *be* to make an affirmative or negative statement.

EXAMPLES I **'m** from the capital city.

I ___**'m not**___ from a small town.

1. I _____ happy with the government of my country.
2. I _____ from the capital city.
3. American cars _____ common in my country.
4. Teachers _____ strict.

[2]A *strict* teacher has a lot of rules.

5. Most people _____ rich.

6. Gas _____ cheap.

7. Apartments _____ expensive.

8. Bicycles _____ a popular form of transportation.

9. Public transportation _____ good.

10. A college education _____ free.

11. The president/prime minister _____ a woman.

12. My hometown _____ in the mountains.

13. My hometown _____ very big.

14. It _____ very cold in the winter in my hometown.

15. Cell phones _____ popular in my country.

EXERCISE 19 **Use the words in parentheses ( ) to change each sentence into a negative statement.**

EXAMPLE My teacher is American. (Canadian)

<u>He isn't Canadian.</u> _____

1. Los Angeles and Chicago are cities. (states)

_____

2. I'm from Guatemala. (Mexico)

_____

3. The U.S. is a big country. (Guatemala)

_____

4. We're in class now. (in the library)

_____

5. You're an English teacher. (a math teacher)

_____

6. Chicago and Springfield are in Illinois. (Miami)

_____

7. January is a cold month in Chicago. (July and August)

_____

EXERCISE 20 **ABOUT YOU** **Fill in the blanks with the affirmative or negative of the verb *be* to make a true paragraph.**

My name ___<u>is</u>___ _____. I _____ from an
            (example)   *(your name)*   *(1)*

English-speaking country. I _____ a student at a community college.
                            (2)

I _____ in my English class now. The class _____
(3)   (4)

big. My teacher _____ a man. He/She _____ very
(5)   (6)

young. The classroom _____ very nice. It _____ clean.
(7)   (8)

My classmates _____ all very young students. We _____
(9)   (10)

all from the same country. We _____ all immigrants.
(11)

Conversation About College

Before You Read

1. Is your family in this city?

2. How do you communicate with your family and friends from other cities?

CD 1, TR 04

Read the following conversation between Mohammad (M), a student in the U.S., and Ali (A), his brother back home. Pay special attention to questions.

A: Hi, Mohammad.

M: Hi, Ali. **How are you?**

A: I'm fine.

M: **Where are you now?**

A: I'm in the college computer lab. **Are you at home?**

M: Yes, I am. It's late.

A: It's 4:15 P.M. here. **What time is it there?**

M: It's 1:15 A.M. here.

A: **Why are you still up?**[3]

M: I'm not sleepy.

[3]To be up means to be awake.

A: Why aren't you sleepy?

M: I'm nervous about my test tomorrow.

A: Why are you nervous?

M: Because my class is very hard.

A: How's college life in the U.S.? Is it very different from here?

M: Yes, it is. But it's exciting for me. My new classmates are so interesting. They're from many countries and are all ages. One man in my class is very old.

A: How old is he?

M: He's 75.

A: Are you serious?

M: Of course, I'm serious. He's an interesting man and a great student.

A: Where's he from?

M: Korea.

A: All my classmates are young.

M: Where are Mom and Dad?

A: They're at work.

M: Are they worried about me?

A: A little.

M: Why?

A: Because there's so much freedom in the U.S.

M: Tell them I'm a good student. I'm on the dean's list.

A: What's that?

M: It's a list of students with a high grade point average.

A: That's great. Bye for now.

M: Bye.

1.10 *Be* in *Yes/No* Questions and Short Answers

Compare statements, *yes/no* questions, and short answers.

STATEMENT	YES/NO QUESTION	SHORT ANSWER	EXPLANATION
I am a student.	**Am I** a good student?	Yes, you are.	• In a *yes/no* question, we put *am, is,* or *are* before the subject. • We usually answer a *yes/no* question with a short answer. A short answer contains a pronoun.
You are in bed.	**Are you** sleepy?	No, I'm not.	
He is old.	**Is he** a good student?	Yes, he is.	
She is from Africa.	**Is she** from Nigeria?	No, she isn't.	
It is cold today.	**Is it** windy?	Yes, it is.	
We are here.	**Are we** late?	No, you aren't.	
They are worried.	**Are they** angry?	No, they aren't.	

Language Note: We don't use a contraction for a short *yes* answer. We usually use a contraction for a short *no* answer.

Pronunciation Note: We usually end a *yes/no* question with rising intonation. Listen to your teacher pronounce the questions above.

EXERCISE **21** **Answer the questions based on the conversation on pages 18 to 19.**

EXAMPLES
Is Ali in the U.S.?
No, he isn't.

Is Mohammad in the U.S.?
Yes, he is.

1. Is Mohammad tired?

2. Are Ali's parents at work?

3. Are they worried about Mohammad?

4. Is it the same time in the U.S. and in Mohammad's native country?

5. Is Mohammad a good student?

6. Are all the students in Mohammad's class from the same country?

7. Is Ali at home?

EXERCISE **22** **ABOUT YOU** **Close your book. The teacher will ask you some questions. Answer with a true short answer. If the answer is negative, you may add more information.**

EXAMPLE
Is your book new?
Yes, it is.

1. Is your hometown big?

2. Is Spanish your native language?

3. Is English hard for you?

4. Are you a citizen of the U.S.?

5. Is my pronunciation clear to you?

6. Am I a strict teacher?

7. Are all of you from the same country?

8. Are all of you the same age?

EXERCISE 23 Ask and answer questions about this school and this class. Use the words given. Use the correct form of *be*.

EXAMPLE school/big

A: Is this school big?
B: Yes, it is.

1. it/near public transportation
2. the cafeteria/on this floor
3. it/open now
4. the library/in this building
5. it/closed now
6. this course/free
7. the textbooks/free
8. the teacher/strict
9. this room/clean
10. it/big

EXERCISE 24 **ABOUT YOU** Ask another student questions about his or her country with the words given.

EXAMPLE movie stars/rich

A: Are movie stars rich in your country?
B: Yes, they are. They're very rich.

1. a high school education/free
2. college books/free
3. medical care/free
4. doctors/rich
5. jeans/popular
6. houses/expensive
7. people/friendly
8. Japanese cars/popular
9. fast-food restaurants/popular
10. movie tickets/cheap

1.11 *Wh-* Questions with *Be*

EXAMPLES				EXPLANATION
Wh- Word	*Be*	Subject	Complement	A *wh-* question asks for information.
Where	**are**	Mom and Dad?		
Why	**are**	they	worried?	
How old	**is**	the teacher?		
Where	**is**	he	from?	
Why	**aren't**	you	sleepy?	

Study the question words below.

QUESTION	ANSWER	MEANING OF QUESTION WORD
Who is your teacher? **Who** are those people?	My teacher is Rich Weiss. They're my parents.	Who = person
What is your classmate's name? **What** is that?	His name is Park. It's a cell phone.	What = thing
When is your test? **When** is the class over?	It's on Friday. It's over at 10 o'clock.	When = time
Why are they worried? **Why** aren't you in bed?	They're worried because you're alone. I'm not in bed because I'm not tired.	Why = reason
Where is your classmate from? **Where** are Mom and Dad now?	He's from Korea. They're at work.	Where = place
Which is your book, the green or the red? **Which** class is your favorite?	The green one is my book. English is my favorite class.	Which = specific thing
How is your life in the U.S.? **How** are you? **How** is the weather?	It's great! I'm fine. It's cold today.	How = description, health, or weather

Language Notes:
1. The *wh-* word + *is* can form a contraction: *who's, what's, when's, where's, how's, why's.*
   We can't make a contraction for *which is.*
   We can't make a written contraction for a *wh-* word + *are.*
2. We usually end a *wh-* question with falling intonation. Listen to your teacher say the questions in the boxes above.

EXERCISE 25 It's the first day of school and two students, Maya and Ricardo, are talking. Fill in the blanks with the correct question word and a form of *be*. Make contractions, if possible.

R: You're in my math class, right?

M: Yes, I am. __**What's**__ your name?

　　　　　　　(example)

R: Ricardo Gomez. _____ your name?

　　　　　　　　　　　(1)

M: Maya Levina. I think we're in the same English class too.

R: _____ your English teacher?

　　(2)

M: Rich Weiss.

R: He's my English teacher too. _____ your class?

　　　　　　　　　　　　　　(3)

M: It's at 7:30 P.M. on Monday and Wednesday.

R: That's my class, too!

M: I'm from Russia. _____(4) you from?

R: I'm from Costa Rica.

M: _____(5) Costa Rica?

R: It's in Central America.

M: _____(6) you here?

R: I'm here to learn English and get my degree in engineering.

M: I'm here to learn English too.

R: _____(7) that big book with the funny letters?

M: That's my Russian/English dictionary.

The Russian alphabet is different.

R: English is hard. But my

alphabet is the same.

M: I'm late for my computer class.

See you later in English class.

R: Bye now.

EXERCISE 26 **Test your knowledge. Circle the correct answer to the following questions. Use the map in Appendix K to help with some items. The answers are at the end of the exercise. You may work with a partner.**

1. Where's Dallas?
   a. in California   **b.** in Texas   **c.** in Illinois

2. When is American Independence Day?
   a. July 4   **b.** May 31   **c.** December 25

3. It's 8 A.M. in New York. What time is it in Los Angeles?
   a. 11 A.M.   **b.** 5 A.M.   **c.** 10 A.M.

4. On what day is Thanksgiving?
   a. on Friday   **b.** on Sunday   **c.** on Thursday

5. Which one of these is the name of a Great Lake?
   a. Mississippi   **b.** Missouri   **c.** Michigan

6. Where is the Statue of Liberty?
   a. in San Francisco   **b.** in New York City   **c.** in Los Angeles

7. What is the first day of summer?

    a. June 1   **b.** June 21   **c.** June 30

8. When is Labor Day in the U.S.?

    a. in May   **b.** in June   **c.** in September

9. What's the biggest state?

    a. Alaska   **b.** Texas   **c.** New York

Answers: 1b, 2a, 3b, 4c, 5c, 6b, 7b, 8c, 9a

1.12 Comparing Statements and Questions with *Be*

Affirmative Statements and Questions

Wh- Word	*Be*	Subject	*Be*	Complement	Short Answer
		Mom and Dad	are	out.	
	Are	they		at the store?	No, they aren't.
Where	are	they?			
		It	is	late.	
	Is	it		1 A.M.?	No, it isn't.
What time	is	it?			

Negative Statements and Questions

Wh- Word	*Be* + *n't*	Subject	*Be* + *n't*	Complement
		You	aren't	in bed.
Why	aren't	you		sleepy?
		He	isn't	in the U.S.
Why	isn't	he		with his parents?

EXERCISE 27   **Respond to each statement with a question.**

EXAMPLE   Mom and Dad are not here. Where _____*are they?*_____

1. Mom and Dad are worried about you. Why _____

2. I'm not sleepy. Why _____

3. My teacher is great. Who _____

4. My classes are early. When _____

5. My roommate's name is hard to pronounce.

    What _____

6. My cell phone isn't on. Why _____

7. Mom isn't in the kitchen. Where _____

1.13 Questions with *What* and *How*

EXAMPLES	EXPLANATION
What is a verb? It's an action word. **What** is the dean's list? It's a list of the best students.	*What* can ask for a definition.
What nationality is the teacher? She's American. **What day** is today? It's Friday. **What time** is it? It's 4:15 P.M. **What color** is the dictionary? It's yellow. **What kind of book** is this? It's a grammar book.	A noun can follow *what*: • *what nationality* • *what day* • *what time* • *what color* • *what kind of* _____ • *what month*
How is your new class? It's great. **How** is the weather today? It's cool. **How** is your sister? She's fine.	We can use *how* to ask for a description. We use *how* to ask about the weather. We can use *how* to ask about health.
How old is your brother? He's 16 (years old). **How tall** are you? I'm 5 feet, 3 inches tall. **How long** is this course? It's 16 weeks long. **How long** is the table? It's 3 feet long. **How much** is the tuition at this college? It's $75 per credit hour.	An adjective or adverb can follow *how*: • *how old* • *how tall* • *how long* • *how much* • *how big* • *how fast*

Usage Notes:
1. For height, Americans use feet (') and inches (").
   He's 5 feet, 8 inches tall. OR He's five-eight. OR He's 5'8".[4]
2. *How are you?* is often just a way to say hello. People usually answer, "Fine, thanks. How are you?"

[4]See Appendix G for conversion from feet and inches to meters and centimeters.

The Present Tense of the Verb *Be*; Prepositions of Place; *This, That, These, Those* 25

EXERCISE **28** **Fill in the blanks to complete the questions.**

EXAMPLE   How ___old are___ your parents? They're in their 50s.

1. What _____ it?
   It's 3 o'clock.

2. What _____ car _____ that?
   That's a Japanese car.

3. What _____ words _____ *tall, old,*
   new, and *good*?
   They're adjectives.

4. What _____ your new car?
   It's dark blue.

5. How _____?
   My son is 10 years old.

6. How _____?
   My brother is 6 feet tall.

7. How _____?
   I'm 25 years old.

8. How _____?
   That car is $10,000.

9. How _____?
   The movie is 2 ½ hours long.

EXERCISE **29**   **ABOUT YOU** **Fill in the blanks to make true statements about yourself. Then find a partner from a different country, if possible, and interview your partner by asking questions with the words in parentheses ( ).**

EXAMPLE   I'm from ___Bosnia___. (Where)

A: I'm from Bosnia. Where are you from?
B: I'm from Taiwan.

1. My name is _____. (What)

2. I'm from _____. (Where)

3. The president/prime minister of my country is _____
   _____. (Who)

4. The flag from my country is _____. (What colors)

5. My country is in _____. (Where)
   (continent or region)

6. I'm _____ feet, _____ inches tall. (How tall)

7. My birthday is in _____. (When)
   (month)

8. My favorite TV show is _____. (What)

EXERCISE 30 **Complete the following phone conversation between Cindy (C) and Maria (M).**

CD 1, TR 05

C: Hello?

M: Hi, Cindy. This is Maria.

C: Hi, Maria. ___How are you___?
(example)

M: I'm fine.

C: _____ your first
(1)
day of class?

M: Yes, it is. I'm at school now, but I'm not in class.

C: Why _____ in class?
(2)

M: Because it's break time now.

C: How _____ the break?
(3)

M: It's 10 minutes long.

C: How _____ ?
(4)

M: My English class is great. My classmates are very interesting.

C: Where _____ from?
(5)

M: They're from all over the world.

C: _____ American?
(6)

M: Yes. My teacher is American. What time _____ ?
(7)

C: It's 3:35.

M: Oh, I'm late.

C: Let's get together soon. Are you free this weekend?

M: I'm free on Saturday afternoon.

C: I have a class on Saturday.

M: When _____ free?
(8)

C: On Sunday afternoon.

M: Sunday's fine. Talk to you later.

In the School Cafeteria

Before
You Read

1. Do you like American food?

2. Do you eat in the school cafeteria?

CD 1, TR 06

Read the following conversation between an American student (A) and his Chinese roommate (C). Pay special attention to *this, that, these,* and *those*.

A: Is **this** your first time in an American college?

C: Yes, it is.

A: Let me show you around the cafeteria. **This** is the cafeteria for students. **That's** the cafeteria for teachers. The vending machines are in **that** room. When the food service is closed, **that** room is always open.

C: The food is in a machine?

A: Yes. And **that's** the change machine. **This** is the line for hot food.

C: What are **those**?

A: They're tacos.

C: Tacos? What are tacos?

A: They're Mexican food.

C: What's **that**?

A: It's pizza. It's Italian food.

C: What's **this**?

A: It's chop suey. It's a Chinese dish.

C: I'm from China, and I'm sure **this** is not a Chinese dish. Where's the American food in America?

A: **This** *is* American food—Mexican, Italian, Chinese—it's all American food.

C: Where are the chopsticks?

A: Uh . . . chopsticks? **Those** are the forks and knives, but there are no chopsticks here.

1.14 *This, That, These, Those*

EXAMPLES		EXPLANATION
Singular	**This** is pizza.	Use *this* and *these* to identify near objects and people.
Plural	**These** are tacos.	
Singular	**That** is the change machine.	Use *that* and *those* to identify far objects and people.
Plural	**Those** are forks and knives.	
This is pizza. **It's** an Italian food. **Those** are knives and forks. **They're** clean. **That's** my teacher. **She's** a nice woman.		After we identify a noun, we can use subject pronouns.
That room is for the teachers. **Those forks** are clean.		A noun can follow *this*, *that*, *these*, and *those*.

Language Note: Only *that is* can form a contraction in writing: ***That's*** the change machine.

EXERCISE **31** **Imagine that you are showing a new student the school cafeteria. Use *this, that, these,* and *those,* and a form of *be* to complete each statement. The arrows indicate if the item is near or far.**

EXAMPLES   _____<u>This is</u>_____ the school cafeteria. ⟶

           _____<u>Those are</u>_____ the clean dishes. ⟶⟶

1. _____ the trays. ⟶
2. _____ today's special. ⟶
3. _____ the napkins. ⟶⟶
4. _____ the forks, knives, and spoons. ⟶⟶⟶
5. _____ the cashier. ⟶
6. _____ the vending machines. ⟶
7. _____ the eating area. ⟶⟶
8. _____ the teachers' section. ⟶⟶

The Present Tense of the Verb *Be*; Prepositions of Place; *This, That, These, Those*   **29**

Summary of Lesson 1

1. **Uses of *Be***

DESCRIPTION:	Chicago **is** big.
IDENTIFICATION/CLASSIFICATION:	This **is** Chicago. It **is** a city.
LOCATION:	Chicago **is** in Illinois.
PLACE OF ORIGIN:	The teacher **is** from Chicago.
AGE:	I **am** 25 (years old).
PHYSICAL OR MENTAL CONDITION:	He **is** hungry. I **am** thirsty. She **is** worried.
TIME:	It **is** 6 P.M.
WEATHER:	It **is** warm today.

2. **Subject Pronouns**

   I   we   he   she   it   you   they

3. **Contractions**

   Subject pronoun + form of *be*:
   I'm, you're, he's, she's, it's, we're, they're
   Subject noun + *is*: the teacher's, Tom's, Mary's
   Is or *are* + *not*: isn't, aren't
   Wh- word + *is*: what's, when's, where's, why's, how's, who's

4. **Articles *a/an***

   Chicago is **a** big city.
   Puerto Rico is **an** island.

5. **Statements and Questions with *Be***

AFFIRMATIVE:	She **is** busy.
NEGATIVE:	She **isn't** lazy.
YES/NO QUESTION:	**Is** she busy on Saturday?
SHORT ANSWER:	No, she **isn't**.
WH- QUESTION:	When **is** she busy?
NEGATIVE QUESTION:	Why **isn't** she busy on Saturday?
AFFIRMATIVE:	You **are** late.
NEGATIVE:	You **aren't** on time.
YES/NO QUESTION:	**Are** you OK?
SHORT ANSWER:	Yes, I **am**.
WH- QUESTION:	Why **are** you late?
NEGATIVE QUESTION:	Why **aren't** you on time?

6. ***This/That/These/Those***

   This is an English book.
   That is a pen.
   These are pencils.
   Those are pens.

Editing Advice

1. Don't repeat the subject with a pronoun.

   My father ~~he~~ lives in Australia.

2. Use the correct word order. Put the subject at the beginning of the statement.

   Cuba is small.
   ~~Is small Cuba.~~

3. Use the correct word order. Put the adjective before the noun.

   small country.
   Cuba is a ~~country small~~.

4. Use the correct word order in a question.

   is he
   Where ~~he is~~ from?

5. Every sentence has a verb. Don't omit *be*.

   is
   My sister ^ a teacher.

6. Every sentence has a subject. For time and weather, the subject is *it*.

   It's
   ~~Is~~ 6 o'clock now.
   It's
   ~~Is~~ very cold today.

7. Don't confuse *this* and *these*.

   This
   ~~These~~ is my coat.
   These
   ~~This~~ are my shoes.

8. Use *the* before *U.S.* and *United States*.

   the
   My sister is in ^ U.S.

9. Don't use a contraction for *am not*.

   I'm not
   ~~I amn't~~ an American.

10. Put the apostrophe in place of the missing letter.

    isn't
    She ~~is'nt~~ here today.

---

11. Use an apostrophe, not a comma, for a contraction.

I'm
~~I,m~~ a good student.

12. Use the article *a* or *an* before a singular noun.

a
New York is ᴧ big city.

an
San Francisco is ᴧ interesting city.

13. Don't use *a* before plural nouns.

July and August are ~~a~~ warm months.

14. Don't use the article *a* before an adjective with no noun.

New York is ~~a~~ big.

15. For age, use a number only or a number + *years old*.

He's 12 ~~years.~~ OR He's 12 years old.

16. Don't use a contraction for a short *yes* answer.

I am
Are you from Mexico? Yes, ~~I'm.~~

17. Don't separate *how* from the adjective or adverb.

old is he?
How ~~is he old?~~

18. Don't make a contraction with *is* after *s, z, sh,* or *ch* sounds.

is
Los Angeles~~'s~~ ᴧ a big city.

Editing Quiz

Some of the shaded words and phrases have mistakes. Find the mistakes and correct them. If the shaded words are correct, write C.

C   I'm
A: Hi. My name's Leo. ~~I,m~~ from Latvia. What's your name?
(example)   *(example)*   *(1)*

B: My name's Diane.
           (2)

A: Nice to meet you, Diane. Where you are from?
                                            (3)

B: I from Burundi.
(4)

A: Where Burundi is?
(5)

B: Its in Central Africa. Burundi is a country very small.
(6)   (7)

What's Latvia? It is a city or a country?
(8)   (9)

A: Latvia is country. It's in Europe. Tell me more about Burundi.
(10)   (11)

What's the language of Burundi?

B: My native language is Kirundi. French's also a language in Burundi.
(12)   (13)

Whats your native language?
(14)

A: Latvian. Russian's also a language in Latvia.
(15)

B: We both speak several languages! Cool!

A: You are married?
(16)

B: Yes, I'm. My husband he is'nt from Burundi. He's from Congo.
(17)   (18) (19)   (20)

Are you married?
(21)

A: No, I amn't. I'm only 18 years. I'm in U.S. with my parents and sister.
(22)   (23)   (24)

B: How your sister is old?
(25)

A: She's 16.
(26)

B: Is in high school your sister?
(27)

A: Yes, she is.
(28)

B: This are pictures of my kids, Joseph and Jimmy.
(29)

A: Are they a twins?
(30)

B: No. Jimmy has eight and Joseph has seven years.
(31)   (32)

A: They're a cute.
(33)

B: This is a interesting exercise, but is time to go. Fun talking to you.
(34)   (35)

A: Same here.

Lesson 1 Test/Review

PART 1 Fill in the blanks to complete this conversation. Use contractions, if possible. Not all blanks need a word. If the blank doesn't need a word, write Ø.

A: Where are you ___*from*___?
   _(example)

B: I'm from ___Ø___ Mexico.
   _(example)

A: Are you happy in _____ U.S.?
   ₍₁₎

B: Yes, I _____. The U.S. is _____ great country.
   ₍₂₎   ₍₃₎

A: _____ from _____ big city?
   ₍₄₎   ₍₅₎

B: Yes. I'm from Mexico City. It's _____ very big city. This city is
   ₍₆₎

_____ big too. But _____ cold in the winter.
   ₍₇₎   ₍₈₎

A: _____ from Mexico too?
   ₍₉₎

B: No. My roommate _____ from Taiwan. I'm happy in the
   ₍₁₀₎

U.S., but he _____ happy here.
   ₍₁₁₎

A: Why _____ happy?
   ₍₁₂₎

B: He _____ homesick. His parents _____ in Taiwan.
   ₍₁₃₎   ₍₁₄₎

He _____ alone here.
   ₍₁₅₎

A: How _____ ?
   ₍₁₆₎

B: He's very young. He _____ only 18 years _____.
   ₍₁₇₎   ₍₁₈₎

A: What _____ his name?
   ₍₁₉₎

B: His name _____ Lu.
   ₍₂₀₎

PART 2 Write a contraction of the words shown. If it's not possible to write a contraction, put an *X* in the blank.

she is ____she's____

English is ____X____

1. we are _____
2. you are not _____
3. I am not _____
4. they are _____
5. this is _____

6. Los Angeles is _____
7. Mary is not _____
8. he is not _____
9. what is _____
10. what are _____

PART 3 Read the conversation between two students, Sofia (S) and Danuta (D). They are talking about their classes and teachers. Fill in the blanks. Use contractions, if possible.

D: Hi, Sofia. How's your English class?

S: Hi, Danuta. It 's_____ wonderful. I _____ very happy with it.
       (example)   *(1)*

D: _____'m in level 3. What level _____ in?
       (2)   *(3)*

S: I' _____ in level 2.
       (4)

D: My English teacher _____ Ms. Kathy James. _____ a very
                          (5)   *(6)*

   good teacher. Who _____?
                     (7)

S: Mr. Bob Kane is my English teacher. _____ very good too.
                                          (8)

D: _____ an old man?
       (9)

S: No, he _____. He's _____ young man. He _____
              (10)   *(11)*   *(12)*

   about 25 years _____. How _____?
                  (13)   *(14)*

D: Ms. James _____ about 50 years old.
                 (15)

S: How _____?
           (16)

D: She's about 5 feet, 6 inches tall.

S: Is she American?

D: Yes, she _____. She's from New York.
                (17)

S: _____?
       (18)

D: Yes. My class is very big. The students _____(19) from many

countries. Ten students _____(20) from Asia, six students

_____(21) from Europe, one student _____(22) from Africa, and

five are _____(23) Central America. Is your class big?

S: No, it _____(24).

D: Where _____(25)?

S: The students _____(26) all from the same country. We _____(27)

all from Russia.

D: _____(28) Russian?

S: No. Mr. Kane isn't Russian. He's from Canada, but he's _____(29)

American citizen now.

D: _____(30)?

S: No. That's not Mr. Kane. That _____(31) my husband. I _____(32)

late! See you later.

Expansion

Classroom Activities

1 **Write a few sentences about yourself. Give your height, a physical description, your nationality, your occupation, your age (optional), and your gender (man or woman). Put the papers in a box. The teacher will read each paper. Guess which classmate is described.**

EXAMPLE   I'm 5 feet, 8 inches tall.
I'm Mexican.
I'm thin.
I'm 21 years old and male.

② Work with a partner. Describe a famous person (an actor, a singer, an athlete, a politician, etc.). Report your description to the class. Do not give the person's name. See if your classmates can guess who it is.

EXAMPLE   He is a former basketball player.
He's tall.
He's famous.
He's African-American.

③ Check the words that describe you. Find a partner and ask each other questions using these words. See how many things you have in common. Tell the class something interesting you learned about your partner.

a. _____ happy

b. _____ from Africa

c. _____ from Asia

d. _____ from Europe

e. _____ interested in politics

f. _____ under 20 years old

g. _____ afraid to speak English

h. _____ an only child[5]

i. _____ an American citizen

j. _____ hungry

k. _____ married

l. _____ athletic

④ Work with a partner from the same country, if possible. Fill in a few items for each category. Report some information to the class.

EXAMPLE   Typical of the U.S.

Common last names	Popular tourist attractions	Popular sports	Language(s)	Capital city	Other big cities
Johnson Wilson	Disneyland Grand Canyon	baseball basketball football	English	Washington	New York Los Angeles Chicago

Typical of _____ (name of country)

Common last names	Popular tourist attractions	Popular sports	Language(s)	Capital city	Other big cities

[5]An *only child* has no sisters or brothers.

Talk

About It

Give your opinion. Fill in the blanks and discuss your answers.

1. Colleges/schools in the U.S. are _____

2. Students in the U.S. are _____

3. Parking at this school is _____

4. The textbook for this course is _____

5. The teachers at this college/school are _____

6. The location of this college/school is _____

Write

About It

Write a paragraph using Exercise 20 as a model. For every negative statement that you write, add an affirmative statement. You may add other information, too.

EXAMPLE

> ### About Me
>
> My name is Mohammad. I'm not from an English speaking country. I'm from Iran. I'm not a student at City College. I'm a student at Roosevelt University. I'm in English class now . . .

 For more practice using grammar in context, please visit our Web site.

Grammar
The Simple Present Tense

Context
The United States

The White House, Washington, D.C.

Washington, D.C.

1. What capital cities do you know?

2. What do you know about Washington, D.C.?

CD 1, TR 07

Read the following magazine article. Pay special attention to the present-tense verbs.[1]

Did You Know?

The first location of the U.S. capital was New York City.

Washington, D.C., is the capital of the United States. "D.C." means District of Columbia. The District of Columbia **is** not a state; it **is** a special government district. It **is** very small. It **is** only 61 square miles (158 square kilometers). More than half a million people **live** in Washington. Washington **doesn't have** factories. Government and tourism **are** the main businesses of Washington. Washington **doesn't have** tall buildings like other big cities.

Some people who **work** in Washington **don't live** there. They **live** in the nearby states: Virginia and Maryland. Washington **has** a good subway (Metro) system. It **connects** Washington to nearby cities in Virginia and Maryland.

The Capitol, the building where Congress **meets, is** on a hill. Senators and representatives from each state **work** on Capitol Hill. They **make** the country's laws.

Tourists from all over the United States and many other countries **visit** Washington. They **come** to see the White House and the Capitol building. Many visitors **want** to see

The Capitol

the Vietnam War Memorial. This wall of dark stone **lists** all the names of American soldiers who died in the war in Vietnam.

Besides government buildings, Washington also **has** many important museums and monuments. The Smithsonian Institution **has** a zoo and 19 museums.

Tourists **don't pay** to see government buildings and museums. However, they **need** tickets to see many places because these places **are** crowded.

A trip to Washington **is** an enjoyable and educational experience.

[1]See the map in Appendix K to find the location of Washington, D.C.

2.1 Simple Present Tense—Forms

A simple present-tense verb has two forms: the base form and the *-s* form.

EXAMPLES			EXPLANATION
Subject I You We They My friends	**Base Form** **live**	**Complement** in Washington.	We use the base form when the subject is *I, you, we, they,* or a plural noun.
Subject He She It The president My family	***-s* Form** **lives**	**Complement** in Washington.	We use the *-s* form when the subject is *he, she, it,* or a singular noun. *Family* is a singular subject.
I **have** friends in Washington, D.C. Washington **has** many museums.			*Have* is an irregular verb. have ⟶ has

EXERCISE **1** **Fill in the blanks with the correct form of the verb.**

EXAMPLE Visitors ___*like*___ the museums.
(like/likes)

1. The president _____ in the White House.
(live/lives)

2. Many people in Washington _____ for the government.
(work/works)

3. Washington _____ many beautiful museums.
(have/has)

4. Millions of tourists _____ Washington every year.
(visit/visits)

5. The Metro _____ Washington to nearby cities.
(connect/connects)

6. The Vietnam War Memorial _____ the names of men and

women who died in the war.
(list/lists)

7. "D.C." _____ District of Columbia.
(mean/means)

2.2 Simple Present Tense—Uses

EXAMPLES	USES
The president **lives** in the White House. Washington **has** a good subway system (the Metro).	With general truths, to show that something is consistently true
The president **shakes** hands with many people. He **waves** to people.	With customs
We **take** a vacation every summer. We sometimes **go** to Washington.	To show regular activity (a habit) or repeated action
I **come** from Bosnia. He **comes** from Pakistan.	To show place of origin

EXERCISE 2 **ABOUT YOU** Write the correct form of the verb. Add more words to give facts about you and your country.

EXAMPLE   I _come from Colombia._
(come)

1. In my native city, I especially _____
(like)

2. My family _____
(live)

3. The capital of my country _____
(have)

4. Most people in my country _____
(speak)

5. Tourists in my country _____
(visit)

6. My native city _____
(have)

7. The president _____
(live)

8. Many people in my country _____
(want)

2.3 Spelling of the -s Form

RULE	BASE FORM	-S FORM
Add -**s** to most verbs to make the -s form.	hope eat	hopes eats
When the base form ends in *ss, sh, ch,* or *x,* add -**es** and pronounce an extra syllable.	miss wash catch mix	misses washes catches mixes
When the base form ends in a consonant + *y,* change the *y* to *i* and add -**es**.	carry worry	carries worries
When the base form ends in a vowel + *y,* add -**s**. Do not change the *y*.	pay enjoy	pays enjoys
Add -**es** to *go* and *do*.	go do	goes does

EXERCISE **3** **Write the -s form of the following verbs.**

EXAMPLES   eat _____*eats*_____

study _____*studies*_____

watch _____*watches*_____

1. try _____
2. play _____
3. have _____
4. go _____
5. worry _____
6. finish _____
7. do _____
8. push _____
9. enjoy _____
10. think _____

11. say _____
12. change _____
13. brush _____
14. obey _____
15. reach _____
16. fix _____
17. work _____
18. raise _____
19. charge _____
20. see _____

2.4 Pronunciation of the -s Form

PRONUNCIATION	RULE	EXAMPLES	
/s/	Pronounce /s/ after voiceless sounds: /p, t, k, f/.	hope—hopes eat—eats	pick—picks laugh—laughs
/z/	Pronounce /z/ after voiced sounds: /b, d, g, v, m, n, ŋ, l, r/ and all vowel sounds.	grab—grabs read—reads hug—hugs live—lives hum—hums run—runs	sing—sings fall—falls hear—hears see—sees borrow—borrows play—plays
/əz/	Pronounce /əz/ when the base form ends in ss, ce, se, sh, ch, ge, x.	miss—misses dance—dances use—uses wash—washes	watch—watches change—changes fix—fixes

Pronunciation Note: The following verbs have a change in the vowel sound. Listen to your teacher pronounce these examples.

do/du/—does/dʌz/
say/sei/—says/sɛz/

EXERCISE 4 Go back to Exercise 3 and pronounce the base form and -s form of each verb.

EXERCISE 5 Fill in the blanks with the -s form of the verb in parentheses ( ). Pay attention to the spelling rules on page 43. Then say each sentence.

EXAMPLE A teacher ___tries___ to help students learn.
(try)

1. A pilot _____ an airplane.
(fly)

2. A dishwasher _____ dishes.
(wash)

3. A babysitter _____ children.
(watch)

4. A soldier _____ an officer.
(obey)

5. A citizen _____ taxes.
(pay)

6. A mechanic _____ machines.
(fix)

7. A student _____.
(study)

8. A student _____ homework.
(do)

9. A carpenter _____ a hammer.
(use)

10. A teacher _____ students.
(teach)

Write at least three sentences to tell what the president of the U.S. does. You may work with a partner.

_____

_____

_____

_____

2.5 Comparing Affirmative Statements—*Be* and Other Verbs

EXAMPLES	EXPLANATION

I **am** a student.
I **study** English.
You **are** right.
You **know** the answer.
He **is** busy.
He **works** hard.
	Don't include a form of *be* with a simple present-tense verb.
	    Wrong: I'm study English.
	    Wrong: You're know the answer.
	    Wrong: He's works hard.

EXERCISE 7 A student is comparing himself to his friend. Fill in the blanks with the correct form of the underlined verb.

EXAMPLES My friend and I are very different.

I <u>get</u> up at 7 o'clock. He _____**gets**_____ up at 10 o'clock.

He's a lazy student. I __**'m**_____ a good student.

1. I <u>study</u> every day. He _____ only before a test.

2. I always <u>get</u> an A on my tests. He _____ a C.

3. I <u>have</u> a scholarship. He _____ a government loan.

4. He <u>lives</u> in a dormitory. I _____ in an apartment.

5. He's from Japan. I _____ from the Philippines.

6. He <u>studies</u> with the radio on. I _____ in a quiet room.

7. He <u>watches</u> a lot of TV. I _____ TV only when I have free time.

8. He <u>eats</u> a lot of meat. I _____ a lot of fish.

9. He <u>uses</u> a laptop computer. I _____ a desktop computer.

2.6 Negative Statements with the Simple Present Tense

EXAMPLES	EXPLANATION
The president **lives** in the White House. The vice president **doesn't live** in the White House. Washington **has** many government buildings. It **doesn't have** tall buildings.	Use *doesn't* + the base form with *he, she, it,* or a singular noun. **Compare:** lives ——→ doesn't **live** has ——→ doesn't **have** *Doesn't* is the contraction for *does not*.
Visitors **pay** to enter museums in most cities. They **don't pay** in Washington museums. We **live** in Maryland. We **don't live** in Washington.	Use *don't* + the base form with *I, you, we, they,* or a plural noun. **Compare:** pay ——→ don't **pay** live ——→ don't **live** *Don't* is the contraction for *do not*.

Usage Note: American English and British English use different grammar to form the negative of *have*. Compare:

American: He *doesn't have* a dictionary.
British: He *hasn't* a dictionary. OR He *hasn't got* a dictionary.

EXERCISE 8 Fill in the blanks with the negative form of the underlined verb.

EXAMPLE You <u>need</u> tickets for some museums. You _____don't need_____ money for the museums.

1. Washington <u>has</u> tourism. It _____ factories.

2. Visitors <u>pay</u> to enter museums in most cities. They _____ to enter museums in Washington, D.C.

3. The Metro <u>runs</u> all day. It _____ after midnight on weeknights.

4. You <u>need</u> a car in many cities. You _____ a car in Washington.

5. Washington <u>has</u> a subway system. Miami _____ a subway system.

6. My friend <u>lives</u> in Virginia. He _____ in Washington.

7. I <u>like</u> American history. I _____ geography.

8. The president <u>lives</u> in Washington. He _____ in New York.

9. The president <u>serves</u> a four-year term. He _____ a six-year term.

10. We <u>have</u> a president. We _____ a prime minister.

11. The U.S. Congress <u>makes</u> the laws. The president _____ the laws.

EXERCISE 9 Tell if the city or town you live in has the following items.

EXAMPLES a lake
This city has a lake.
OR
This city doesn't have a lake.

1. tall buildings
2. an art museum
3. a subway
4. a large university
5. factories

6. government buildings
7. monuments
8. parks
9. modern buildings
10. movie theaters

EXERCISE 10 Make an affirmative statement or a negative statement with the words given to state facts about the teacher. Use the correct form of the verb.

EXAMPLES speak Arabic
The teacher speaks Arabic.
OR
The teacher doesn't speak Arabic.

1. talk fast
2. speak English well
3. speak my language
4. give a lot of homework
5. give tests

6. pronounce my name correctly
7. wear glasses
8. wear jeans to class
9. teach this class every day
10. watch the students during a test

EXERCISE 11 **ABOUT YOU** Check (✓) the items that describe you and what you do. Exchange your book with another student. Make statements about the other student.

EXAMPLES _____ I have children.
Marta doesn't have children.

✓ I like cold weather.
Marta likes cold weather.

1. _____ I speak Chinese.
2. _____ I live alone.
3. _____ I live near school.
4. _____ I walk to school.
5. _____ I speak Spanish.

6. _____ I like summer.
7. _____ I like hot weather.
8. _____ I have a laptop.
9. _____ I use the Internet.
10. _____ I have a dog.

2.7 Comparing Negative Statements—*Be* and Other Verbs

EXAMPLES	EXPLANATION

I**'m not** from Washington.
I **don't work** for the government.
The museums **aren't** open on Christmas Day.
They **don't have** tours on Christmas Day.
Washington, D.C. **isn't** a very big city.
It **doesn't have** tall buildings.
	Don't use *be* to make the negative of a simple present-tense verb.
	   Wrong: I*'m not* work for the government.
	         They *aren't* have tours.
	         It *isn't* have tall buildings.

EXERCISE **12**   **ABOUT YOU** Check (✓) the items that describe you and what you do. Exchange your book with another student. Make statements about the other student.

EXAMPLES   _____ I'm an immigrant.   ✓ I have a computer.
Margarita isn't an immigrant.   Margarita has a computer.
She comes from Puerto Rico.

1. _____ I'm married.
2. _____ I have children/a child.
3. _____ I have a laptop.
4. _____ I'm an American citizen.
5. _____ I like this city.
6. _____ I have a job.
7. _____ I'm a full-time student.
8. _____ I have a pet.[2]
9. _____ I'm an immigrant.
10. _____ I'm happy in the U.S.
11. _____ I like baseball.
12. _____ I understand Americans.

EXERCISE **13**   Choose one of the items from the list below. Write sentences telling what this person does or is. Include negative statements. You may work with a partner. Read some of your sentences to the class.

EXAMPLES   a good teacher

A good teacher explains the lesson.

A good teacher doesn't get angry at students.

A good teacher doesn't walk away after class if students have questions.

A good teacher is patient.

1. a good friend
2. a good mother or father
3. a good doctor
4. a good son or daughter

_____

_____

_____

_____

[2]A *pet* is an animal that lives in someone's house. Dogs and cats are common pets.

EXERCISE 14 **Fill in the blanks with the correct form of the verb in parentheses ( ).**

CD 1, TR 08

Sara Harris ___is___ a 30-year-old woman. She _____ in
Example: (be)   (1 live)

Arlington, Virginia. She _____ in Washington because
                              (2 not/live)

rent is cheaper in Arlington. Arlington _____ far from
                                              (3 be/not)

Washington. Sara _____ a car because her apartment
                      (4 not/need)

_____ near a Metro stop. She
    (5 be)

_____ the Metro to go to work
    (6 use)

every day. Sara works in Washington,

but she _____ for the
              (7 not/work)

government. She _____ a tour guide.
                      (8 be)

She _____ groups on tours of the Capitol. Tour groups
      (9 take)

_____ to pay to enter the Capitol, but they do _____
          (10 not/need)   (11 need)

a reservation.

Sara _____ married. She _____ two roommates.
          (12 be/not)   (13 have)

They _____ in government offices. Sara and her roommates
        (14 work)

_____ hard, so they _____ much time to visit
    (15 work)   (16 not/have)

the museums. When Sara's friends _____ from out of town, Sara
                                          (17 visit)

_____ them to museums and other tourist attractions.
    (18 take)

One Country, Many Differences

1. Does your country have a national language?
2. Do citizens of your country pay income tax?

CD 1, TR 09

Read the following questions and answers about the U.S. Pay special attention to *yes/no* questions and short answers.

Q: **Does** the U.S. **have** a national language?

A: No, it **doesn't**. About 81 percent of Americans speak English at home. Spanish is the second most common language.

Q: **Does** the U.S. **have** a national religion?

A: No, it **doesn't**. Americans have freedom of religion.

Q: **Do** Americans **have** to vote?

A: No, they **don't**.

Q: **Does** the U.S. **control** education?

A: No, it **doesn't**. Each state makes its own decisions about education.

Q: **Do** all citizens **pay** income tax to the U.S. government?

A: Yes, they **do**. But they don't all pay the same amount.

Q: **Does** every state **have** a sales tax?

A: No. Some states, like California and Illinois, have a high sales tax. Some states, like Alaska and Montana, have no sales tax.

Q: **Does** the U.S. **have** one time zone or more?

A: The U.S. has six time zones.

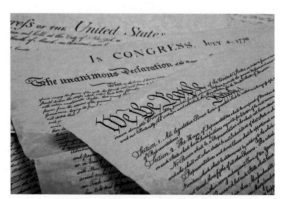

The United States Constitution

2.8 Yes/No Questions and Short Answers with the Simple Present Tense

EXAMPLES	EXPLANATION
Does **Subject** **Verb** **Complement** **Does** Sara **have** a car? **Does** everyone **pay** taxes? **Does** your family **visit** you?	To form a question with *he, she, it, everyone, family,* or a singular subject, use: *Does* + subject + base form...? *Wrong:* Does she *works* in Washington?
Do **Subject** **Verb** **Complement** **Do** you **work** hard? **Do** Americans **vote** for the president? **Do** they **pay** taxes?	To form a question with *I, you, we, they,* or a plural noun, use: *Do* + subject + base form...?

Does the U.S. have a national religion?
No, it doesn't.
Does the U.S. have six time zones?
Yes, it does.
	We usually answer a *yes/no* question with a short answer.
	
	Short answer:
	    Yes, + subject pronoun + *do/does.*
	    No, + subject pronoun + *don't/doesn't.*

Usage Note: American English and British English use different grammar to form a question with *have.* Compare:
      American: Does she *have* a car? Yes, she *does.*
      British: *Has* she a car? OR *Has* she *got* a car? Yes, she *has.*

Compare statements and questions.

Do/Does	Subject	Verb	Complement	Short Answer
Does	The U.S. the U.S.	has have	a president. an official language?	No, it doesn't.
Do	You you	pay pay	taxes. a lot?	Yes, I do.

EXERCISE 15   Go back and read Exercise 14 on page 49. Then answer with a short answer.

EXAMPLE   Does Sara work in Washington, D.C.? _____Yes, she does._____

     1. Does Sara live in Washington, D.C.? _____

     2. Does she work for the government? _____

     3. Does the Metro go to Virginia? _____

     4. Does Sara need a car? _____

     5. Do Sara and her roommates often visit museums? _____

     6. Do her roommates work for the government? _____

     7. Does Sara have out-of-town visitors? _____

EXERCISE 16 **Ask your teacher a question with "Do you . . .?" and the words given. Your teacher will respond with a short answer.**

EXAMPLE   drive to school
A: Do you drive to school?
B: Yes, I do.   OR   No, I don't.

1. like your job
2. teach in the summer
3. have another job
4. speak another language
5. travel a lot
6. know my language

7. like to read students' homework.
8. live far from the school
9. have a fax machine
10. have trouble with English spelling
11. have a scanner
12. like soccer

EXERCISE 17 **ABOUT YOU** **Put a check (✓) next to customs from your native country. Then make an affirmative or negative statement about your native country or culture. Ask another student if this is a custom in his or her native country or culture.**

EXAMPLES   ✓ People take off their shoes before they enter a house.

A: Russians take off their shoes before they enter a house. Do Mexicans take off their shoes before they enter a house?
B: No, we don't.

✓ Schoolchildren study English.

A: Romanian schoolchildren don't study English. They study French. Do German schoolchildren study English?
B: Yes, they do.

1. _____ People take off their shoes before they enter a house.
2. _____ People bow when they say hello.
3. _____ People shake hands when they say hello.
4. _____ People bring a gift when they visit a friend's house.
5. _____ People eat with chopsticks.
6. _____ On the bus, younger people stand up to let an older person sit down.
7. _____ High school students wear a uniform.
8. _____ People visit friends without calling first.
9. _____ Men open doors for women.
10. _____ Men give flowers to women for their birthdays.
11. _____ People celebrate Children's Day.
12. _____ Women wear a veil.

EXERCISE ▮18▮ **A tourist in Washington, D.C., has a lot of questions. Fill in the blanks to make questions.**

EXAMPLE   Most big cities have tall buildings. <u>Does Washington have</u> tall buildings? No, it doesn't.

1. The Metro trains run all day. _____ 24 hours a day? No, they don't. On weekdays they run only from early morning to midnight. On weekends they run later.

2. In my city, all passengers pay the same fare on the subway. _____ the same fare on the Metro in Washington? No, they don't. Passengers pay according to the distance they ride.

3. You need a ticket to enter museums in my hometown. _____ a ticket to enter museums in Washington? Yes, you do, but the museums are free.

4. The Washington Monument is very tall. _____ an elevator? Yes, it has an elevator.

5. The president works in Washington. _____ on Capitol Hill? No, he doesn't. He works in the White House.

6. _____ the laws? No, he doesn't. The president doesn't make the laws. Congress makes the laws.

Washington Monument

EXERCISE ▮19▮ **Two students are comparing teachers. Fill in the blanks to complete this conversation.**

A: Do you ___like___ your English class?
        (example: like)

B: Yes, I _____. I _____ a very good teacher.
            (1)   (2 have)

Her name is Ms. Lopez.

A: _____ Spanish?
        (3)

B: No, she doesn't. She comes from the Philippines.

She _____ English and Tagalog.
      (4 speak)

A: My teacher is very good too. But he _____ fast, and sometimes
                                          (5 talk)

I _____ him. He _____ a lot of homework.
    (6 not/understand)   (7 give)

_____ a lot of homework?
      (8)

B: Yes, she does. And she _____ a test once a week.
                            (9 give)   (continued)

A: My teacher _____ jeans to class. He's very informal.
(10 wear)

_____ jeans to class?
(11)

B: No, she doesn't. She always wears a dress.

A: My teacher always _____ to us about American culture.
(12 talk)

_____ you about American culture?
(13)

B: Yes, she _____. She also teaches us about American government.
(14)

2.9 Comparing *Yes/No* Questions—*Be* and Other Verbs

EXAMPLES		EXPLANATION
Are you lost?	No, I'm not.	Don't use *be* to make a question with a simple present-tense verb.
Do you **need** help?	No, I **don't**.	*Wrong: Are* you need help?
Am I right?	Yes, you **are**.	*Wrong: Am* I have the answer?
Do I **have** the answer?	Yes, you **do**.	*Wrong: Is* he speak French?
Is he from Haiti?	Yes, he **is**.	
Does he **speak** French?	Yes, he **does**.	

EXERCISE **20**   Read each statement. Write a *yes/no* question about the words in parentheses ( ). Then write a short answer.

EXAMPLES   California has a sales tax. (Alaska) (no)

<u>Does Alaska have a sales tax? No, it doesn't.</u>

Washington, D.C., is on the East Coast. (New York) (yes)

<u>Is New York on the East Coast? Yes, it is.</u>

1. Sara works from Monday to Friday. (on the weekend) (no)

_____

2. You are interested in American culture. (American government)

_____

3. The president lives in the White House. (the vice president) (no)

_____

4. The museums are free. (the Metro) (no)

_____

5. Washington has government buildings. (tall buildings) (no)

_____

6. The U.S. doesn't have a national language. (a national religion) (no)

_____

7. Washington, D.C. is in the eastern time zone. (Los Angeles) (no)

_____

8. The Metro runs all day. (after midnight on weeknights) (no)

_____

9. The Metro is clean. (quiet) (yes)

_____

2.10 *Or* Questions

EXAMPLES	EXPLANATION

Do you study English **or** French?
  I study English.
Is Washington, D.C., on the East Coast **or**
the West Coast?
  It's on the East Coast.
	An *or* question gives a choice of answers.

Pronunciation Note: The first part of an *or* question has rising intonation; the second part has falling intonation. Listen to your teacher pronounce the examples above.

EXERCISE **21** **ABOUT YOU** Circle the words that are true for you. Then ask an *or* question. Another student will answer.

EXAMPLE   I drink (coffee / tea) in the morning.

A: I drink coffee in the morning. Do you drink coffee or tea in the morning?
B: I drink coffee too.

1. I speak (*English / my native language*) at home.

2. I prefer (*classical music / popular music*).

3. I'm a (*resident of the U.S. / a visitor*).

4. I'm (*married / single*).

5. I live in (*a house / an apartment / a dormitory*).

6. I write with my (*right hand / left hand*).

7. I'm from (*a big city / a small town*).

8. I prefer (*morning classes / evening classes*).

9. I prefer to (*eat out / eat at home*).

10. English is (*easy / hard*) for me.

11. I live (*with someone / alone*).

The National Museum of the American Indian

Before
You Read

1. Do you like to visit museums?

2. What kind of museums do you like?

CD 1, TR 10

Read the following conversation. Pay special attention to *wh-* questions.

A: **Where do you plan** to go on your next vacation?

B: We want to go to Washington, D.C.

A: **What do you want** to see and do there?

B: We want to visit the government buildings, of course. And the museums. My daughter's very interested in American Indians, so we plan to go to the NMAI.

A: **What does "NMAI" mean?**

B: It's the National Museum of the American Indian.

National Museum of the American Indian, Washington, D.C.

A: **What kind of exhibits do they have** there?

B: Some exhibits show the history of the American Indian. Others show their life and culture. They also have a theater.

A: **What do they show** in the theater?

B: Different things like the storytelling, dance, and music of American Indians. They also have a garden with native American plants, like corn and beans.

A: It sounds like a big museum.

B: It is. It has four levels.

A: Wow! That's big. **How long does it take** to see everything?

B: They recommend that you visit for about two hours.

A: Is the museum new?

B: Yes. It's one of the newest museums. It opened in 2004.

A: **How much does it cost** to enter?

B: Like all the museums in Washington, D.C., it's free.

A: Really? Nothing's free! All the museums in this city charge a lot of money. **Why don't they charge** any money in Washington?

B: We pay with our taxes. And museums have members too.

A: **What do the members do?**

B: Members make contributions to the museum.

A Sioux Indian

2.11 *Wh-* Questions with the Simple Present Tense

EXAMPLES					EXPLANATION
***Wh-* Word**	***Does***	**Subject**	**Verb**	**Complement**	To form a question with *he, she, it, everyone, family,* or a singular subject, use:
What	does	the museum	have?		*Wh-* word + *does* + subject + base form
What	does	the theater	show?		Use the base form after *do* or *does*.
How often	does	the Metro	run	on Saturdays?	*Wrong*: Where does the Metro *goes*?
Where	does	it	go?		
***Wh-* Word**	***Do***	**Subject**	**Verb**	**Complement**	To form a question with *I, you, we, they,* or a plural subject, use:
When	do	you	plan	to go?	*Wh-* word + *do* + subject + base form
Why	do	I	need	a ticket?	
Where	do	we	enter	the museum?	
How much	do	you	need	to pay?	
***Wh-* Word**	***Do/ Does***	**Subject**	**Verb**	**Preposition**	In informal written and spoken English, we usually put the preposition at the end of a *wh-* question.
Where	do	you	come	from?	
Who	does	she	live	with?	
What floor	do	you	live	on?	
Prep.	***Wh-* Word**	***Do/ Does***	**Subject**	**Verb**	In formal written and spoken English, we put the preposition before the question word.
With	whom	does	she	live?	
On	what floor	do	you	live?	

Language Note: We use *whom,* not *who,* after a preposition. We often use *who* when the preposition is at the end of the sentence. Compare:

> **Formal: With whom** do you travel?
> **Informal: Who** do you travel **with**?

EXERCISE 22 **Answer the questions.**

1. Where does the president of the U.S. live?
2. What state does he come from?
3. Why does Washington, D.C. get a lot of visitors?
4. What kind of transportation does Washington, D.C. have?
5. What kinds of museums does Washington, D.C. have?
6. Why don't museums in Washington, D.C. charge money?

2.12 Comparing Statements and Questions with the Simple Present Tense

Affirmative Statements and Questions

Wh- Word	Do/Does	Subject	Verb	Complement	Short Answer
		Sara	works	in Washington.	
	Does	she	work	at the museum?	No, she doesn't.
Where	does	she	work?		
		You	pay	taxes.	
	Do	you	pay	income tax?	Yes, I do.
Why	do	you	pay	taxes?	

Negative Statements and Questions

Wh- Word	Don't/Doesn't	Subject	Verb	Complement
		Museums	don't charge	money.
Why	don't	they	charge	money?
		Sara	doesn't live	in D.C.
Why	doesn't	she	live	in D.C.?

EXERCISE **23** **ABOUT YOU** Ask and answer questions with the words given. First, ask another student a *yes/no* question. Then use the words in parentheses ( ) to ask a *wh-* question, if possible.

EXAMPLE like to travel (why)

A: Do you like to travel?

B: Yes, I do.

A: Why do you like to travel?

B: I like to see new places and learn new things.

1. like museums (what kind)
2. like to learn about American history (why)
3. visit museums in this city (which museums)
4. know a lot about American Indians (which American Indians)
5. plan to take a vacation (where/go)
6. travel with someone (who OR whom/with)

EXERCISE 24 **Read each statement. Write a question with the words in parentheses ( ).**

EXAMPLE The museum has several floors. (how many)
<u>How many floors does it have?</u>

1. It has a garden with native American plants. (what kinds)

   _____

2. We don't have to pay to go into the museum. (why)

   _____

3. They have programs in the theater. (what kinds of programs)

   _____

4. The museum opens at 9 A.M. (what time/close)

   _____

5. The U.S. doesn't have an official language. (why)

   _____

EXERCISE 25 **Fill in the blanks to complete the conversation.**

CD 1, TR 11

A: Let's do something fun this weekend.

B: What _____<u>do you want to</u>_____ do?

       (example)

A: I want to go to a museum.

B: I don't like museums.

A: Really? Why _____ museums?

                    (1)

B: They're boring.

A: No, they're not. You learn a lot when you go to a museum. Come on. Let's go.

B: Which museum _____ visit?

                         (2)

A: How about the history museum? It's free on Fridays.

B: I don't like history.

A: Why _____?

                (3)

B: History is just a bunch of facts and dates.

A: No, it's not. History is a very interesting story. It's a true story.

B: I prefer to go to the movies.

A: Come with me to the museum. Please?

B: What _____ this museum _____?
(4)   (5)

A: It has exhibits about American life in the past.

B: What time _____?
(6)

A: The museum closes at 5 P.M.

B: OK. Let's go at 4 P.M., and then we can go to a movie, okay? I

have a good one in mind.

A: What time _____?
(7)

B: It starts at 6:10. We can leave the museum, get something to eat,

and then see the movie.

A: Fine.

2.13 Questions About Meaning, Spelling, Cost, and Time

Wh- Word	Do/Does	Subject	Verb	Complement	Explanation
What	does	"D.C."	mean?		*Mean, spell, say,* and *cost* are verbs and should be in the verb position of a question.
How	do	you	spell	"government"?	
How	do	you	say	"government" in your language?	
How much	does	a Metro ticket	cost?		
How long	does	it	take	to see the museum?	We use the verb *take* with time. The subject is *it*.

EXERCISE 26 **Read each statement. Then write a question beginning with the words given.**

EXAMPLE The museum isn't free. How much _____**does it cost**_____ to enter?

1. It takes a long time to see everything in the museum. How long

_____?

2. The spelling of "government" is difficult. How _____
"government"?

3. IRS means "Internal Revenue Service." What _____
"D.C." _____?

4. In English, we say "museum." In Spanish, we say "*museo.*" How

_____ "museum" in your language?

EXERCISE 27 **Fill in the blanks in the conversation below with the missing words.**

A: What 's _____ your name?
(example)

B: My name is Martha Gomez.

A: How _____ spell "Gomez"?
(1)

B: G-O-M-E-Z. It's a Spanish name.

A: Are you _____ Spain?
(2)

B: No, I'm _____.
(3)

A: What country _____ you come _____?
(4)   (5)

B: I come from Guatemala.

A: What language _____ they _____ in Guatemala?
(6)   (7)

B: They speak Spanish in Guatemala.

A: _____ your family here?
(8)

B: No. My family is still in Guatemala. I call them once a week.

A: Isn't that expensive?

B: No, it _____. I use a phone card.
(9)

A: How much _____ cost?
(10)

B: It _____ five dollars. We can talk for 35 minutes. I like
(11)
to say hello to my family every week.

A: How _____ "hello" in Spanish?
(12)

B: We say "*hola*." Please excuse me now. I'm late for my class. *Hasta luego.*

A: What _____ "*hasta luego*" _____?
(13)   (14)

B: It means "see you later" in Spanish.

2.14 Comparing *Wh-* Questions—*Be* and Other Verbs

EXAMPLES	EXPLANATION

Where **is** the museum?
 How many floors **does** it **have**?
 What **do** you **want** to see?
 What **are** you interested in?
 When **is** the museum free?
 How much **does** it **cost** to enter?
	Don't forget to use *do* or *does* in a question with a simple present-tense verb.
	    Wrong: How many floors it has?
	    Wrong: What you want to see?
	 Don't use *be* to form a simple present-tense question.
	    Wrong: How much is it costs?

EXERCISE 28   **Read this conversation between two students. Fill in the blanks with the missing words.**

CD 1, TR 12

A: Are these your children?

B: Yes, they are.

A: How old _____are they_____?
                     (example)

B: Jessica's 23 and Brian's 29.

A: Do they live with you?

B: Oh, no. Jessica lives in New York, and

    Brian lives in Washington, D.C.

A: _____ for the government?
             (1)

B: Yes, he does. He works at the IRS.

A: What _____ at the IRS?
              (2)

B: He audits people's taxes.

A: What _____ "audit" _____?
          (3)   *(4)*

B: It means he checks to see if people pay all their taxes.

A: _____ in D.C.?
         (5)

B: No, he doesn't. He takes the Metro into D.C. every day.

A: Where _____?
           (6)

B: He lives in Maryland with his wife. I plan to visit them next month.

A: How long _____ to fly from here to D.C.?
                (7)

B: It only takes an hour and a half. But I plan to drive there. It takes about

    five hours from here.

                                             (continued)

A: You know, my niece lives in Maryland, too.

B: Where _____ in Maryland?

(8)

A: She lives in Fallston.

B: I don't know that city. How _____?

(9)

A: F-A-L-L-S-T-O-N.

B: What _____ do? _____ for the

(10) (11)

government?

A: No. She's a teacher in Fallston.

B: I'm late for an appointment. *Ciao.*

A: What _____?

(12)

B: It means "good-bye" in Italian. How _____ "good-bye"

(13)

in Spanish?

A: We say "*hasta luego.*"

Summary of Lesson 2

1. The simple present tense has two forms: the base form and the *-s* form:

Base Form		-s Form	
I You We They (Plural noun)	eat.	Everyone He She It (Singular noun)	eats.

2. Simple present-tense patterns with the *-s* form:

AFFIRMATIVE:	The president **lives** in Washington, D.C.
NEGATIVE:	He **doesn't live** in New York.
YES/NO QUESTION:	**Does** he **live** in the White House?
SHORT ANSWER:	Yes, he **does**.
WH- QUESTION:	Where **does** the vice president **live**?
NEGATIVE QUESTION:	Why **doesn't** the vice president **live** in the White House?

3. Simple present-tense patterns with the base form:

AFFIRMATIVE:	We **study** English in class.
NEGATIVE:	We **don't study** American history in class.
YES/NO QUESTION:	**Do** we **study** grammar?
SHORT ANSWER:	Yes, we **do**.
WH- QUESTION:	Why **do** we **study** grammar?
NEGATIVE QUESTION:	Why **don't** we **study** history?

4. Present-tense patterns with the verb *be*:

AFFIRMATIVE:	The teacher **is** absent.
NEGATIVE:	She **isn't** here today.
YES/NO QUESTION:	**Is** she sick?
SHORT ANSWER:	No, she **isn't**.
WH- QUESTION:	Where **is** she?
NEGATIVE QUESTION:	Why **isn't** she here?

5. We use the simple present tense with:

General truths and facts	Washington, D.C., **has** over half a million people. Americans **speak** English.
Customs	Japanese people **take** off their shoes when they enter a house. Americans **don't visit** friends without an invitation.
Regular activities (*more on this use in Lesson 3*)	He **visits** his parents every summer. I **play** soccer once a week.

Editing Advice

1. Don't forget to use the -s form when the subject is *he, she, it,* or a singular noun.

He need⟨s⟩ more money.

This school ~~have~~ ⟨has⟩ a big library.

2. Use the base form after *does* and *doesn't*.

My father doesn't ~~has~~ ⟨have⟩ a car.

Does your mother speaks English well?

3. Don't forget *do/does* in a question.

Where ⟨do⟩ your parents live? Where ⟨does⟩ your mother work?

4. Use the correct word order in a question.

your brother live
Where does ~~live your brother~~?

does your father have
What kind of car ~~has your father~~?

don't you
Why ~~you don't~~ like pizza?

5. Don't use *be* with another verb to form the simple present tense.

I
~~I'm~~ have three brothers.

She's lives in New York.

I don't
~~I'm not~~ have a car.

6. Don't use *be* in a simple present-tense question that uses another verb.

Does
~~Is~~ your college have a computer lab?

Do
~~Are~~ you speak French?

7. Use the correct spelling for the *-s* form.

studies
She ~~studys~~ in the library.

watches
He ~~watchs~~ TV every evening.

8. Use the correct negative form.

doesn't
He ~~not~~ know the answer.

don't
They ~~no~~ speak English.

9. Don't use an *-ing* form for the simple present tense.

write
I ~~writing~~ a letter to my family once a week.

10. *Family* is a singular word. Use the *-s* form.

s
My family live in Germany.

11. Use the same auxiliary verb in a short answer as in a *yes/no* question.

am
Are you hungry? Yes, I ~~do~~.

do
Do you like baseball? Yes, I ~~am~~.

12. Use correct question formation for meaning, spelling, cost, and time.

does "wonderful" mean
What ~~means "wonderful"~~?

do bananas cost
How much ~~cost bananas~~ this week?

do you
How ⌃spell "opportunity"?

do you
How ⌃say "opportunity" in your language?

does
How long ⌃it takes to finish this lesson?

Editing Quiz

PART A **Some of the shaded words and phrases have mistakes. Find the mistakes and correct them. If the shaded words are correct, write C.**

I live   *C*
~~I'm live~~ in Chicago. Chicago has many tourist attractions. My family
(example)   *(example)*

like to go to the zoo in the summer. We going there at least three times every
(1)   *(2)*

summer. The zoo have all kinds of animals, but it doesn't has any elephants.
(3)   *(4)*

I don't know why. My daughter really like the monkeys. She watchs them very
(5)   *(6)*   *(7)*

carefully. But she doesn't likes the reptiles. She's afraid of snakes. She crys when
(8)   *(9)*

we want to see the snakes. We not want to make her unhappy so we don't go
(10)   *(11)*

there anymore. She's likes the giraffes too. They eating from tall trees. A trip to
(12)   *(13)*

the zoo is a very enjoyable time for my family.

do
PART B **A:** Where ⌃you live? You live near the college?
(example)   *(1)*

B: I live on the north side of town.

A: How long it takes you to get to school?
(2)

B: It takes me about half an hour.

A: How you get to school?
(3)

B: I take the bus, but I need a transfer.

A: What means "transfer"?
  (4)

B: It's a paper I use to change buses.

A: How much costs the transfer?
  (5)

B: It costs 25 cents extra.

A: I have a car, but I walk to school. It's about two miles.

B: Why you don't drive to school?
  (6)

A: Parking is expensive. And there's a lot of traffic.

B: How much costs parking at school?
  (7)

A: It's $100 per semester. It's easier to take the bus. I come with my friend.

B: Where your friend lives? Does he lives with you?
  (8)   (9)

A: No, he isn't. He lives in the same building, but in a different apartment.
  (10)

B: What's your friend's name? Do I know him?
  (11)

A: His name is Dmitry.

B: How spell Dmitry?
  (12)

A: D-M-I-T-R-Y. I don't think you know him. He's from Russia, like me.

B: How say "see you later" in Russian?
  (13)

A: We say "*da svidanya.*"

B: That's hard. I'll just say "see you later."

Lesson 2 Test/Review

PART 1 Write the -s form of the following verbs. Use correct spelling.

EXAMPLE take ___*takes*___

1. go _____

2. carry _____

3. mix _____

4. drink _____

5. play _____

6. study _____

7. catch _____

8. say _____

PART **2** **Fill in the first blank with the affirmative form of the verb in parentheses ( ). Then write the negative form of this verb.**

EXAMPLES   A monkey _____lives_____ in a warm climate.
            (live)

It _____doesn't live_____ in a cold climate.

Brazil ____is____ a big country.
       (be)

Haiti _____isn't_____ a big country.

1. The English language _____ the Roman alphabet.
                          (use)

   The Chinese language _____ the Roman alphabet.

2. We _____ English in class.
      (speak)

   We _____ our native languages in class.

3. March _____ 31 days.
         (have)

   February _____ 31 days.

4. Mexico and Canada _____ in North America.
                     (be)

   Colombia and Ecuador _____ in North America.

5. You _____ the "k" in "bank."
       (pronounce)

   You _____ the "k" in "knife."

6. The teacher _____ the English language.
               (teach)

   He/She _____ American history.

7. A green light _____ "go."
                 (mean)

   A yellow light _____ "go."

8. I _____ from another country.
     (come)

   I _____ from the U.S.

9. English _____ hard for me.
           (be)

   My language _____ hard for me.

The Simple Present Tense   **69**

PART 3   Write a *yes/no* question about the words in parentheses ( ).
Then write a short answer.

EXAMPLE   China is in Asia. (Korea) (yes)

Is Korea in Asia? Yes, it is.

1. The U.S. has 50 states. (Mexico) (no)

_____

2. The post office sells stamps. (the bank) (no)

_____

3. San Francisco is in California. (Los Angeles) (yes)

_____

4. Americans pay sales tax. (income tax) (yes)

_____

5. January and March have 31 days. (April and June) (no)

_____

6. Senators work on Capitol Hill. (the president) (no)

_____

7. Americans speak English. (Canadians) (yes)

_____

8. We come to class on time. (the teacher) (yes)

_____

PART 4   Read each statement. Then write a *wh-* question about the words in
parentheses ( ). You don't need to answer the question.

EXAMPLES   February has 28 days. (March)

How many days does March have?

Mexico is in North America. (Venezuela)

Where is Venezuela?

1. Mexicans speak Spanish. (Canadians)

_____

2. Washington, D.C. has one zoo. (museums)

_____

3. The president meets with foreign leaders. (how often)

_____

4. Thanksgiving is in November. (Christmas)

_____

5. You spell "occasion" O-C-C-A-S-I-O-N. ("tomorrow")

_____

6. "Occupation" means job or profession. ("occasion")

_____

7. The president doesn't make the laws. (why)

_____

8. Marek comes from Poland. (you)

_____

PART 5 **Read this interview. Fill in the blanks with the missing word(s).**

A: How old _____**are you**_____?
                        (example)

B: I'm 30 years old.

A: _____ married?
            _(1)_
B: No I'm single.

A: _____ with your parents?
            _(2)_
B: No, I don't live with my parents.

A: Why _____ with your parents?
                _(3)_
B: I don't live with my parents because they live in another city.

A: Where _____?
                _(4)_
B: They live in Chicago.

A: _____ you _____ Washington?
        _(5)_   _(6)_
B: Yes, I like it very much.

A: Why _____ Washington?
                _(7)_
B: I like it because it has so many interesting museums and galleries. But I
       don't have time to visit these places very often. I work every day. When
       my parents visit, we go to galleries and museums.

A: When _____?
                _(8)_
B: They visit me in the spring. They love Washington.

(continued)

A: Why _____ Washington?
      (9)

B: They love it because it's a beautiful, interesting city. And they love it because I'm here.

A: What kind of job _____?
      (10)

B: I have a job with the government. I work in the Department of Commerce.

A: What _____?
      (11)

B: Commerce means "business."

A: How _____?
      (12)

B: C-O-M-M-E-R-C-E.

A: _____ your job?
      (13)

B: Yes, I like my job very much.

A: _____?
      (14)

B: I live a few blocks from the White House.

A: _____ have a car?
      (15)

B: No, I don't. I don't need a car.

A: How _____ to work?
      (16)

B: I go to work by Metro. If I'm late, I take a taxi.

A: How much _____?
      (17)

B: A taxi ride from my house to work costs about $12.

A: _____ clean?
      (18)

B: Oh, yes. The Metro is very clean.

A: _____ all night?
      (19)

B: No, the trains don't run all night. They run until midnight.

A: In my city, we don't say "the metro." We use a different word.

B: What _____ in your city?
      (20)

A: We say "subway."

Expansion

Classroom Activities

❶ Check (✓) all the items below that are true for you. Find a partner and compare your list to your partner's list. Write three sentences telling about differences between you and your partner. You may read your list to the class.

a. _____ I have a cell phone.

b. _____ I own a home.

c. _____ I live in an apartment.

d. _____ I exercise regularly.

e. _____ I'm a vegetarian.

f. _____ I live with my parents.

g. _____ I play a musical instrument.

h. _____ I sing well.

i. _____ I'm a good driver.

j. _____ I like pizza.

k. _____ I use an electronic calendar.

l. _____ I write with my left hand.

❷ Game: One student thinks of the name of a famous person and writes this person's initials on the board. Other students ask questions and try to guess the name of this person.

SAMPLE QUESTIONS

Is he an athlete?
Where does he come from?

Is he tall?
How old is he?

❸ Game: One student comes to the front of the room. He or she thinks of an animal and writes the name of this animal on a piece of paper. The other students try to guess which animal it is by asking questions. The person who guesses the animal is the next to come to the front of the room.

EXAMPLE

lion
Does this animal fly? No, it doesn't.
Does it live in water? No, it doesn't.
What does it eat? It eats meat.
Does this animal live in Africa? Yes, it does.

❹ In a small group, discuss differences between classes and teachers in this school and another school that you know about.

EXAMPLES

In my college back home, students stand up when they speak.
This class has some older people. In my native country, only young people study at college.

Talk

About It

1 Talk about taxes. What kind of taxes do we pay? What do we get for our tax money?

2 Talk about the public transportation in this city. Do you think it's good?

3 Talk about the language(s) in your native country. Does your country have an official national language? Does everyone speak that language?

4 Talk about elections in your native country. Does your country have free elections? Does everyone vote?

Write

About It

Write about a tourist attraction in your country (or in another country you know something about).

EXAMPLE

The Hermitage Museum

The Hermitage is a popular tourist attraction in my country, Russia. It is a big museum in St. Petersburg. It has art from all over the world. Many people visit this museum . . .

 For more practice using grammar in context, please visit our Web site.

Grammar
Frequency Words with the Simple Present Tense

Prepositions of Time

Context
American Holidays

Three Special Days in the United States

Before
You Read

1. What is your favorite holiday? When is it?

2. Do you celebrate Mother's Day? When?

3. Do you send cards for special occasions?

CD 1, TR 13

Read the following Web article. Pay special attention to the frequency words.

http://www.website*reading.com

Did You **Know?**

Some people believe that Valentine's Day began in ancient Rome to honor Juno, the Roman goddess of women and marriage.

Valentine's Day is a day of love. It is **always** on February 14. On this day, people **often** give flowers or candy to their spouses or sweethearts. Candy manufacturers make candy or candy boxes in the shape of a heart. People **sometimes** send cards, called valentines, to close friends and relatives. Red is the color associated with Valentine's Day. A valentine **usually** has a red heart and a message of love. It **often** has a picture of Cupid, a symbol of romantic love. Florists sell a lot of red roses on Valentine's Day. Young children **usually** have a party at school and exchange cards.

Another special day is Saint Patrick's Day. It is **always** on March 17. It is really an Irish holiday, but many Americans like St. Patrick's Day even if they are not Irish. We **sometimes** say that on St. Patrick's Day, everybody is Irish. In New York City, there is **always** a parade on St. Patrick's Day. Green is the color associated with St. Patrick's Day. People **often** wear green clothes on this day. One symbol of St. Patrick's Day is the shamrock.

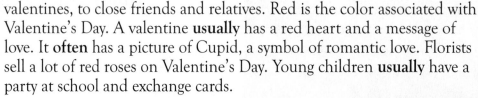

Businesses are **never** closed for Valentine's Day or St. Patrick's Day. People **never** take a day off from work for these days. Schools and government offices are **always** open (except if these days fall on a Sunday).

Another special day is Mother's Day. It is **always** in May, but it isn't **always** on the same date. It is **always** on the second Sunday in May. People **usually** buy presents for their mothers and grandmothers or send special cards. Families **often** have dinner in a restaurant. Florists sell a lot of flowers on Mother's Day.

People enjoy these holidays. Greeting card companies also enjoy these holidays. They **always** sell a lot of cards and make a lot of money at these times.

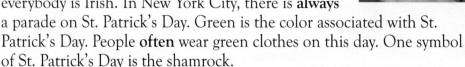

3.1 Frequency Words with the Simple Present Tense

FREQUENCY WORD	FREQUENCY	EXAMPLES
Always	100%	Mother's Day is **always** in May.
Usually	↑	I **usually** take my mother out to dinner.
Often		People **often** wear green on St. Patrick's Day.
Sometimes		I **sometimes** watch the parade.
Rarely/Seldom	↓	We **rarely** give flowers to children.
Never	0%	Businesses are **never** closed for Valentine's Day.

EXERCISE 1   Choose the correct word to fill in the blanks.

EXAMPLE   People _____*often*_____ give flowers or candy on Valentine's Day.
(never/seldom/often)

1. Valentine's Day is _____ on February 14.
(always/sometimes/never)

2. People _____ send valentine cards to their sweethearts.
(rarely/often/never)

3. A valentine card _____ has a red heart and a
(never/rarely/usually)

   message of love.

4. Young children _____ have a
(usually/always/never)

   Valentine's Day party at school.

5. Saint Patrick's Day is _____ on
(always/sometimes/never)

   March 17.

6. A St. Patrick's Day card _____
(always/usually/never)

   has a red heart.

St. Patrick's Day Parade

7. In New York City, there is _____
(always/seldom/never)

   a parade on Saint Patrick's Day.

8. Card companies _____ do a lot of business before
(never/always/seldom)

   holidays.

9. Businesses are _____ closed for St. Patrick's Day.
(always/usually/never)

10. Mother's Day is _____ on a Saturday in the U.S.
(always/never/sometimes)

EXERCISE 2 **Fill in the blank with an appropriate frequency word about this class or this school.**

EXAMPLE   We _____*sometimes*_____ use a dictionary in class.

1. The teacher _____ wears a suit to class.

2. The school is _____ closed on Labor Day.

3. The students _____ ask questions in class.

4. The windows of the classrooms are _____ open.

5. The students _____ talk to each other during a test.

6. The door of the classroom is _____ open.

7. We _____ write a composition in class.

8. The teacher _____ writes on the board.

9. The students _____ write on the board.

10. The students _____ stand up when the teacher enters the room.

3.2 Position of Frequency Words and Expressions

EXAMPLES	EXPLANATION
Businesses *are* **never** closed for St. Patrick's Day. Mother's Day *is* **always** in May.	The frequency word comes after the verb *be*.
I **usually** *buy* a card for my mother. I **sometimes** *wear* green on St. Patrick's Day.	The frequency word comes before other verbs.
Sometimes I take my mother to a restaurant. **Usually** the weather is nice in May. **Often** we give gifts.	*Sometimes*, *usually*, and *often* can come at the beginning of the sentence too.

EXERCISE 3   **ABOUT YOU** **Add a frequency word to each sentence to make a true statement about yourself.**

EXAMPLE   I eat fish.
I usually eat fish on Fridays.

1. I cook the meals in my house.

2. I stay home on Sundays.

3. I buy the Sunday newspaper.

4. I read the newspaper in English.

5. I use public transportation.

6. I'm tired in class.

7. I use my dictionary to check my spelling.

8. I buy greeting cards.

EXERCISE **4** **Add a verb phrase to make a true statement about people from your country or cultural group.**

EXAMPLE people / often
Russian people often go to the forest on the weekends to pick berries.

1. people / often

_____

2. people / seldom

_____

3. women / usually

_____

4. women / rarely

_____

5. men / usually

_____

6. men / rarely

_____

EXERCISE **5** **ABOUT YOU** Add a verb phrase to make a true statement about yourself.

EXAMPLE   I / never

I never go to bed after 11 o'clock.

OR

I'm never in a good mood in the morning.

1. I / never

_____

2. I / always / in the morning

_____

3. I / usually / on Sunday

_____

4. I / often / on the weekend

_____

5. I / sometimes / in class

_____

EXERCISE **6** **Use the words below to make sentences.**

EXAMPLE   Americans / often

Americans often send greeting cards on holidays.

1. American doctors / rarely

_____

2. American teachers / sometimes

_____

3. students at this school / often

_____

4. this classroom / never

_____

5. American hospitals / always

_____

6. American children / often

_____

The Fourth of July

1. Do you like to see fireworks?

2. Do you celebrate any American holidays? What's your favorite American holiday?

CD 1, TR 14

Read the following student composition. Pay special attention to prepositions of time.

My Favorite American Holiday

My favorite holiday in the U.S. is American Independence Day. We celebrate it **on** July 4. In fact, we often call this holiday "the Fourth of July."

In the morning, my family and I prepare hamburgers for a barbecue. Our guests arrive **in** the afternoon, and we cook hamburgers and hot dogs on the grill in the backyard. We usually start to eat **at** about three o'clock. We have a lot of barbecues **in** the summer, but my favorite is **on** the Fourth of July.

We usually stay in our yard **from** about two o'clock **to** six o'clock. Then, **in** the evening, we usually go to the park. Most of our town goes there too, so we visit with each other while we wait for the fireworks. Finally, **at** night when it's completely dark, the fireworks show begins.

This is an exciting time for all of us. We celebrate our nation's independence, and we have a lot of fun.

3.3 Prepositions of Time

PREPOSITION	EXAMPLES	EXPLANATION
in	We prepare for the barbecue **in the morning.** We eat **in the afternoon.** We go to the park **in the evening.**	Use *in* with morning, afternoon, and evening.
in	Americans elect a president every four years: **in 2012, 2016, 2020,** and so on.	Use *in* with years.
in	We often have a barbecue **in the summer.** It's too cold to have a barbecue **in the winter.**	Use *in* with seasons: summer, fall, winter, spring.
in	We celebrate Independence Day **in July.** We celebrate Mother's Day **in May.**	Use *in* with months.
on	We celebrate Independence Day **on July 4.** This year the holiday is **on a Tuesday.**	Use *on* with dates and days.
at	We start to eat **at 3 o'clock.** We start the grill **at noon.** We go to bed **at midnight.**	Use *at* with a specific time of day.
at	The fireworks show starts **at night.**	Use *at* with night.
from . . . to from . . . till from . . . until	We stay in the backyard **from 2 to 6 o'clock.** The fireworks show lasts **from 9 till 10.** We stay there **from 6 until midnight.**	Use *from . . . to* or *till* or *until* with a beginning and an ending time.

EXERCISE **7** **ABOUT YOU** **Answer these questions. Use the correct preposition.**

1. What time do you get up in the morning?

2. What time do you go to bed at night?

3. What time does your English class begin?

4. What days does your English class meet?

5. What time do you get to school?

6. When do students have vacation?

7. When do you do your homework?

8. What hours do you go to school?

9. When is your birthday?

3.4 Questions with *Ever*

We use *ever* in a question when we want an answer that has a frequency word.

Do/Does	Subject	*Ever*	Verb	Complement	Short Answer
Do	you	**ever**	cook	outside?	Yes, we **sometimes** do.
Does	your brother	**ever**	work	on a holiday?	Yes, he **often** does.

Be	Subject	*Ever*	Complement	Short Answer
Are	the stores	**ever**	open on a holiday?	Yes, they **sometimes** are.
Is	the park	**ever**	crowded on the Fourth of July?	Yes, it **always** is.

Language Notes:
1. In a short answer, the frequency word comes between the subject and the verb.
2. If the frequency word is *never*, don't use a negative verb.

      Is the school **ever** open on the Fourth of July?
           No, it **never** is.
      Do you **ever** eat hot dogs?
           No, I **never** do.

EXERCISE **8** **ABOUT YOU** Add *ever* to ask these questions. Another student will answer.

EXAMPLES Do you eat in a restaurant?

A: Do you ever eat in a restaurant?
B: Yes, I often do.

Are you bored in class?

A: Are you ever bored in class?
B: No, I never am.

1. Do you use public transportation?
2. Do you drink coffee at night?
3. Do you drink tea in the morning?
4. Do you speak English at home?
5. Do you watch TV at night?
6. Do you rent DVDs?
7. Are you late to class?
8. Do you drive and use your cell phone at the same time?
9. Are you homesick?
10. Are you lazy on Saturdays?
11. Does it snow in March?
12. Do you ask for directions on the street?

EXERCISE **9**   **Add *ever* to these questions to ask about Americans. Another student will answer.**

EXAMPLES   Do Americans eat fast food?

A: Do Americans ever eat fast food?
B: Yes, they sometimes do.

Are Americans friendly to you?

A: Are Americans ever friendly to you?
B: Yes, they usually are.

1. Do Americans eat with chopsticks?

2. Are American drivers rude?

3. Do Americans say, "Have a nice day"?

4. Do Americans kiss when they meet?

5. Do Americans pronounce your name incorrectly?

6. Are Americans impolite to you?

7. Do Americans shake hands when they meet?

8. Do Americans ask you what country you're from?

9. Are Americans curious about your native country?

EXERCISE **10**   **ABOUT YOU** **Fill in the blanks with a frequency word to make a statement about yourself. Then ask a question with *ever*. Another student will answer.**

EXAMPLE   I ____*never*____ jog in the morning.

A: Do you ever jog in the morning?
B: No, I never do.

1. I _____ ride a bike in the summer.

2. I _____ visit relatives on Sunday.

3. I _____ go to sleep before 9 p.m.

4. I _____ eat meat.

5. I _____ take a nap in the afternoon.

6. I _____ eat in a restaurant.

7. I _____ use cologne or perfume.

8. I _____ check my e-mail in the morning.

9. I _____ borrow money from a friend.

10. I _____ leave a light on when I sleep.

11. I _____ buy the newspaper.

3.5 Questions with *How Often* and Answers with Frequency Expressions

We ask a question with *how often* when we want to know the frequency of an activity.

EXAMPLES	EXPLANATION

How often do you eat hamburgers?
    Once in a while.
How often do you go to the park?
    Every week.
How often does the park have fireworks?
    Once a year.
	Expressions that show frequency are:
	• every day, week, month, year
	• every other day, week, month, year
	• from time to time
	• once in a while

I learn more about life in America **every day**. **Every day** I learn more about life in America. **From time to time**, I eat hamburgers. I eat hamburgers **from time to time**.	Frequency expressions can come at the beginning or the end of the sentence.

EXERCISE **11** **ABOUT YOU** Ask a question with "How often do you . . . ?" and the words given. Another student will answer.

EXAMPLE   get a haircut

    A: How often do you get a haircut?
    B: I get a haircut every other month.

1. come to class
2. shop for groceries
3. wash your clothes
4. use your cell phone
5. go out to dinner
6. use public transportation
7. use your dictionary
8. buy the newspaper
9. go to the movies
10. check your e-mail

EXERCISE 12 Linda has a list to remind her of the things she has to do on a regular basis. Write questions and answers about her activities.

- drive daughter to ballet lessons—Tu, Th
- pick up son at baseball practice—Mon, Wed
- shop for groceries—Sat
- take the dog for a haircut—3rd day of every month
- go to the beauty salon—5th day of every month
- visit Mom—Fri
- go to the gym—Mon, Wed, Fri morning
- prepare the kids' lunches—Mon to Fri
- change the oil in the car—Jan, April, July, Oct

EXAMPLE How often does she drive her daughter to ballet lessons?

She drives her daughter to ballet lessons twice a week.

1. _____
   _____

2. _____
   _____

3. _____
   _____

4. _____
   _____

5. _____
   _____

6. _____
   _____

7. _____
   _____

8. _____
   _____

EXERCISE 13 **ABOUT YOU** Write a few sentences about a member of your family or another person you know. Use frequency words.

EXAMPLE   My sister never helps with the housework.

She sometimes leaves dirty dishes in the sink.

She always gets good grades.

_____

_____

_____

_____

EXERCISE 14 Use the words in parentheses ( ) to complete this conversation. Put the words in the correct order. Use the correct form of the verb.

CD 1, TR 15

A: Let's go to a movie tonight.

B: I can't. My mother ____**always makes**____ dinner for me on Fridays.

(example: make/always)

If I don't visit her, she _____. And if I don't call her,

(1 complain/usually)

she worries.

A: _____ her?

(2 do/how/often/you/call)

B: _____.

(3 I/every day/call her)

A: Why do you call her so often?

B: She's old now, and she _____ lonely.

(4 often/be)

A: Well, invite your mother to go to the movies.

B: Thanks, but she has a favorite TV show on Friday

nights. She _____ it.

(5 watch/always)

A: _____ go out?

(6 do/ever/she)

B: She _____. She prefers to stay home.

(7 rarely/do)
She likes to cook, knit, and watch TV.

A: Is she a good cook?

B: Not really. She _____ the same

(8 usually/cook)

thing every week: chicken on Friday, fish on Saturday,

meatloaf on Sunday . . . Her routine _____.

(9 change/never)

Only Mother's Day is different.

(continued)

A: What _____ on Mother's Day?
(10 you/do/usually)

B: My sister and I _____ her flowers and take her to a
(11 usually/buy)

restaurant.

A: Does she like that?

B: Not really. She _____, "Don't waste your money.
(12 usually/say)

Flowers _____ in a day or two. And my cooking is
(13 die/always)

better than restaurant food."

A: _____ hard to please?
(14 be/she/always)

B: Yes, she is.

A: _____ satisfied?
(15 be/she/ever)

B: Not usually. She _____, "I don't want Mother's Day
(16 always/say)

once a year. I want it every day."

EXERCISE 15 **A student wrote a composition about the Fourth of July. The teacher underlined the student's mistakes. Correct these mistakes.**

My favorite holiday in the U.S. is the Fourth of July. My

           always puts
family ~~puts always~~ an American flag in front of the house.
     (example)

Always my friends and I get together for a barbecue. We cook usually
        (1)   (2)

hamburgers and hot dogs on the grill. Sometimes we cook fried chicken

and steaks. The men in the family usually cooking. (Rarely they cook
                           (3)   (4)

the rest of the year!) We usually have the barbecue at my house, but

sometimes we're have the barbecue in a park. We always has a wonderful
        (5)   (6)

dinner; everyone brings a different dish. My mother always bake a
                                     (7)

delicious apple pie.

Our city always has a parade at the Fourth of July from noon at
                        (8)   (9)

one o'clock. In the night, we usually go to see the fireworks at the main
        (10)

park. The park always is crowded. The weather is usually nice, but it's
          (11)   (12)

sometimes rains and the fireworks show is canceled. When that happen, we are very disappointed. Luckily, that seldom happens.

Most businesses and schools is closed on the Fourth of July. The library, banks, and offices always are closed. I'm never work on this holiday, but my brother is a police officer and he sometimes work on the Fourth of July. Some businesses, such as supermarkets, stays open for half the day. People often forgets to buy something and need to get some last-minute items.

I always look forward to this holiday because I see all my family and we has a lot of fun together. Also my birthday is on July and I get a lot of presents.

Summary of Lesson 3

1. Frequency Words:

Most Frequent	always	100%
	usually	
	often	
	sometimes	
	rarely/seldom	
Least Frequent	never	0%

2. The Position of Frequency Words:

AFTER THE VERB *BE*: He is **always** late.

BEFORE A MAIN VERB: I **usually** walk to work.

3. The Position of Frequency Expressions:
> **Every day** I watch TV.
> I watch TV **every day**.

4. Frequency Questions and Answers:
> Do you **ever** wear a suit? I **seldom** do.
> Are you **ever** bored in class? Yes, I **sometimes** am.
> **How often** do you go to the library? About **once a month**.

5. Review prepositions of time on page 82. Review the simple present tense in Lessons 1 and 2.

Editing Advice

1. Put the frequency word in the correct place.

> *am never*
> I ~~never am~~ bored in class.

> *I always*
> ~~Always I~~ drink coffee in the morning.

2. Don't separate the subject and the verb with a frequency phrase.

> *once in a while*
> She ~~once in a while~~ visits her grandmother.

> *Every other day we*
> ~~We every other day~~ write a composition.

3. Don't use a negative verb with *never*.

> *do*
> Do you ever take the bus to school? No, I never ~~don't~~.

> We never ~~don't~~ eat in class.

4. Use *ever* in questions. Answer the question with a frequency word.

> *sometimes*
> Do you ever listen to the radio in the morning? Yes, I ~~ever~~ do.

Editing Quiz

Some of the shaded words and phrases have mistakes. Find the mistakes and correct them. If the shaded words are correct, write C.

I'm not married and I don't have a boyfriend, but ~~I'm always celebrate~~ *I always celebrate*
                                                                        (example)

Valentine's Day. It's always a special day for me: a day of friendship.
        C
        (example)

I never don't buy cards. I usually make my own cards. I'm never mail the
    (1)   (2)   (3)

cards. Always I visit my friends and give them my cards personally. It's
        (4)

important to tell friends that we love them. What often do you tell
                                                (5)

your friends that you love them? Do you once in a while tell them?
                                    (6)

Do you tell them every day? Probably not. Once a year, it's a good idea
(7)   (8)

to tell them. Do you think ever about this? I always am.
              (9)   (10)

Lesson 3 Test/Review

PART 1 **This is a conversation between two students. Fill in the blanks to complete the conversation.**

A: Who ___*is*___ your English teacher?
                (example)

B: His name _____ David.
                    (1)

A: _____ David?
          (2)

B: Yes. I like him very much.

A: _____ he wear a suit to class?
          (3)

B: No, he _____. He always _____ jeans and running shoes.
              (4)   (5)

A: _____ ?
          (6)

B: He _____ about 60 years old.
          (7)

(continued)

A: _____ your language?
(8)

B: No. He doesn't speak Spanish. But he _____ Polish and Russian.
(9)
And English, of course.

A: _____ often does your class meet?
(10)

B: It meets three days a week: Monday, Wednesday, and Friday.

A: My class _____ two days a week: Tuesday and Thursday.
(11)

B: Tell me about your English teacher.

A: Her name _____ Dr. Misko. She never _____ jeans to class.
(12)   (13)
She _____ wears a dress or suit. She _____ my
(14)   (15)
language. She only _____ English.
(16)

B: Do you like her?

A: Yes, but she _____ a lot of homework and tests.
(17)

B: _____ does she give a test?
(18)

A: Once a week. She gives a test every Friday. I _____ like tests.
(19)

B: My teacher sometimes teaches us American songs. _____ your
(20)
teacher _____ _____ you American songs?
(21)   (22)

A: No, she never _____.
(23)

B: What book _____ ?
(24)

A: My class uses *Grammar in Context*.

B: What _____ ?
(25)

A: "Context" means the words that help you understand a new word or idea.

B: How _____ ?
(26)

A: C-O-N-T-E-X-T.

PART **2** **Fill in the blanks with the correct preposition.**

EXAMPLE Many people go to church ___*on*___ Sundays.

1. We have classes _____ the evening.

2. Valentine's Day is _____ February.

3. Valentine's Day is _____ February 14.

4. A news program begins _____ 6 o'clock.

5. I watch TV _____ night.

6. We have vacation _____ the summer.

7. Many Americans work _____ 9 _____ 5 o'clock.

8. I drink coffee _____ the morning.

9. I study _____ the afternoon.

PART 3 Review the Editing Advice sections in Lessons 1 and 2. Then read this student's composition for mistakes with the shaded words. If the shaded words are correct, write *C*. Add the verb *be* where necessary.

                               is   **teaches**

My English teacher ^ Barbara Nowak. She ~~teach~~ grammar and
     (example)   *(example)*

composition at City College. She very nice, but she's very strict. She give
                                 (1)   *(2)*   *(3)*

a lot of homework, and we take a lot of tests. English's hard for me.
                            (4)   *(5)*

    Every day, at the beginning of the class, she takes attendance and
        (6)   *(7)*

we hand in our homework. Then she's explains the grammar. We do
   (8)   *(9)*   *(10)*

exercises in the book. The book have a lot of exercises. Most exercises is
                            (11)   *(12)*

easy, but some are hard. Sometimes we says the answers out loud, but
                                     (13)

sometimes we write the answers. Sometimes the teacher asks a student to
           (14)   *(15)*

write the answers on the board.

    The students like Barbara because she make the class interesting. She
             (16)   *(17)*

brings often songs to class, and we learn the words. Sometimes we watch
  (18)   *(19)*   *(20)*

a movie in class. Always I enjoy her lessons.
               (21)

    After class I sometimes going to her office if I want more help.
                  (22)

She very kind and always try to help me.
 (23)   *(24)*

    Barbara dresses very informally. Sometimes she wears a skirt, but
          (25)   *(26)*

she wears usually jeans. She about 35 years old, but she's looks like a
   (27)   *(28)*   *(29)*

teenager. (In my country, never a teacher wear jeans.)
                         (30)

I very happy with my teacher. She understand the problems of a
(31)   (32)
foreigner because she's also a foreigner. She's comes from Poland, but she
(33)   (34)
speaks English very well. She know it's hard to learn another language.
(35)   (36)

Expansion

Classroom
Activities

❶ **Find a partner. Interview your partner about one of his or her teachers, friends, or relatives. Ask about this person's usual activities.**

EXAMPLE
A: What's your math teacher's name?

B: Her name is Kathy Carlson.

A: Does she give a lot of homework?

B: No, she doesn't.

A: What does she usually wear to class?

B: She usually wears a skirt and blouse.

A: Does she ever wear jeans to class?

B: No, she never does.

❷ **In a small group or with the entire class, use frequency words to talk about the activities of a famous person (the president, a singer, an actor, etc.).**

EXAMPLE
The president of the U.S. often meets with leaders of other countries.

❸ **Find a partner. Talk about a special holiday that you and your family celebrate. Ask your partner questions about the date of the holiday, food, clothing, preparations, activities, and so on.**

EXAMPLE
A: We celebrate the Lunar New Year.

B: Do you wear special clothes?

A: Yes, we do.

B: What kind of clothes do you wear?

❹ **Look at the list of Linda's activities on page 86. Write a list to remind yourself of things you do on a regular basis. Find a partner. Compare your list to your partner's list.**

Talk

About It

In the left column in the following table is a list of common customs in the U.S. Do people in your native country or cultural group have similar customs? If so, put a check (✓) in Column A. If not, put a check (✓) in Column B. Discuss your answers in a group.

AMERICAN CUSTOMS	A SIMILAR CUSTOM IN MY NATIVE COUNTRY OR CULTURAL GROUP	B DIFFERENT CUSTOM IN MY NATIVE COUNTRY OR CULTURAL GROUP
1. Americans often say, "Have a nice day."		
2. When someone sneezes, Americans usually say, "Bless you."		
3. Americans often ask, "How are you?" People usually reply, "I'm fine, thanks. How are you?"		
4. Americans rarely visit their friends without calling first.		
5. Americans are often in a hurry. They rarely have free time.		
6. Americans often eat popcorn in a movie theater.		
7. Americans often eat in fast-food restaurants.		
8. Americans often say, "OK."		
9. Americans often wear shorts and sandals in the summer.		
10. Americans often listen to MP3 players.		
11. Banks in the U.S. often have a time/temperature sign.		
12. American restaurants usually have salt and pepper shakers on the table.		
13. When a radio or TV breaks down, Americans often buy a new one. They rarely try to repair it.		
14. Americans often send greeting cards to close friends and relatives for birthdays, anniversaries, holidays, and illnesses.		
15. The Sunday newspaper often has store coupons.		
16. There is a special day for sweethearts.		

Write
About It

1 Write about one of your teachers. Describe your teacher and write about his or her classroom behavior and activities.

2 Write about a holiday that you celebrate. Explain how you celebrate this holiday. Or write about how you celebrate your birthday or another special day.

EXAMPLE

The Day of the Dead

The Day of the Dead is an important holiday in my country, Mexico. On this day, we go to the cemetery to visit the graves of our dead relatives. We clean the graves and bring flowers. We also bring food and eat at the cemetery . . .

For more practice using grammar in context, please visit our Web site.

Grammar

Singular and Plural

There + *Be* + Noun

Articles and Quantity Words

Context

Americans and Where They Live

Americans and Where They Live[1]

1. Do you know anyone who lives alone?

2. Does your family own a house or rent an apartment?

CD 1, TR 16

Read the following Web article. Pay special attention to plural nouns.

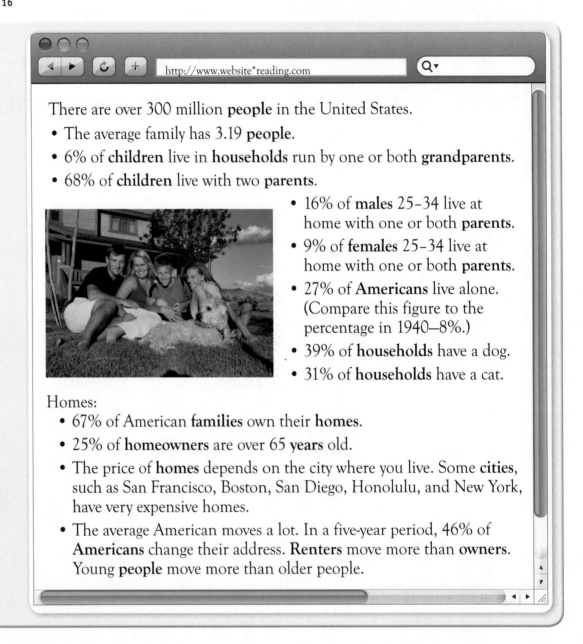

There are over 300 million **people** in the United States.

- The average family has 3.19 **people**.
- 6% of **children** live in **households** run by one or both **grandparents**.
- 68% of **children** live with two **parents**.

- 16% of **males** 25–34 live at home with one or both **parents**.
- 9% of **females** 25–34 live at home with one or both **parents**.
- 27% of **Americans** live alone. (Compare this figure to the percentage in 1940—8%.)
- 39% of **households** have a dog.
- 31% of **households** have a cat.

Homes:

- 67% of American **families** own their **homes**.
- 25% of **homeowners** are over 65 **years** old.
- The price of **homes** depends on the city where you live. Some **cities**, such as San Francisco, Boston, San Diego, Honolulu, and New York, have very expensive homes.
- The average American moves a lot. In a five-year period, 46% of **Americans** change their address. **Renters** move more than **owners**. Young **people** move more than older people.

[1]Statistics are from the 2007 American Community Survey conducted by the U.S. Census Bureau.

4.1 Singular and Plural—An Overview

EXAMPLES	EXPLANATION
Some kids live with one **parent**. Some kids live with two **parents**. Everyone pays **taxes**.	Singular means one. Plural means more than one. Plural nouns usually end in -s or -es.

Some young **men** and **women** live with their parents.
Some **children** live with their grandparents.
	Some plural forms are irregular. They don't end in -s or -es.
	    man ⟶ men
	    woman ⟶ women
	    child ⟶ children

EXERCISE **1** **Tell whether the statement is true (T) or false (F).**

EXAMPLE Homes in Boston are very expensive.   T

1. Most American children live with their grandparents.
2. More Americans live alone now than in 1940.
3. Most people rent an apartment.
4. Americans stay in the same house for their entire lives.
5. Cats are more popular than dogs in American homes.
6. Families in the U.S. are small (fewer than five people).
7. Most children live with both parents.
8. The price of homes depends on where you live.
9. Most homeowners are over 65 years old.
10. More males 25–34 than females 25–34 live with their parents.
11. Homes in San Francisco are very expensive.

4.2 Spelling of Regular Noun Plurals

WORD ENDING	EXAMPLE WORDS	PLURAL ADDITION	PLURAL FORM
Vowel	bee banana pie	+ -s	bees bananas pies
Consonant	bed pin month	+ -s	beds pins months
ss, sh, ch, x	class dish church box	+ -es	classes dishes churches boxes
Vowel + y	boy day monkey	+ -s	boys days monkeys
Consonant + y	lady story party	y̶ + -ies	ladies stories parties
Vowel + o	patio stereo radio	+ -s	patios stereos radios
Consonant + o	mosquito tomato potato	+ -es	mosquitoes tomatoes potatoes
Exceptions: photos, pianos, solos, altos, sopranos, autos, avocados			
f or fe	leaf calf knife	f̶ + -ves f̶e̶ + -ves	leaves calves knives
Exceptions: beliefs, chiefs, roofs, chefs			

EXERCISE **2** **Write the plural form of each noun.**

EXAMPLES   leaf ___*leaves*___

             toy ___*toys*___

1. dish _____
2. country _____
3. half _____
4. book _____
5. boy _____

6. girl _____
7. bench _____
8. box _____
9. shark _____
10. stereo _____

11. knife _____
12. story _____
13. sofa _____
14. key _____
15. movie _____
16. squirrel _____
17. mosquito _____
18. lion _____
19. fly _____
20. cow _____
21. table _____

22. roach _____
23. fox _____
24. house _____
25. turkey _____
26. chicken _____
27. wolf _____
28. dog _____
29. bath _____
30. pony _____
31. duck _____
32. moth _____

4.3 Pronunciation of Plural Nouns

The plural ending has three pronunciations: /s/, /z/, and /əz/.

PRONUNCIATION	RULE	EXAMPLES	
/s/	Pronounce /s/ after voiceless sounds: /p, t, k, f, θ/.	lip—lips cat—cats rock—rocks cuff—cuffs month—months	
/z/	Pronounce /z/ after voiced sounds: /b, d, g, v, m, n, ŋ, l, r/ and all vowels.	cab—cabs lid—lids bag—bags stove—stoves sum—sums	can—cans thing—things bill—bills car—cars bee—bees
/əz/	Pronounce /əz/ when the base form ends in s, ss, ce, se, sh, ch, ge, and x.	bus—buses class—classes place—places cause—causes	dish—dishes beach—beaches garage—garages tax—taxes

EXERCISE 3 **Go back to Exercise 2 and pronounce the plural form of each word.**

4.4 Irregular Noun Plurals

SINGULAR	PLURAL	EXPLANATION
man woman tooth foot goose	men women teeth feet geese	Some nouns have a vowel change in the plural form. **Singular:** Do you see that old **woman**? 　　**Plural:** Do you see those young **women**?
sheep fish deer	sheep fish deer	Some plural forms are the same as the singular form. **Singular:** I have one **fish** in my tank. 　　**Plural:** She has ten **fish** in her tank.
child person mouse	children people mice	For some plurals, we change to a different form. **Singular:** She has one **child**. 　　**Plural:** They have two **children**.
	pajamas clothes pants/slacks (eye)glasses scissors	Some words have no singular form. **Examples:** My **pants** are new. Do you like them? 　　My **glasses** are dirty. I can't see with 　　them.
dozen hundred thousand million		Exact numbers use the singular form. **Examples:** The U.S. has over 300 **million** people. 　　I need to buy two **dozen** eggs.
	dozens hundreds thousands millions	The plural form of a number is *not* an exact number. **Examples:** **Thousands** of people live alone. 　　**Millions** of people live in New York City.

Pronunciation Note:
　You hear the difference between *woman* (singular) and *women* (plural) in the first syllable.
　Listen to your teacher pronounce *one woman* and *two women*.
Language Note:
　The plural of *person* can also be *persons*, but *people* is more common.

EXERCISE 4 The following nouns have an irregular plural form. Write the plural.

EXAMPLE　man _____*men*_____

1. foot _____

2. woman _____

3. policeman _____

4. child _____

5. fish _____

6. mouse _____

7. sheep _____

8. tooth _____

EXERCISE 5   **Fill in the blanks with the correct plural form of the noun in parentheses ( ).**

EXAMPLE   Some _____**people**_____ like to live alone.
(person)

1. Most _____ in the U.S. own a house.
(family)

2. The U.S. has over 300 million _____.
(person)

3. Americans move many _____.
(time)

4. Some _____ earn more money than their
(woman)

_____.
(husband)

5. _____ are very expensive in some
(Home)

_____.
(city)

6. Divorce is very high in some _____.
(country)

7. Some _____ live with only one parent.
(child)

8. How many square _____ does your house or
(foot)

apartment have?

9. Some _____ live with _____.
(kid)   (grandparent)

10. The average family has 3.19 _____.
(person)

11. Some apartments have a problem with _____.
(mouse)

12. _____ are popular in the U.S.
(pet)

13. _____ are more common than
(dog)

_____.
(cat)

14. _____ are interesting to watch.
(fish)

Finding an Apartment

1. Do you live in a house, an apartment, or a dorm?[2] Do you live alone?

2. Do you like the place where you live? Why or why not?

CD 1, TR 17

Read the following Web article. Pay special attention to *there + be* followed by singular and plural nouns.

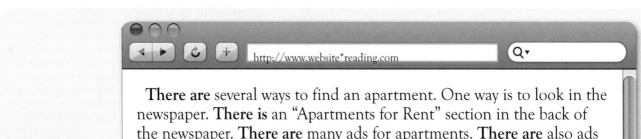

There are several ways to find an apartment. One way is to look in the newspaper. **There is** an "Apartments for Rent" section in the back of the newspaper. **There are** many ads for apartments. **There are** also ads for houses for rent and houses for sale. Many newspapers also put their listings online.

Another way to find an apartment is by looking at the buildings in the neighborhood where you want to live. **There are** often "For Rent" signs on the front of the buildings. **There is** usually a phone number on the sign. You can call and ask for information about the apartment that you are interested in. You can ask:

- How much is the rent?
- Is heat included?
- What floor is the apartment on?
- **Is there** an elevator?
- How many bedrooms **are there** in the apartment?
- How many closets **are there** in the apartment?
- Is the apartment available[3] now?

If an apartment interests you, you can make an appointment to see it. When you go to see the apartment, you should ask some more questions, such as the following:

- **Is there** a lease?[4] How long is the lease?
- **Is there** a janitor or manager?

Did You Know?

Nowadays, people search for apartments online using Web sites such as Craigslist.org.

---

[2]*Dorm* is short for *dormitory*, a building where students live.
[3]*Available* means ready to use now.
[4]A *lease* is a contract between the owner (landlord or landlady) and the renter (tenant). It tells how much the rent is, how long the tenant can stay in the apartment, and other rules.

renovated kitchen

bathroom

bedroom

air-conditioning

hardwood floors

- **Is there** a parking space for each tenant? Is it free, or do I have to pay extra?
- **Are there** smoke detectors? (In many places, the law says that the landlord must put a smoke detector in each apartment and in the halls.)
- **Is there** a laundry room in the building? Where is it?

The landlord may ask you a few questions, such as:

- How many people **are there** in your family?
- Do you have any pets?

You should check over the apartment carefully before you sign the lease. If **there are** some problems, you should talk to the landlord to see if he will take care of them before you move in.

4.5 Using *There* + *Is/Are*

We use *there* + *is* or *there* + *are* to introduce a subject into the conversation when we show location or time.

	EXAMPLES				
Affirmative Singular	*There*	*is*	*a/an/one*	**Singular Subject**	**Location/Time**
	There	is	a	janitor	in my building.
	There	is	an	air conditioner	in the bedroom.
	There	is	one	dryer	in the basement.
	There	is	a	rent increase	this year.
	Note: *There's* is the contraction for *there is*.				
Negative Singular	*There*	*isn't*	*a/an*	**Singular Subject**	**Location/Time**
	There	isn't	a	back door	in my apartment.
	There	isn't	an	elevator	in the building.
	There's	*no*		**Singular Subject**	**Location/Time**
	There's	no		balcony	in my apartment.
	There's	no		heat	this month.
Affirmative Plural	*There*	*are*	**Plural Word**	**Plural Subject**	**Location/Time**
	There	are	several	windows	in the bedroom.
	There	are	many	children	in the building.
	There	are	some	cats	in the building.
	There	are	two	closets	in the hall.
	There	are	—	curtains	on the windows.
	Note: We don't write a contraction for *there are*.				
Negative Plural	*There*	*aren't*	*any*	**Plural Subject**	**Location/Time**
	There	aren't	any	shades	on the windows.
	There	aren't	any	new tenants	this month.
	There	*are*	*no*	**Plural Subject**	**Location/Time**
	There	are	no	cabinets	in the kitchen.

Language Note:

1. When two nouns follow *there*, use a singular verb (*is*) if the first noun is singular. Use a plural verb (*are*) if the first noun is plural.

   There is a closet in the bedroom and two closets in the hall.

   There are two closets in the hall and one closet in the bedroom.

   There is a washer and dryer in the basement.

2. *There* never introduces a specific or unique noun. The definite article (*the*) indicates a specific or unique noun.

   Wrong: *There's* the Eiffel Tower in Paris.

   Right: The Eiffel Tower is in Paris.

EXERCISE **6** **ABOUT YOU** Use the words given to make a statement about the place where you live (house or apartment). If you live in a dorm, use Exercise 7 instead.

EXAMPLES
carpet / in the living room
There's a carpet in the living room.

trees / in front of the building
There are no trees in front of the building.

porch

fireplace

1. porch
2. blinds / on the windows
3. door / in every room
4. window / in every room
5. lease
6. closet / in the living room
7. number / on the door of the apartment or house
8. overhead light / in every room
9. microwave oven / in the kitchen
10. back door
11. fireplace
12. smoke detector

blinds

smoke detector

EXERCISE **7** **ABOUT YOU** Make a statement about your dorm and dorm room with the words given. (If you live in an apartment or house, skip this exercise.)

EXAMPLES
window / in the room
There's a window in the room.

curtains / on the window
There are no curtains on the window.
There are shades.

window shades

1. closet / in the room
2. two beds / in the room
3. private bath / for every room
4. men and women / in the dorm
5. cafeteria / in the dorm
6. snack machines / in the dorm
7. noisy students / in the dorm
8. numbers / on the doors of the rooms
9. elevator(s) / in the dorm
10. laundry room / in the dorm

4.6 Questions and Short Answers Using *There*

Compare statements and questions with *there*. Observe short answers.

	EXAMPLES	EXPLANATION

Singular Statement
 	
Yes/No **Question**
 	
Short Answer
	There is a laundry room in the building.
	
	Is there an elevator in the building?
	
	Yes, there is.
		Question word order:
		Is + *there* + *a/an* + singular noun...?
		
		Short answers:
		    Yes, there is. (no contraction)
		    No, there isn't. OR No, there's not.

Plural Statement
 	
Yes/No **Question**
 	
Short Answer
	There are some children in the building.
	
	Are there (any) children on your floor?
	
	No, there aren't.
		Question word order:
		Are + *there* + (*any*) + plural noun...?
		We often use *any* to introduce a plural noun in a *yes/no* question.
		
		Short answers:
		    Yes, there are.
		    No, there aren't.

Plural Statement **Information Question** **Short Answer**	**There are** ten apartments in my building. **How many** apartments **are there** in your building? Thirty.	**Question word order:** *How many* + plural noun + *are there*...?

EXERCISE 8   **ABOUT YOU** Ask and answer questions with *there* and the words given to find out about another student's apartment and building. (If you live in a dorm, use Exercise 9 instead.)

EXAMPLES   a microwave oven / in your apartment

   A: Is there a microwave oven in your apartment?
   B: No, there isn't.

   closets / in the bedroom

   A: Are there any closets in the bedroom?
   B: Yes. There's one closet in the bedroom.

   1. children / in your building

   2. a dishwasher / in the kitchen

3. a yard / in front of your building

4. trees / in front of your building

5. a basement / in the building

6. a laundry room / in the basement

7. a janitor / in the building

8. noisy neighbors / in the building

9. nosy[5] neighbors / in the building

10. an elevator / in the building

11. parking spaces / for the tenants

12. a lot of closets / in the apartment

13. how many apartments / in your building

14. how many parking spaces / in front of your building

EXERCISE 9 **ABOUT YOU** Ask and answer questions with *there* and the words given to find out about another student's dorm. (If you live in an apartment or house, skip this exercise.)

EXAMPLE   a bicycle room

A: Is there a bicycle room in your dorm?
B: No, there isn't.

1. married students

2. private rooms

3. a bicycle room

4. a computer room

5. an elevator

6. a bulletin board

7. graduate students

8. a quiet place to study

9. an air conditioner / in your room

10. parking lot / for your dorm

11. how many rooms / in your dorm

12. how many floors / in your dorm

---

[5]A *nosy* person is a person who wants to know everyone's business.

EXERCISE 10 Use the words given to ask the teacher a question about his or her office. Your teacher will answer.

EXAMPLES pencil sharpener

A: Is there a pencil sharpener in your office?
B: No, there isn't.

books

A: Are there any books in your office?
B: Yes. There are a lot of books in my office.

1. phone
2. file cabinet
3. photos of your family
4. radio
5. copy machine
6. windows
7. calendar
8. bookshelves
9. plants
10. pictures
11. fax machine
12. computer

EXERCISE 11 A student is calling about an apartment for rent. Fill in the blanks with *there is, there are, is there, are there,* and other related words to complete this phone conversation between the student (S) and the landlord (L).

CD 1, TR 18

S: I'm calling about an apartment for rent on Grover Street.

L: We have two apartments available. _____There's_____ a four-room
   (example)
   apartment on the first floor and a three-room apartment on the fourth
   floor. Which one are you interested in?

S: I prefer the smaller apartment. _____ an elevator in
   (1)
   the building?

L: Yes, there is. How many people _____ in your family?
   (2)

S: It's just for me. I live alone. I'm a student. I need a quiet apartment. Is
   this a quiet building?

L: Oh, yes. _____ no kids in the building. This is a very
   (3)
   quiet building.

S: That's good. I have a car. _____ parking spaces?
   (4)

L: Yes. _____ twenty spaces in the back of the building.
   (5)

S: How _____ apartments _____ in the
   (6)   *(7)*
   building?

110   Lesson 4

L: _____ 30 apartments.
         (8)

S: Twenty parking spaces for thirty apartments? Then _____
         (9)
enough spaces for all the tenants.

L: Don't worry. Not everyone has a car. Parking is on a first-come,
first-served basis.[6] And _____ plenty of[7] spaces on the
                            (10)
street.

S: _____ a laundry room in the building?
         (11)

L: Yes. There are washers and dryers in the basement.

S: How much is the rent?

L: It's $850 a month.

S: I hear a dog. Is that your dog?

L: Yes, but don't worry. I don't live in the building. _____
                                                              (12)
no dogs in the building.

S: When can I see the apartment?

L: How about tomorrow at six o'clock?

S: That'll be fine. Thanks.

4.7 *There* vs. *They* and Other Pronouns

EXAMPLES		EXPLANATION
There's a *janitor* in the building.	**He's** in the basement.	To introduce a new noun, we use *there + is/are*. When we use this noun again as the subject of another sentence, we use *he, she, it,* or *they*.
There's a little *girl* in the next apartment.	**She's** cute.	
There's an empty *apartment* on the first floor.	**It's** available now.	
There are two washing *machines*.	**They're** in the basement.	

Pronunciation Note: We pronounce *there* and *they're* exactly the same.
Spelling Note: Don't confuse *there* and *they're*.
   There are dogs in the next apartment.
   They're very friendly.

---

[6]A *first-come, first-served* basis means that people who arrive first will get something first (parking spaces, theater tickets, classes at registration etc.).
[7]*Plenty of* means "a lot of."

EXERCISE 12 Fill in the blanks with *there's, there are, it's,* or *they're.*

EXAMPLE   __There's__ a small apartment for rent in my building.

__It's__ on the fourth floor.

1. _____ two apartments for rent. _____ not on the same floor.

2. _____ a laundry room in the building. _____ in the basement.

3. The parking spaces are in the back of the building. _____ for the tenants with cars.

4. The parking spaces don't cost extra. _____ free for the tenants.

5. The apartment is small. _____ on the fourth floor.

6. The building has 30 apartments. _____ a big building.

7. The student wants to see the apartment. _____ on Grover Street.

8. The building is quiet because _____ no kids in the building.

9. How much is the rent? _____ $850 a month.

10. Is the rent high? No, _____ not high.

11. _____ no dogs in the building.

12. _____ a quiet building.

EXERCISE 13 Ask a question about this school using *there* and the words given. Another student will answer. If the answer is "yes," ask a question with *where.*

EXAMPLE   lockers

A: Are there any lockers at this school?
B: Yes, there are.
A: Where are they?
B: They're near the gym.

1. a library
2. vending machines
3. public telephones
4. a computer room
5. a cafeteria
6. a gym
7. a swimming pool

8. tennis courts
9. dormitories
10. a parking lot
11. a bookstore
12. copy machines
13. a student lounge
14. an auditorium

Calling About an Apartment

1. Does your neighborhood have more apartment buildings or houses?

2. Do you prefer to live alone, with a roommate, or with your family? Why?

CD 1, TR 19

Read the following phone conversation between a student (S) and the manager (M) of a building. Pay special attention to the definite article (*the*), the indefinite articles (*a, an*), and indefinite quantity words (*some, any*).

S: Hello? I want to speak with **the landlord**.

M: I'm **the manager** of **the building**. Can I help you?

S: I need to find **a** new **apartment**.

M: Where do you live now?

S: I live in **a** big **apartment** on Wright Street. I have **a roommate**, but he's graduating, and I need **a** smaller **apartment**. Are there **any** small **apartments** for rent in your building?

M: There's one.

S: What floor is it on?

M: It's on **the** third **floor**.

S: Does it have **a bedroom**?

M: No. It's **a** studio **apartment**. It has **a living room** and **a kitchen**.

S: Is **the living room** big?

M: So-so.[8]

S: Does **the kitchen** have **a stove** and **a refrigerator**?

M: Yes. **The refrigerator** is old, but it works well. **The stove** is pretty new.

S: Can I see **the apartment**?

M: I have **a question** for you first. Do you have **a dog**? We don't permit dogs. **Some dogs** make a lot of noise.

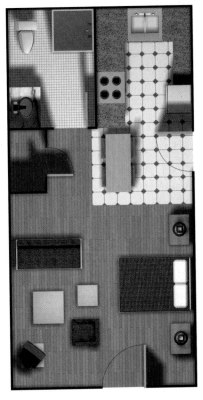

[8]*So-so* means medium or average.

(continued)

S: I don't have **a dog**.

M: I'm happy to hear that.

S: But I have **a snake**.

M: **A snake?**

S: **Snakes** are quiet.

M: Yes, but . . .

S: Don't worry. I keep **the snake** in **a glass box**.

M: I hope **the box** is always closed.

S: It is. I only open it to feed **the snake**. I feed it **mice**.

M: Oh.

S: When can I see **the apartment?**

M: I have to speak to **the landlord**. I'm not sure if you can have **snakes** and **mice** in **the apartment**.

4.8 Articles with Definite and Indefinite Nouns

Singular

INDEFINITE	DEFINITE	EXPLANATION
I live in **a** big building. There's **a** janitor in the building.	**The** building is near the college. **The** janitor lives on the first floor.	We introduce a singular noun with the indefinite articles (*a* or *an*). When we refer to this noun again, we use the definite article *the*.
	May I speak to **the** landlord? He lives on **the** third floor. **The** basement is dirty.	We use *the* before a singular noun if this noun is the only one or if the speaker and listener share an experience and are referring to the same one. (In this case, they are talking about the same building.)

Plural

INDEFINITE	DEFINITE	EXPLANATION
My building has **(some)** washing machines. Are there **(any)** dryers?	**The** washing machines are in the basement. Where are **the** dryers?	We introduce a plural noun with *some, any,* or no article. When we refer to this noun again, we use the definite article *the*.
	The tenants are angry. **The** washing machines don't work.	We use *the* before a plural noun if the speaker and the listener share the same experience. (In this case, they are talking about the same building.)

EXERCISE 14 **Fill in the blanks in the conversations between two students. Use *the, a, an, some,* or *any*.**

CONVERSATION 1 **A:** Is there ____*a*____ cafeteria at this school?

      (example)

       B: Yes, there is.

       A: Where's _____ cafeteria?

              (1)

       B: It's on _____ first floor.

            (2)

       A: Are there _____ snack machines in _____ cafeteria?

               (3)   *(4)*

       B: Yes, there are.

       A: I want to buy _____ sandwich.

               (5)

       B: _____ sandwich machine is out of order today.

         (6)

CONVERSATION 2 **A:** Is there _____ bookstore for this college?

              (7)

       B: Yes, there is.

       A: Where's _____ bookstore?

             (8)

       B: It's on Green Street.

       A: I need to buy _____ English dictionary.

             (9)

       B: Today's _____ holiday. _____ bookstore is closed today.

         (10)   *(11)*

EXERCISE 15 **Fill in the blanks in the conversation about apartment problems. Use *the, a, an, some,* or *any.***

CD 1, TR 20

A: I have _____*a*_____ problem in my apartment.
(example)

B: What's _____ problem?
(1)

A: _____ landlord doesn't provide enough
(2)
heat. I have to wear _____ sweater or
(3)
_____ overcoat all the time in the
(4)
apartment.

B: Why don't you talk to _____ building
(5)
manager? Maybe _____ heating system is
(6)
broken. If he doesn't solve _____ problem,
(7)
you can send _____ letter to _____
(8) (9)
Department of Housing.

A: That's _____ good idea. There's one more problem.
(10)
I have _____ neighbor who has _____ small dog.
(11) (12)
_____ dog barks all the time when _____ neighbor isn't
(13) (14)
home. We share _____ wall, and I can hear _____ dog
(15) (16)
barking through _____ wall.
(17)

B: Talk to _____ neighbor. Tell him there are dog services. For
(18)
_____ price, someone can go to his house every day and play
(19)
with _____ dog and take it out for a walk.
(20)

A: I don't think he wants to pay for this service.

B: Then talk to _____ landlord. Tell him about _____ problem.
(21) (22)

A: Do you have _____ problems in your apartment?
(23)

B: Of course we have _____ problems. But we have _____ very
(24) (25)
nice landlady. She lives in _____ building. If there's _____
(26) (27)
problem, I send her _____ e-mail, and she usually takes care of it
(28)
right away.

4.9 Making Generalizations

A generalization says that something is true of all members of a group.

SINGULAR	PLURAL	EXPLANATION
A snake is quiet. **A dog** makes noise.	**Snakes** are quiet. **Dogs** make noise.	To make a generalization about the **subject**, use the indefinite article (*a* or *an*) with a singular subject or no article with a plural subject.
	I don't like **snakes**. Snakes eat **mice**.	To make a generalization about the **object**, use the plural form with no article.

EXERCISE 16 The following sentences are generalizations. Change the subject from singular to plural. Make other necessary changes.

EXAMPLE A single parent has a difficult life.
<u>Single parents have a difficult life.</u>

1. A house in San Diego is expensive.

2. A homeowner pays property tax.

3. A dog is part of the family.

4. A renter doesn't have the freedom to make changes.

5. An owner has the freedom to make changes.

EXERCISE 17 Use the noun in parentheses ( ) to give general information about your native country or hometown. Use the plural form with no article.

EXAMPLE (woman)
Generally, women don't work outside the home in my native country.

1. young (person)   **5.** (house)

2. old (person)   **6.** poor (person)

3. (woman)   **7.** (car)

4. (man)   **8.** (doctor)

EXERCISE 18 Add a plural subject to make a generalization.

EXAMPLE _____*Students*_____ need a cheap apartment.

1. _____ need a big apartment.
2. _____ don't want to rent to people with pets.
3. _____ sometimes make a lot of noise in an apartment.
4. _____ need an apartment with an elevator.
5. _____ are sometimes noisy and sometimes nosy.
6. _____ like houses with a garden.
7. _____ move a lot from place to place.
8. _____ are expensive in the U.S.

EXERCISE 19 **ABOUT YOU** Use the plural form of each noun to tell if you like or don't like the following in the place where you live.

EXAMPLE tall building
I like tall buildings.

1. white wall
2. curtain on the window
3. picture on the wall
4. plant
5. friendly neighbor

6. blind on the window
7. high ceiling
8. bright light
9. rug
10. hardwood floor

curtains

hardwood floors

EXERCISE 20   **ABOUT YOU** Ask *Do you like* + the plural form of the noun. Another student will answer.

EXAMPLES   child

A: Do you like children?
B: Yes, I do.

snake

A: Do you like snakes?
B: No, I don't.

1. cat
2. dog
3. hamburger
4. American car
5. American movie
6. fashion magazine

7. comic book
8. computer
9. computer game
10. strict teacher
11. American supermarket
12. American textbook

EXERCISE 21   This is a conversation between two students. Fill in the blanks with *the, a, an, some, any,* or *X* for no article.

A: Is there _____**a**_____ copy machine in our library?
           (example)

B: Yes. There are several copy machines in _____ library.
                                             (1)

A: Are _____ copy machines free?
        (2)

B: No. You need to use _____ nickel[9] for _____ copy machines.
                      (3)   *(4)*
What do you want to copy?

A: I want to copy my classmate's textbook.

B: The whole thing? Why?

A: _____ textbooks in the U.S. are too expensive.
      (5)

B: There's _____ law against copying an entire book.
              (6)

A: What's _____ law?
         (7)

B: You can't copy _____ books without permission from the publisher.
                (8)

A: In my country, we copy _____ books all the time.
                    (9)

B: But it's illegal. People who copy _____ books, CDs, and movies
                                      (10)
without permission are called "pirates."

[9]A *nickel* is a five-cent coin.

Summary of Lesson 4

1. Singular and Plural

REGULAR	IRREGULAR
boy–boys	man–men
box–boxes	woman–women
story–stories	child–children
tomato–tomatoes	foot–feet
wife–wives	fish–fish

2. *There + be*

There's an empty apartment in my building.
There are two washing machines in the basement.
Are there any parking spaces?

3. Articles

- To introduce a new noun into the conversation:
SINGULAR	I have **a dog**.
PLURAL	I have **(some) turtles**.
	I don't have **(any) birds**.

- To talk about a previously mentioned noun:
SINGULAR	I have a dog. **The dog** barks when the letter carrier arrives.
PLURAL	I have some turtles. I keep **the turtles** in the bathroom.

- To talk about specific items or people from our experience:
SINGULAR	**The janitor** cleans the basement once a week.
PLURAL	**The tenants** have to take out their own garbage.

- To talk about the only one:
  The president lives in Washington, D.C.
  The Statue of Liberty is in New York.

- To make a generalization:
SINGULAR	**A dog** has good hearing.
PLURAL	**Dogs** have good hearing.
	I like **dogs**.

Statue of Liberty

Editing Advice

1. *People* is a plural noun. Use a plural verb form.

   People in my country ~~is~~ *are* very poor.

2. Don't use *the* with a generalization.

   ~~The~~ *D*ogs are friendly animals.

3. Don't confuse *there* with *they're*.

   I have two brothers. ~~There~~ *They're* in Florida.

4. Use *there + is/are* to introduce a new subject.

   In my class *there are* five students from Haiti.

5. Don't confuse *it's* and *there's*.

   ~~It's~~ *There's* a closet in my bedroom.

6. Don't confuse *have* and *there*.

   ~~Have~~ *There's* a closet in my bedroom.

7. Don't use *the* + a unique noun after *there*.

   ~~There's~~ *T*he Golden Gate Bridge *is* in California.

8. Don't use *the* with the first mention of a noun when you and the listener do not share a common experience with this noun.

   I have ~~the~~ *a* new watch.

Golden Gate Bridge

9. Don't use an apostrophe for a plural ending.

   She has three ~~brother's~~ *brothers*.

Editing Quiz

Some of the shaded words and phrases have mistakes. Find the mistakes and correct them. If the shaded words are correct, write *C*.

A: Let me show you around my new apartment.

B: It's a big apartment.
(example) — *C*

A: It's big enough for my family. ~~They're~~ **There** are four bedrooms and two
(example)

bathrooms. Has a large closet in each bedroom. Let me show you my
(1)

kitchen too.

B: Oh. It's a new dishwasher in your kitchen.
(2)

A: It's wonderful. You know how I hate to wash dishes.
(3)

B: Is there a microwave oven?
(4)

A: No, there isn't.
(5)

B: Are any washers and dryers for clothes?
(6)

A: Oh, yes. They're in the basement. In the laundry room are five
(7) *(8)*

washers and five dryers. I never have to wait.

B: There are a lot of people in your building?
(9)

A: In my building 30 apartments.
(10)

B: Is a janitor in your building?
(11)

A: Yes. There's a very good janitor. He keeps the building very clean.
(12)

B: I suppose this apartment costs a lot.

A: Well, yes. The rent is high. But I share the apartment with my cousins.
(13) *(14)*

Lesson 4 Test/Review

PART **1** **Write the plural form for each noun.**

box ___boxes___   month _____   child _____

card _____   match _____   desk _____

foot _____   shelf _____   key _____

potato _____   radio _____   story _____

woman _____   mouse _____   bush _____

PART **2** **Fill in the blanks with *there, is, are, it,* or *they* or a combination of these words.**

A: ___Are there___ any people from your country in your building?
(example)

B: Yes. _____ a few people from my country in my
(1)

building._____ very friendly.
(2)

A: _____ a laundry room in your building?
(3)

B: Yes, _____.
(4)

A: Where _____ the laundry room?
(5)

B: _____ on the third floor.
(6)

A: _____ any lockers in your apartment building?
(7)

B: Yes, there are. _____ in the basement.
(8)

A: _____ a bicycle room in your building?
(9)

B: Yes, there is. _____ in the basement.
(10)

A: How many floors _____ in your building?
(11)

B: _____ four floors and a basement.
(12)

A: _____ an elevator in your building?
(13)

B: Yes, _____, but _____ very slow.
(14)   *(15)*

I usually walk up the stairs.

PART 3 Fill in the blanks with *the*, *a*, *an*, *some*, *any*, or *X* for no article.

A: Do you like your apartment?

B: No, I don't.

A: Why not?

B: There are many reasons. First, I don't like ___the___ janitor.
(example)
He's impolite.

A: Anything else? Are there _____ other problems?
(1)

B: Yes. I want to get _____ dog.
(2)

A: So?

B: It's not permitted. _____ landlord says that _____ dogs
(3)   *(4)*
make a lot of noise.

A: Can you get _____ cat?
(5)

B: Yes, but I don't like _____ cats.
(6)

A: Is your building quiet?

B: No. There are _____ children in _____ building. When
(7)   *(8)*

I try to study, I can hear _____ children in the next apartment.
(9)
They watch TV all the time.

A: You need to find _____ apartment in a different building.
(10)

B: I think you're right.

Classroom Activities

1 Make a list of things you have, things you don't have but would like to have, and things you don't need. Choose from the list below and add any other items you can think of. Then find a partner and compare lists.

a computer	a house	a credit card
a DVD player	a diamond ring	a speaker phone
a digital camera	a CD player	a cell phone
an encyclopedia	an electric can opener	a flat-screen TV
an electric toothbrush	a microwave oven	a letter opener
a pet	a waterbed	a hair dryer
a scale	an electronic calendar	an orange juice squeezer

bathroom scale

orange juice squeezer

I have:	I don't have, but I would like to have:	I don't need:

Discuss your chart with a partner. Tell why you need or don't need some things. Tell why you want some things that you don't have.

② People often use the newspaper to look for an apartment. The Sunday newspaper has the most ads. Bring in a copy of the Sunday newspaper. Look at the section of the newspaper that has apartments for rent. Ask the teacher to help you understand the abbreviations.

③ What other sections are there in the Sunday newspaper? Work with a partner and make a list of everything you can find in the Sunday paper.

EXAMPLE   There's a TV schedule for this week's programs.
There are a lot of ads and coupons.
There's a crossword puzzle.

④ Look at the information about two apartments for rent below. What are some of the advantages and disadvantages of each one? Discuss your answers with a partner or with the entire class.

Apartment 1	Apartment 2
a view of a park	on a busy street
rent = $950	rent = $750
fifth floor (an elevator in the building)	third floor walk-up
a new kitchen with a dishwasher	old appliances in the kitchen
pets not allowed	pets allowed
hardwood floors	a carpet in the living room
the janitor lives in the building	the owner lives in the building on the first floor
management controls the heat	the tenant controls the heat
no air conditioners	air conditioners in the bedroom and living room
faces north only	faces east, south, and west
a one-year lease	no lease
a large building—50 apartments	a small building—6 apartments
washers and dryers on each floor	a laundry room in the basement
parking spaces on first-come, first-served basis	a parking space for each tenant

5 Do you have a picture of your house, apartment, or apartment building? Bring it to class and talk about it.

6 Find a partner and pretend that one of you is looking for an apartment and the other person is the landlady, landlord, or manager. Ask and answer questions about the apartment, the building, parking, laundry, and rent. Write your conversation. Then read it to the class.

Talk
About It
In a small group or with the entire class, discuss the following:

a. How do people rent apartments in your hometown? Is rent high? Is heat usually included in the rent? Does the landlord usually live in the building?

b. What are some differences between a typical apartment in this city and a typical apartment in your hometown?

Write
About It
1 Write a description of a room or place that you like very much. (Review prepositions in Lesson 1.)

2 Write a comparison of your apartment in this city and your apartment or house in your hometown.

> ### Two Apartments
> There are many differences between my apartment here and my apartment in Kiev, Ukraine. In my Kiev apartment, there is a door in every room. In my apartment here, only the bedrooms and bathrooms have doors . . .

For more practice using grammar in context, please visit our Web site.

Grammar
Possession

Object Pronouns

Questions About the Subject

Context
Families and Names

Names

1. What is your complete name? What do your friends call you?

2. Do you like your name?

CD 1, TR 21

Read the following Web article. Pay special attention to possessive forms.

Did You Know?

The five most common last names in the U.S. are Smith, Johnson, Williams, Brown, and Jones.

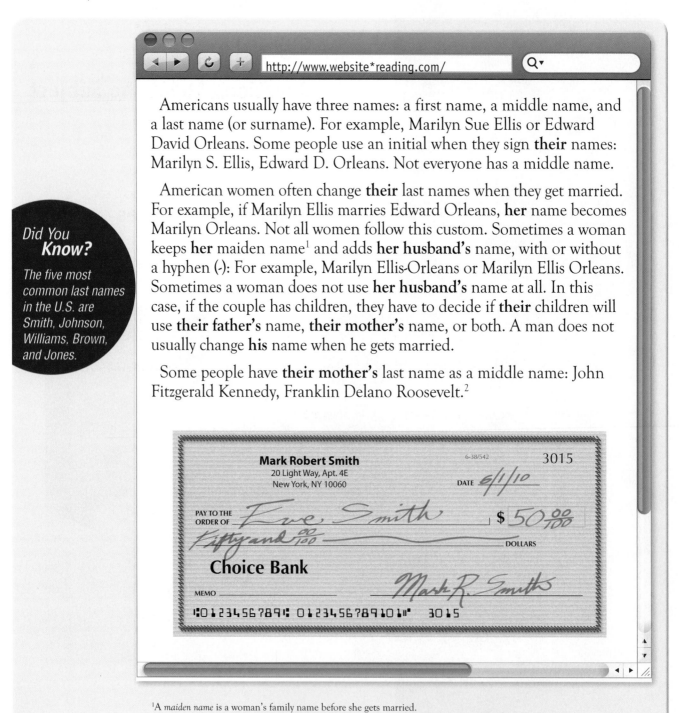

http://www.website*reading.com/

Americans usually have three names: a first name, a middle name, and a last name (or surname). For example, Marilyn Sue Ellis or Edward David Orleans. Some people use an initial when they sign **their** names: Marilyn S. Ellis, Edward D. Orleans. Not everyone has a middle name.

American women often change **their** last names when they get married. For example, if Marilyn Ellis marries Edward Orleans, **her** name becomes Marilyn Orleans. Not all women follow this custom. Sometimes a woman keeps **her** maiden name[1] and adds **her husband's** name, with or without a hyphen (-): For example, Marilyn Ellis-Orleans or Marilyn Ellis Orleans. Sometimes a woman does not use **her husband's** name at all. In this case, if the couple has children, they have to decide if **their** children will use **their father's** name, **their mother's** name, or both. A man does not usually change **his** name when he gets married.

Some people have **their mother's** last name as a middle name: John Fitzgerald Kennedy, Franklin Delano Roosevelt.[2]

Mark Robert Smith
20 Light Way, Apt. 4E
New York, NY 10060

6-38/542   3015

DATE 6/1/10

PAY TO THE ORDER OF Eve Smith $ 50 00/100

Fifty and 00/100   DOLLARS

Choice Bank

MEMO   Mark R. Smith

⑆0123456789⑈ 0123456789⑉0⑆   3015

[1]A *maiden name* is a woman's family name before she gets married.
[2]These are the names of two American presidents.

5.1 Possessive Form of Nouns

We use the possessive form to show ownership or relationship.

NOUN	ENDING	EXAMPLES
Singular Noun father mother dog	Add apostrophe + s	I use my **father's** last name. I don't use my **mother's** last name. My **dog's** name is PeeWee.
Plural Noun Ending in -s parents boys	Add apostrophe only	My **parents'** names are Ethel and Herman. The **boys'** names are Ted and Mike.
Irregular Plural Noun children women	Add apostrophe + s	What are your **children's** names? Marilyn and Sandra are **women's** names.
Names That End in -s Mr. Harris Charles	Add apostrophe + s	Do you know **Mr. Harris's** wife? Do you know **Charles's** daughter? **Note:** Sometimes you will see only an apostrophe when a name ends in s. Do you know Charles' daughter?
Inanimate Objects the classroom the school	Use "the ___ of ___." Do not use apostrophe + s.	**The door of the classroom** is closed. Washington College is **the name of my school**.

EXERCISE ▮1▮ **Fill in the blanks with the possessive form of a noun to make a true statement.**

EXAMPLE   I use my __father's__ last name.

1. I use my _____ last name.
2. I don't use my _____ last name.
3. A married American woman often uses her _____ last name.
4. A married woman in my native culture uses her _____ last name.
5. A single American woman usually uses her _____ last name.
6. An American man rarely uses his _____ last name.
7. President John F. Kennedy had his _____ maiden name as a middle name.

EXERCISE **2** **Some of the following sentences can show possession with 's or '. Rewrite these sentences only. Write "no change" for the others.**

EXAMPLES   The teacher knows the names of the students.
<u>The teacher knows the students' names.</u>

The door of the classroom is usually closed.
<u>No change.</u>

1. The teacher always corrects the homework of the students.

_____

2. The name of the textbook is *Grammar in Context*.

_____

3. The job of the teacher is to explain the grammar.

_____

4. What are the names of your parents?

_____

5. The color of this book is blue.

_____

6. Do you use the last name of your father?

_____

7. What is the name of your dog?

_____

8. The names of the children are Jason and Jessica.

_____

5.2 Possessive Adjectives

Possessive adjectives show ownership or relationship.

EXAMPLES	EXPLANATION	
Compare subject pronouns and possessive adjectives. *I* like **my** name. *You* are a new student. What's **your** name? *He* likes **his** name. *She* doesn't like **her** name. Is this your dog? Is *it* friendly? What's **its** name? *We* use **our** nicknames. *They* are my friends. **Their** last name is Jackson.	**Subject Pronouns** I you he she it we they	**Possessive Adjectives** my your his her its our their

Be careful not to confuse *his* and *her*.
 	
My sister loves **her** husband.
 	
My uncle lives with **his** daughter.
	Match the possessive adjective to the preceding noun.
	    Wrong: My sister loves *his* husband.
	    Wrong: My uncle lives with *her* daughter.	

My sister's name is Marilyn. **Her son's** name is David.	We can use a possessive adjective (*my*, *her*) and a possessive noun (*sister's*, *son's*) together.	
My **sister's husband's** name is Edward.	We can use two possessive nouns together (*sister's husband's*).	

EXERCISE **3** Fill in the blanks with the possessive adjective that relates to the subject.

EXAMPLE   I like ___my___ teacher.

1. He loves _____ mother.

2. She loves _____ father.

3. A dog loves _____ master.

4. Many American women change _____ names when they get married.

5. Sometimes a woman keeps _____ maiden name and adds _____ husband's name.

6. American men don't usually change _____ names when they get married.

7. Do you use _____ father's last name?

8. I use _____ middle name.

9. We write _____ names at the top of the page.

10. Do you like _____ name?

11. I use _____ father's last name.

5.3 Questions with *Whose*

***Whose* + noun asks about possession or ownership.**

QUESTIONS					ANSWERS
Whose + Noun	+ Aux. Verb	+ Subject	+ Verb		
Whose name	do	you	use?		I use **my father's** name.
Whose composition	do	you	like?		I like **Lisa's** composition.
Whose + Noun	+ *Be*	+ Subject			
Whose pen	is	this?			It's **Bob's** pen.
Whose glasses	are	those?			They're **my** glasses.

EXERCISE 4 Write a question with *whose* and the words given. Answer with the words in parentheses ( ).

EXAMPLES   wife/that (Robert)

Whose wife is that? That's Robert's wife.

children/these (Robert)

Whose children are these? These are Robert's children.

1. office/this (the dean)

_____

2. offices/those (the teachers)

_____

3. dictionary/that (the teacher)

_____

4. books/those (the students)

_____

5. car/that (my parents)

_____

6. house/this (my cousin)

_____

7. papers/those (Mr. Ross)

_____

8. pencils/these (the teacher)

_____

5.4 Possessive Pronouns

We use possessive pronouns to avoid repetition of a noun.

EXAMPLES	EXPLANATION
You don't know my name. I know **yours**. (*yours = your name*) Your name is easy for Americans. **Mine** is hard. (*mine = my name*) My parents are in the U.S. **Theirs** are in Russia. (*theirs = their parents*)	When we omit the noun, we use the possessive pronoun. **Compare:** <table><tr><td>Possessive Adjectives</td><td>Possessive Pronouns</td></tr><tr><td>my</td><td>mine</td></tr><tr><td>your</td><td>yours</td></tr><tr><td>his</td><td>his</td></tr><tr><td>her</td><td>hers</td></tr><tr><td>our</td><td>ours</td></tr><tr><td>their</td><td>theirs</td></tr></table>
Robert's wife speaks English. **Peter's** doesn't. (*Peter's = Peter's wife*)	After a possessive noun, we can omit the noun.

EXERCISE 5   **Replace the underlined words with a possessive pronoun.**

EXAMPLE   Your name is long. ~~My name~~ is short. *(Mine)*

1. My sister likes her name. I don't like <u>my name</u>.

2. I like my first name. Do you like <u>your first name</u>?

3. My sister uses her middle name. My brother doesn't use <u>his middle name</u>.

4. My wife and I have different last names. My last name is Roberts.

   <u>Her last name</u> is Paulson.

5. Your last name is easy for Americans to pronounce. <u>Their last name</u> is hard.

6. My brother's children are grown-up. <u>Our children</u> are still small.

EXERCISE 6   **Circle the correct word in parentheses ( ) to complete this conversation.**

CD 1, TR 22

A: Do you live with (**your**) / yours) parents?
(example)

B: No, I don't. Do you live with (your / yours)?
(1)

(*continued*)

A: No. I live with (*my / mine*) sister. (*Our / Ours*) parents are back
(2)   (3)

home. They live with (*my / mine*) brother.
(4)

B: (*Your / Yours*) brother is single, then?
(5)

A: No, he's married. He lives with his wife and (*our / ours*) parents.
(6)

B: If he's married, why does he live with (*your / yours*) parents?
(7)

A: In (*our / ours*) country, it's an honor to live with parents.
(8)

B: Not in (*my / mine*). Grown children don't usually want to live with
(9)

(*their / theirs*) parents, and parents don't usually want to live with
(10)

(*their / theirs*) grown children.
(11)

A: Where do (*your / yours*) parents live?
(12)

B: They live in another state.

A: Isn't that hard for you?

B: Not really. I have (*my / mine*) own life, and they have (*their / theirs*).
(13)   (14)

5.5 The Subject and the Object

EXAMPLES	EXPLANATION
S V O Bob likes Mary. We like movies.	The **subject** (S) comes before the **verb** (V). The **object** (O) comes after the verb. The object is a person or a thing.
S V O S V O Bob likes Mary because **she** helps **him**. S V O S V O I like movies because **they** entertain **me**.	We can use pronouns for the **subject** and the **object**.

William Madison's Name

1. What are common American names?

2. What is a very common first name in your country or native culture? What is a very common last name? Is your name common in your country or native culture?

CD 1, TR 23

Read the following conversation. Pay special attention to object pronouns.

A: I have many questions about American names. Can you answer **them** for me?

B: Of course.

A: Tell **me** about your name.

B: My name is William, but my friends call **me** Bill.

A: Why do they call **you** Bill?

B: Bill is a common nickname for William.

A: Is William your first name?

B: Yes.

A: What's your full name?

B: William Michael Madison.

A: Do you ever use your middle name?

B: I only use **it** for very formal occasions. I sign my name William M. Madison, Jr. (junior).

A: What does "junior" mean?

B: It means that I have the same name as my father. His name is William Madison, Sr. (senior).

A: What's your wife's name?

B: Anna Marie Simms-Madison. I call **her** Annie.

(continued)

Possession; Object Pronouns; Questions About the Subject **137**

A: Why does she have two last names?

B: Simms is her father's last name, and Madison is mine. She uses both names with a hyphen (-) between **them**.

A: Do you have any children?

B: Yes. We have a son and a daughter. Our son's name is Richard, but we call **him** Dick. Our daughter's name is Elizabeth, but everybody calls **her** Lizzy.

A: What do your children call **you**?

B: They call **us** Mommy and Daddy, of course.

5.6 Object Pronouns

SUBJECT	OBJECT	EXAMPLES		
		Subject	**Verb**	**Object**
I ⟶	me	You	love	me.
you ⟶	you	I	love	you.
he ⟶	him	She	loves	him.
she ⟶	her	He	loves	her.
it ⟶	it	We	love	it.
we ⟶	us	They	love	us.
they ⟶	them	We	love	them.

They love her. She loves them.

We can use an object pronoun after the verb or after a preposition.

OBJECT NOUN	OBJECT PRONOUN	EXPLANATION
I have a **middle name**.	I use **it** when I sign my name.	We can use an object pronoun to substitute for an object noun.
He loves **his wife**.	The kids love **her** too.	
You know **my son**.	Friends call **him** Dick.	
We have **two children**.	We love **them**.	We use *them* for plural people and things.
I need **my books**.	I use **them** in class.	
I have **two last names**.	I use both *of* **them**.	An object pronoun can follow a preposition (*of, about, to, from, in,* etc.).
My sister has **a son**.	She always talks *about* **him**.	

EXERCISE 7 **Fill in the blanks. Substitute an object pronoun for the underlined words.**

1. I visit my parents, and my parents visit _____.

2. I use my middle name when I sign my name, but I don't use _____ any other time.

3. My parents live far away, so I don't visit _____ often.

4. I miss my mother. I call _____ every day.

5. You are a new student. I don't know _____. What's your name?

6. We are very informal in the U.S. The teacher calls _____ by our first names.

7. My brother is very busy, so I don't see _____ very often.

EXERCISE 8 **This is a conversation between two students, one from China (A), and one from the U.S. (B). Fill in the blanks with an appropriate object pronoun.**

CD 1, TR 24

A: Americans are very informal about names. The teacher calls

___us___ by our first names.
(example)

B: What does the teacher call _____ in your country?
(1)

A: In my country, when a teacher talks to a woman, he calls

_____ "Miss" or "Madam." When he talks to a man, he calls
(2)

_____ "Sir."
(3)

(continued)

B: I like it when the teacher calls _____ by my first name.

(4)

A: I don't. There's another strange thing: In my country, we never use a first name for our teachers. We call _____ "Professor" or "Teacher." Our teacher here gets mad when we call _____

(5)

(6)
"Teacher." She doesn't like _____. She says it's impolite. But in

(7)
my country, "Teacher" is a term of great respect.

B: Only small children in the U.S. call their teacher "Teacher." If you know your teacher's name, use _____.

(8)

A: Do you mean I should call _____ Dawn?

(9)

B: If that's what she likes.

A: I'm sorry. I can't do _____. She's about 50 years old,

(10)
and I'm only 20.

B: Then call _____ Ms. Paskow.

(11)

A: She doesn't like to use her last name. She says everyone mispronounces _____. Sometimes I call _____ Ms. Dawn,

(12)

(13)
but she says no one does that here.

B: We have an expression, "When in Rome, do as the Romans do."[3]

A: It's hard for _____ to change my customs after a lifetime of

(14)
following _____.

(15)

EXERCISE **9** **Fill in the blanks with *I, I'm, my, mine,* or *me.***

EXAMPLES   _____ a foreign student. _____ come from Japan.

  I'm   *I*

  _____ roommate's parents live in the U.S., but _____ live in Japan.

  My   *mine*

1. _____ roommate's name is Kelly. _____ is Yuki.

2. _____ roommate helps _____ with my English.

3. _____ study at the University of Wisconsin.

4. _____ major is engineering.

5. _____ 20 years old.

6. _____ parents don't live in the U.S.

7. _____ parents call _____ twice a week.

---

[3] This expression means that you should follow the customs of the place you are in.

EXERCISE 10   **Fill in the blanks with *he, he's, his,* or *him*.**

EXAMPLE   I have a good friend. ____His____ name is Paul. ____He's____ Puerto Rican.

     ____He____ lives in New York. I like ____him____.

1. _____ married.
2. _____ works in an office.
3. _____ an accountant.
4. _____ son helps _____ in _____ business.
5. _____ 37 years old. _____ wife is 35.
6. My wife and _____ wife are friends.
7. My wife is a doctor. _____ is a computer programmer.

EXERCISE 11   **Fill in the blanks with *she, she's, her,* or *hers*.**

EXAMPLE   I have a friend. ____Her____ name's Diane. ____She's____ American.

     ____She____ lives in Boston. My native language is Korean. ____Hers____

is English.

1. _____ an interesting person.
2. I like _____ very much.
3. _____ married.
4. _____ has two children.
5. My children go to Dewey School. _____ go to King School.
6. _____ a nurse. _____ likes _____ job.
7. _____ husband is a teacher.

EXERCISE 12   **Fill in the blanks with *they, they're, their, theirs,* or *them*.**

EXAMPLE   Diane and Richard are my friends. ____They____ live in Boston. ____Their____

house is beautiful. ____They're____ happy. I see ____them____ on the weekends.

1. _____ Americans.
2. _____ both work.
3. _____ have two children.
4. _____ children go to public school.
5. My house is small. _____ is big.
6. _____ interested in art.
7. I talk to _____ once a week.

EXERCISE 13 Fill in the blanks about a cat. Use *it*, *it's*, or *its*.

EXAMPLE _____It's_____ an independent animal. _____It_____ always lands on

_____its_____ feet.

1. _____ likes to eat fish.
2. _____ a small animal.
3. _____ fur is soft.
4. _____ catches mice.
5. _____ claws are sharp.
6. _____ a clean animal.
7. Do you see that cat? Yes, I see _____.

EXERCISE 14 Fill in the blanks with *we*, *we're*, *our*, *ours*, or *us*.

EXAMPLE _____We_____ study English. _____We're_____ foreign students.

_____Our_____ teacher is American. He helps _____us_____.

1. _____ come from different countries.
2. _____ in class now.
3. _____ classroom is comfortable.
4. The teacher asks _____ a lot of questions.
5. The teacher's textbook has the answers. _____ don't have the answers.
6. _____ interested in English.

EXERCISE 15 Fill in the blanks with *you*, *you're*, *your*, or *yours*.

EXAMPLE _____You're_____ a good teacher. Students like _____you_____. My other teacher's

name is hard to pronounce. _____Yours_____ is easy to pronounce.

1. _____ explain the grammar well.
2. We all understand _____.
3. Our pronunciation is sometimes hard to understand. _____ is clear.
4. _____ a kind teacher.
5. _____ class is very interesting.
6. _____ have a lot of experience with foreign students.

Who Helps Your Parents?

1. At what age should adult children leave home if they're not married?

2. Should adult children take care of their parents?

CD 1, TR 25

Read the following conversation. Pay special attention to *wh-* **questions.**

A: Where does your dad live?

B: He lives back in our country.

A: Is he in good health?

B: His health is so-so.

A: Who takes care of him?

B: My brother and his wife do.

A: Do they go to his house every day?

B: No. They live with him.

A: Why do they live with him?

B: It's the custom in my country. What about in America? Do you live with your parents?

(continued)

A: Of course not. I'm 25. I live with my roommate.

B: Where do your parents live?

A: My parents are divorced. My mother lives just a couple of miles from me. My dad lives in another state.

B: How often do you see your parents?

A: I see my dad a couple of times a year. I see my mom about once or twice a month.

B: Is that all? Who helps them? Who shops for them? Who cooks for them?

A: They're in their 60s and in great health. They can do everything. No one takes care of them. What's wrong with that?

B: What about when they get older?

A: I never think about it. Who knows about the future?

5.7 Questions About the Subject or About the Complement

Compare these statements and related questions about the complement.

Subject	Verb	Complement	Wh-Word	Does/Do	Subject	Verb	
Dad	lives	in Korea.	Where	does	Dad	live?	We use *do* and *does* to ask a question about the complement of the sentence.
Dad	lives	with someone.	Whom*	does	he	live with?	
I	visit	once a month.	When	do	you	visit?	

*Language Note: In formal English, we put the preposition at the beginning and use *whom*.

Compare these statements and related questions about the subject.

Subject	Verb	Complement	Who/What	Verb -s Form	Complement	
Someone	helps	my father.	Who	helps	your father?	When we ask a question about the subject, we don't use *do* or *does*. We can use the *-s* form in the question.
Nobody	knows.		Who	knows	about the future?	
Something	is	wrong.	What	is	wrong with that?	

EXERCISE 16 **ABOUT YOU** Talk about some jobs in your house. Ask another student, "Who _____s in your house?" The other student will answer.

EXAMPLES take out the garbage

    A: Who takes out the garbage in your house?
    B: My brother does.

vacuum the carpet

    A: Who vacuums the carpet in your house?
    B: Nobody does. We don't have carpet.

1. dust the furniture
2. shop for groceries
3. pay the bills
4. wash the dishes
5. make your bed

6. take in the mail
7. wash the clothes
8. cook the meals
9. sweep the floor

EXERCISE 17 **Fill in the blanks to complete this conversation.**

A: _____ *Do you like* _____ going to school in the U.S.?
              (example)

B: Yes, I like it very much. But I miss my parents.

A: Where _____ *do they live* _____?
                (example)

B: They live in Korea.

A: How old _____ *are they* _____?
                (example)

B: They're in their 60s.

A: Who _____ of them?
          (1)

B: No one takes care of them. They're in great health.

A: _____ alone?
       (2)

B: No, they don't. They live with my oldest sister.

A: _____?
       (3)

B: No, she isn't single. She's married. She's a nurse, and her husband is a doctor.

A: How many _____?
              (4)

B: They have three kids. The girl is seven, and the boys are six and three.

A: Who _____ the kids when your sister and her
          (5)
husband go to work?

B: The older two are in school. My parents take care of the youngest.

A: How often _____ your parents?
$\qquad$ (6)

B: I talk to them about once a week.

A: Is it expensive to call your country?

B: Not really. I buy a phone card.

A: How much _____?
$\qquad$ (7)

B: It costs $5.00. We can talk for 30 minutes.

A: Do you plan to see them soon?

B: Who _____? Maybe yes, maybe no. I hope so.
$\qquad$ (8)

5.8 Who, Whom, Who's, Whose

Compare *who*, *whom*, *who's*, and *whose*.

EXAMPLES	EXPLANATION
Who needs the teacher's help? We do.	*Who* = Subject
Who(m) do you love? I love my parents.	*Who(m)* = Object
Who's that man? He's my dad.	*Who's* = Who is
Whose book is this? It's mine.	*Whose* = Possession (ownership)

EXERCISE 18 Fill in the blanks with *who*, *whom*, *who's*, or *whose*.

A: __Whose__ last name do you use? Your mother's or your father's?
$\qquad$ (example)

B: I use my father's last name. But I don't live with my father.

A: Why not?

B: My parents are divorced.

A: _____ do you live with, then? Your mother?
$\qquad$ (1)

B: No. I live with Nina.

A: _____ that?
$\qquad$ (2)

B: That's my sister.

A: Do you get along?[4]

B: Not really. She's so lazy. She never washes the dishes.

---

[4]To get along with someone means to have an easy, peaceful relationship with that person.

A: _____ washes the dishes then?
(3)

B: I do. I have to do everything. When I say, "_____ turn is it?" she
(4)

always says, "I know it's my turn, but I'm so busy today."

B: Then don't ask. Just tell her it's her turn. _____ pays the rent?
(5)

B: We both do.

A: I guess you need her, then.

B: I guess I do—for now.

EXERCISE 19 **Circle the correct word(s) to complete this conversation between two students.**

EXAMPLE **A:** (Who/(Who's)/Whose / Whom) your English teacher?
(example)

CD 1, TR 26

B: (My / Mine / Me) teacher's name is Charles Flynn.
(1)

A: (My / Mine / Me) is Marianne Peters. She's Mr. Flynn's wife.
(2)

B: Oh, really? His last name is different from (she / her / hers).
(3)

A: Yes. She uses (her / hers / his / he's) father's last name,
(4)

not her (husband's / husbands' / husbands / husband).
(5)

B: Do they have children?

A: Yes.

B: (Whose / Who's / Who / Whom) name do the children use?
(6)

A: (They / They're / Their / Theirs) children use both last names.
(7)

B: How do you know so much about (you / you're / your / yours) teacher
(8)

and (she / she's / her / hers) children?
(9)

A: We talk about (we / us / our /ours) names in class. We also talk about
(10)

American customs. She explains her customs, and we explain

(our / ours / us).
(11)

B: Mr. Flynn doesn't talk about (her / his / he's / hers) family in class.
(12)

A: Do you call (her / his / him / he) "mister"?
(13)

B: Of course. (He / He's / His) the teacher. We show respect.
(14)

(continued)

A: But we call Marianne by (*her / hers / she*) first name. (*She / She's / Her*) prefers that.
(15)   (16)

B: I prefer to call (*our / us / ours*) teachers by (*they / they're / their / theirs*) last names. That's the way we do it in my country.
                (17)   (18)

A: In (*me / my / mine*) we just say "Professor." But (*we / we're / us*) in the U.S. now. There's an expression: "When in Rome, do as the Romans do."
        (19)   (20)

Summary of Lesson 5

1. Possessive Forms of Nouns
   Jack's car is old.
   His **parents'** car is new.
   The **children's** toys are on the floor.
   What's the **name of our textbook**?

2. Pronouns and Possessive Forms

SUBJECT PRONOUN	OBJECT PRONOUN	POSSESSIVE ADJECTIVE	POSSESSIVE PRONOUN
I	me	my	mine
you	you	your	yours
he	him	his	his
she	her	her	hers
it	it	its	—
we	us	our	ours
they	them	their	theirs
who	whom	whose	whose

SUBJECT	**I** come from Cuba	**They** come from Korea.	**Who** comes from Poland?
OBJECT	The teacher helps **me.**	The teacher helps **them.**	**Who(m)** does the teacher help?
POSSESSIVE ADJECTIVE	**My** name is Rosa.	**Their** names are Kim and Park.	**Whose** name do you use?
POSSESSIVE PRONOUN	Your book is new. **Mine** is used.	Your book is new. **Theirs** is used.	This is your book. **Whose** is that?

Editing Advice

1. Don't confuse *you're* (you are) and *your* (possessive form).

   You're
   ~~Your~~ a good person.

   your
   Where's ~~you're~~ book?

2. Don't confuse *he's* (he is) and *his* (possessive form).

   His
   ~~He's~~ name is Paul.

   He's
   ~~His~~ a good student.

3. Don't confuse *it's* (it is) and *its* (possessive form).

   It's
   ~~Its~~ a beautiful day today.

   its
   A monkey uses ~~it's~~ tail to climb trees.

4. Don't confuse *his* and *her*.

   his
   My brother loves ~~her~~ daughter.

   her
   My sister loves ~~his~~ son.

5. Don't confuse *my* and *mine*.

   my
   I don't have ~~mine~~ book today.

6. Don't confuse *they're* and *their*.

   Their
   I have two American friends. ~~They're~~ names are Bob and Sue.

   They're
   ~~Their~~ very nice people.

7. Use the correct pronoun (subject or object).

   her
   I have a daughter. I love ~~she~~ very much.

   I
   My father and ~~me~~ like to go fishing.

8. Don't use *the* with a possessive form.

   M
   ~~The~~ my friend is very tall.

   I need ~~the~~ your dictionary.

9. Don't use *do* or *does* in a *who* question about the subject.

has
Who ~~does have~~ a Spanish dictionary?

10. Don't separate *whose* from the noun.

book
Whose is this ~~book~~?

11. Don't confuse *whose* and *who's*.

Whose
~~Who's~~ coat is that?

12. Use the correct word order for possession.

My neighbor's dog
~~Dog my neighbor~~ makes a lot of noise.

13. Put the apostrophe in the right place.

parents'
My ~~parent's~~ car is new.

14. Don't use the possessive form for nonliving things.

name of the book
Grammar in Context is the ~~book's name~~.

15. Don't use an apostrophe for plural nouns.

friends
She has many ~~friend's~~.

Editing Quiz

Some of the shaded words and phrases have mistakes. Find the mistakes and correct them. If the shaded words are correct, write C.

C
A: What's your name?
   (example)

B: Lisa Simms-Evans.

your
A: Do you like ~~you're~~ name?
   (example)

B: No, I don't. Its too long.
   (1)

A: Why do you have two last name's?
   (2)

B: I use both my mother's and my father's last names.
   (3)   *(4)*

A: What are your parent's names?
  (5)   (6)

B: They're names are Mary Simms and Ron Evans.
  (7)

A: Do you have any brothers or sisters?
  (8)   (9)

B: I have one brother. He's name is Leslie. His not happy with him name.
  (10)   (11)   (12)

In fact, he hates it.
  (13)

A: Why?

B: Leslie can be a boys' name or a girls' name. Her wife calls him Les.
  (14)   (15)   (16)   (17)

My parents and me call him "More or Less."
  (18)   (19)

A: That's funny.

B: And I have a sister too. Hers name is Holly. She doesn't like his name either.
  (20)   (21)

A: In your family, who does have a good name?
  (22)

B: My goldfish! It's name is Goldie.
  (23)

A: The dog my neighbor has that name. She's a Golden Retriever. But I
  (24)

don't like hers. She's barks all the time.
  (25)   (26)

B: My Goldie doesn't make any noise. It just quietly swims around in it's bowl.
  (27)   (28)

A: Well, class is over. Whose is that coat? Is it your's?
  (29)   (30)

B: It's not my. I think it's the teacher's.
  (31)   (32)

A: And that book on the floor. Is it yours or mines?
  (33)   (34)

B: What's the book's name?
  (35)

A: *Biology Today.* It's not my.
  (36)

B: Its not mine either. Who's name is in the book?
  (37) (38)   (39)

A: John Park. Let's take it and give it to him next time.
  (40)   (41)

Lesson 5 Test/Review

PART 1 **Choose the correct word(s) to complete these sentences.**

EXAMPLE Most American women change _____c_____ names when they get married, but not all do.

    a. her   **b.** hers   **c.** their   **d.** theirs

1. I have two _____.
   a. sisters   **b.** sister's   **c.** sisters'   **d.** sister

2. _____ names are Marilyn and Charlotte.
   a. Their   **b.** Theirs   **c.** They're   **d.** They   **e.** Hers

3. _____ both married.
   a. Their   **b.** They're   **c.** They   **d.** Them   **e.** There

4. Marilyn uses _____.
   a. the last name her husband
   b. the last name of his husband
   c. her husband's last name
   d. his husband's last name

5. Charlotte uses _____ father's last name.
   a. we   **b.** our   **c.** ours   **d.** us

6. I have one brother. _____ married.
   a. He's   **b.** His   **c.** He   **d.** Him

7. _____ wife is very nice.
   a. Him   **b.** Her   **c.** His   **d.** He's

8. _____ first name is Sandra.
   a. My   **b.** Mine   **c.** I'm   **d.** Me

9. My friends call _____ "Sandy."
   a. me   **b.** my   **c.** mine

10. My sister often uses her middle name, but I rarely use _____.
   a. my   **b.** mine   **c.** me   **d.** I'm

11. You have a dog, but I don't know _____ name.
   a. it   **b.** it's   **c.** its

12. _____ your teacher?

    a. Whom   **b.** Who   **c.** Whose   **d.** Who's

13. Her _____ names are Ricky and Eddie.

    a. childs'   **b.** children's   **c.** childrens   **d.** childrens'

14. _____ has the newspaper?

    a. Whom   **b.** Whose   **c.** Who   **d.** Who's

15. Who _____ more time with the test?

    a. need   **b.** does need   **c.** needs   **d.** does needs

16. The teacher's name is on _____.

    a. the door of her office

    b. her office's door

    c. the door her office

    d. her the office's door

17. _____

    a. Who's is that office?

    b. Whose is that office?

    c. Who's office is that?

    d. Whose office is that?

PART 2 **Two women are talking about names. Fill in the blanks with possessive forms, subject pronouns, or object pronouns. Some blanks need an apostrophe or an apostrophe + _s_.**

A: What's your last name?

B: It's Woods.

A: Woods sounds like an American name. But ___*you're*___ Polish, aren't you?
                                 (example)

B: Yes, but Americans have trouble pronouncing _____ name, so I
                                         _(1)_

    use the name "Woods."

A: What's _____ real last name?
              _(2)_

B: Wodzianicki.

A: My name is hard for Americans too, but _____ like my
                                           _(3)_

    name, and I don't want to change _____. I'm proud of it.
                                        _(4)_

B: What's _____ last name?
            _(5)_

A: Lopez Hernandez.

B: Why do _____ have two last names?
(6)

A: I come from Mexico. Mexicans have two last names. Mexicans use both parents _____ names.
(7)

B: What happens when a woman gets married? Does she use _____ parents _____ names and _____ husband _____ name too?
(8)　(9)　(10)　(11)

A: No. When a woman gets married, she usually drops _____ mother _____ name. She adds "of" (in Spanish, "de") and _____ husband _____ name. My sister is married. _____ name is Maria Lopez de Castillo. Lopez is _____ father _____ name and Castillo is her husband _____ name. _____ kids _____ last name is Castillo Lopez.
(12)　(13)　(14)　(15)　(16)　(17)　(18)　(19)　(20)　(21)

B: That's confusing. Everybody in the family has a different last name.

A: It's not confusing for us. You understand your customs, and we understand _____.
(22)

B: Do your sister _____ kids have American first names?
(23)

A: My sister gave _____ Spanish names, but _____ friends gave them American names. Her daughter _____ name is Rosa, but _____ friends call her Rose. _____ son _____ name is Eduardo, but _____ friends call _____ Eddie. Ricardo is the youngest one. _____ still a baby, but when he goes to school, _____ friends will probably call _____ Rick.
(24)　(25)　(26)　(27)　(28)　(29)　(30)　(31)　(32)　(33)　(34)

Expansion

1 **Find a partner. Compare yourself to your partner. Compare physical characteristics, clothes, family, home, job, car, etc. Report some interesting facts to the class.**

EXAMPLE My hair is straight. Mark's is curly.
His eyes are blue. Mine are brown.
My family lives in this city. Mark's family lives in Romania.

2 **One student will ask these *who* questions. Raise your hand if this is a fact about you. The first student will answer the question after he or she sees raised hands.**

EXAMPLE Who has kids?
Ben, Maria, and Lidia have kids.
Who has a pet bird?
No one has a pet bird.

1. Who has kids?
2. Who likes cartoons?
3. Who plays soccer?
4. Who has a laptop computer?
5. Who is a sports fan?
6. Who likes to swim?
7. Who is a vegetarian?
8. Who wants a grammar test?
9. Who has American friends?
10. Who has a pet?
11. Who lives in a house?
12. Who is over 6 feet tall?
13. Who has a motorcycle?
14. Who has an e-mail address?
15. Who gets a lot of junk mail?
16. Who exercises every day?
17. Who watches TV in the morning?
18. Who has a middle name?
19. Who wants to become an American citizen?
20. Who plays a musical instrument?

❸ Think of something unusual that you do or are. Write a sentence telling what you do or are. Then ask a question to find out who else does or is this.

EXAMPLES   I have a pet snake. Who else has a pet snake?
I play volleyball. Who else plays volleyball?
I am a baseball fan. Who else is a baseball fan?

(Variation: On a piece of paper, write something unusual that you do or are. Give the papers to the teacher. The teacher reads a statement. Other students—and the teacher—try to guess who wrote it.
Example: Someone has a pet snake. Who has a pet snake?)

Talk
About It

❶ What are some popular first names in your native country or culture?

❷ How do people choose a first name for their babies in your native country or culture?

Write
About It

Write about naming customs in your native culture. Do people have a middle name? Do fathers and sons ever have the same name? Tell about your name. Does it mean something?

My Name

My name is Yelena Ivanova Galinsky. I'm from

Russia. Yelena is my first name, but in the U.S.

everyone calls me Ellen. My father's name is Ivan.

"Ivanova" means that I'm Ivan's daughter. In Russia, we

always use our father's name as our middle name . . .

For more practice using grammar in context, please visit our Web site.

Grammar
The Present Continuous Tense[1]

Context
Observations About American Life

[1]The present continuous tense is sometimes called the present progressive tense.

Observations in the Park

Before You Read

1. Do you ever write in a journal?

2. Do you ever compare the behavior of Americans to the behavior of people from your native culture?

CD 1, TR 27

Read the following entry from Dan's journal. Pay special attention to the present continuous tense.

September 9

    I'm **taking** an ESL course this semester. Our teacher wants us to keep a journal. She wants us to write in it every day. I'm **beginning** my journal now. I'm in the park now. It's a beautiful day. The sun **is shining**. I'm **sitting** on a park bench and **observing** the behavior of people around me.

    It's warm and most of the people **are wearing** shorts, but I'm **wearing** long pants. Even old people **are wearing** shorts. This surprises me. Some people **are jogging**. They **are** all **carrying** MP3 players and **wearing** headphones. They **are** all **jogging** alone. A lot of people **are going** by on roller skates. Some young kids **are using** skateboards. It seems that these are popular activities here.

    A group of young men **is playing** soccer. I don't think they're Americans. I think Americans don't like soccer. Americans prefer baseball. In another part of the park, small children **are playing** baseball. Their parents **are watching** them. This is called Little League. Little League is very popular here.

    One man **is riding** a bike and **talking** on a cell phone at the same time. Some people **are having** a picnic. They **are barbecuing** hamburgers.

    There is a group of teenagers nearby. They **are talking** very loudly. They have a big boombox and **are listening** to hip-hop music. They**'re making** a lot of noise.

    I'm **learning** a lot about the American lifestyle.

6.1 The Present Continuous Tense

To form the present continuous tense, use a form of *be* (*is, am, are*) + verb *-ing*. We use the present continuous tense to describe an action in progress at this moment.

EXAMPLES	EXPLANATION
Subject **Be** **Verb + *-ing*** **Complement** I am **taking** an ESL class. The sun is **shining**. A man is **jogging**. He is **wearing** shorts. You are **reading** Dan's journal. Kids are **listening** to music. They are **talking** very loudly. We are **learning** about Americans.	I ⟶ am He/She/It ⟶ is Singular Subject ⟶ is } + verb *-ing* We/You/They ⟶ are Plural Subject ⟶ are
I'm taking an ESL class this semester. **They're** listening to music. **The sun's** shining.	We can make a contraction with the subject pronoun and a form of *be*. Most nouns can also form a contraction with *is*.[2]

Dan **isn't** writing a composition. He's writing in his journal.
The teenagers **aren't** paying attention to other people. They're listening to music.
	To form the negative, put *not* after the verb *am/is/are*.
	Negative contractions:
	  is not = isn't
	  are not = aren't
	There is no contraction for *am not*.

A man **is riding** his bike **and talking** on his cell phone.	When the subject is doing two or more things, we don't repeat the verb *be* after *and*.

EXERCISE 1   **Fill in the blanks with the missing part of each sentence.**

EXAMPLES   I' <u>m</u>   writing in my journal.

I'm learn <u>ing</u>   about life in the U.S.

1. Most people are wear ＿＿＿＿＿ shorts.

2. Some young men ＿＿＿＿＿ playing soccer.

3. Some children are play ＿＿＿＿＿ baseball.

4. Teenagers ＿＿＿＿＿ listening to music.

5. I' ＿＿＿＿＿ looking at people in the park.

6. The sun ＿＿＿＿＿ shining.

7. A man is riding his bike and talk ＿＿＿＿＿ on his cell phone.

[2]See Lesson 1, page 8 for exceptions.

6.2 Spelling of the *-ing* Form

Forms

RULE	VERBS	*-ING* FORM
Add *-ing* to most verbs. (Note: Do not drop the *y* of the base form.)	eat go study	eat**ing** go**ing** study**ing**
For a one-syllable verb that ends in a consonant + vowel + consonant (CVC), double the final consonant and add *-ing*.	p l a n ↓↓↓ C V C s t o p ↓↓↓ C V C s i t ↓↓↓ C V C	plan**ning** stop**ping** sit**ting**
Do not double a final *w*, *x*, or *y*.	show mix stay	sho**wing** mi**xing** sta**ying**
For a two-syllable verb that ends in CVC, double the final consonant only if the last syllable is stressed.	refér admít begín	refer**ring** admit**ting** begin**ning**
When the last syllable of a two-syllable verb is not stressed, do not double the final consonant.	lísten ópen óffer	listen**ing** open**ing** offer**ing**
If the verb ends in a consonant + *e*, drop the *e* before adding *-ing*.	live take write	liv**ing** tak**ing** writ**ing**

EXERCISE **2** Write the *-ing* form of the verb. (Two-syllable verbs that end in the CVC pattern have accent marks to show which syllable is stressed.)

EXAMPLES play __playing__

make __making__

1. plan _____
2. ópen _____
3. sit _____
4. begín _____
5. hurry _____
6. háppen _____

7. stay _____
8. grow _____
9. marry _____
10. grab _____
11. write _____
12. fix _____

13. wipe _____

14. carry _____

15. drink _____

16. drive _____

17. wait _____

18. serve _____

19. vísit _____

20. occúr _____

EXERCISE **3** Fill in the blanks with the present continuous tense of the verb in parentheses ( ). Use correct spelling.

EXAMPLE Dan ___*is observing*___ people in the park.
(observe)

1. He _____ about his observations.
(write)

2. Some men _____ soccer.
(play)

3. A man _____ a bike.
(ride)

4. Some people _____.
(jog)

5. The sun _____.
(shine)

6. He _____ on a park bench.
(sit)

7. Some people _____ by on roller skates and skateboards.
(go)

8. Some people _____ an MP3 player.
(carry)

6.3 The Present Continuous Tense—Uses

EXAMPLES	EXPLANATION
I **am writing** in my journal now. I **am observing** people in the park. Children **are playing** baseball. Teenagers **are listening** to music.	To show that an action is in progress now, at this moment
I'm **learning** about the American lifestyle. I'm **taking** an ESL course this semester. I'm **keeping** a journal this semester.	To show a long-term action that is in progress. It may not be happening at this exact moment.
Most people **are wearing** shorts. I'm **sitting** on a park bench.	To describe a state or condition, using the following verbs: *sit, stand, wear, sleep*

EXERCISE 4 **ABOUT YOU** **Make a true affirmative statement or negative statement about your activities now with the words given.**

EXAMPLES   wear a watch
I'm not wearing a watch (now).

drink coffee
I'm drinking coffee (now).

1. sit in the back of the room
2. speak my native language
3. pay attention
4. ask questions
5. practice the present continuous tense
6. look out the window
7. look at the board
8. write a composition
9. use my textbook
10. wear jeans

EXERCISE 5 **ABOUT YOU** **Make a true affirmative statement or negative statement about yourself with the words given. Talk about a long-term action.**

EXAMPLES   look for a job
I'm looking for a job.

live in a hotel
I'm not living in a hotel.

1. look for a new apartment
2. learn a lot of English
3. gain weight
4. lose weight
5. spend a lot of money
6. save my money
7. keep a journal
8. try to understand American customs
9. meet Americans
10. learn how to drive
11. live in a dorm
12. plan to return to my hometown

Observations Downtown

1. Do you ever take the bus?

2. Do a lot of people in this city drive and talk on a cell phone at the same time?

CD 1, TR 28

Dan (D) and his friend Peter (P) are waiting for the bus downtown. Read the following conversation. Pay special attention to questions with the present continuous tense.

D: Is the bus **coming**?

P: I don't see it. While we're waiting for the bus, let's talk about life in this city.

D: OK. Look at those women. **Why are they wearing** running shoes with business suits? **Why aren't they wearing** dress shoes? It looks strange.

P: Women in the U.S. want to be comfortable. They change to dress shoes when they get to work.

D: Oh. Now I understand. Look at that guy. **Why is he talking** on the phone **and driving** at the same time? Isn't it dangerous?

P: It seems everyone does that these days. Some places don't permit it.

D: And look at those bicycle riders. They're riding so fast. **Where are they going**? And **why are they riding** between the cars?

P: They're couriers. There are a lot of them downtown. They deliver packages from one office to another downtown.

D: **Are they getting** paid for this?

P: Of course. It's their job.

D: Look at all these people. **Why are they walking** so fast?

P: I guess everyone's in a hurry here. You know what they say: "Time is money."

D: Finally the bus is coming. **Are you going** back home now?

P: No. I'm going to the library to write in my journal about American customs.

6.4 Questions with the Present Continuous Tense

Compare affirmative statements and questions.

Wh- word	Be	Subject	Be	Verb + -ing	Complement	Short Answer
		Women	are	wearing	running shoes.	
	Are	they		wearing	suits?	Yes, they are.
Why	are	they		wearing	running shoes?	
Who	is			wearing	a business suit?	
		A man	is	talking	in his car.	
	Is	he		talking	to a passenger?	No, he isn't.
Why	is	he		talking	on his cell phone?	
Who(m)	is	he		talking	to?	

Language Notes:

1. We can answer a *yes/no* question with a short answer. Use the subject plus a form of *be*.
   Are they riding in a bus? No, they aren't.
   Are they waiting for the bus? Yes, they are. (Don't make a contraction for an affirmative short answer.)
2. When the question is "What ... doing?" we usually answer with a different verb.
   What is Dan *doing*? He's *looking* at people.
   What is the driver *doing*? He's *talking* on his cell phone.
3. Americans often use *who* instead of *whom*.
   Who is he talking to?

Compare negative statements and questions.

Wh- word	Be + n't	Subject	Be + n't	Verb + -ing	Complement
		They	aren't	wearing	dress shoes.
Why	aren't	they		wearing	dress shoes?

EXERCISE **6** **Answer the questions based on the conversation on page 163.**

1. Is Dan writing in his journal now?
2. Are people walking fast downtown?
3. What is the woman wearing?
4. Why is she wearing running shoes?
5. What are the two students waiting for?
6. Who is going to the library?

EXERCISE **7** **Use the words given to ask a question about what people in this class are doing now. Another student will answer.**

EXAMPLE   we/use the textbook now

A: Are we using the textbook now?
B: Yes, we are.

1. the teacher/write on the board
2. the teacher/sit at the desk
3. the teacher/help the students
4. we/practice the past tense
5. we/review Lesson 5
6. where/the teacher/stand or sit
7. what exercise/we/do
8. what/you/think about

EXERCISE **8**   **ABOUT YOU** **Ask a question about a long-term action with the words given. Another student will answer.**

EXAMPLE   you/study math this semester

A: Are you studying math this semester?
B: Yes, I am.

1. you/plan to buy a car
2. you/study biology this semester
3. you/take other courses this semester
4. you/look for a new apartment
5. you/look for a job
6. your English/improve
7. your vocabulary/grow
8. the teacher/help you
9. the students/make progress
10. you/learn about other students' countries

EXERCISE 9 **ABOUT YOU** Fill in the blanks with *I'm* or *I'm not* + the *-ing* form of the verb in parentheses ( ) to tell if you are doing these things now or at this general point in time. Then ask another student if he or she is doing this activity. The other student will answer.

EXAMPLES (plan) _____I'm planning_____ to buy a computer.

A: Are you planning to buy a computer?

B: Yes, I am.

(learn) _____I'm not learning_____ to drive a car.

A: Are you learning to drive a car?

B: No, I'm not.

1. (wear) _____ jeans.

2. (hold) _____ a pencil.

3. (chew) _____ gum.

4. (think) _____ about the weekend.

5. (live) _____ in a dorm.

6. (plan) _____ to take a vacation.

7. (look) _____ for a job.

8. (plan) _____ to buy a new computer.

9. (take) _____ a computer class this semester.

10. (get) _____ tired.

11. (gain) _____ weight.

12. (learn) _____ about the history of the U.S.

13. (learn) _____ how to drive.

EXERCISE 10 Write a question about each statement below. Use the question words given.

EXAMPLE Dan and Peter are studying English.

Where ___are they studying English__ ?

1. Dan and Peter are looking at people.

   Why _____?

2. They are waiting for the bus.

   Where _____?

3. People are walking fast.

   Why _____?

4. A man is talking on his cell phone.

   Who _____ to?

5. The woman in a suit isn't wearing dress shoes.

Why _____?

6. Dan isn't writing in his journal now.

Why _____?

7. Someone is riding a bicycle.

Who _____?

EXERCISE 11 A woman is calling her husband from a cell phone in her car. Fill in the blanks to complete the conversation. Answers may vary.

CD 1, TR 29

A: Hello?

B: Hi. It's Betty.

A: Oh, hi, Betty. This connection is so noisy. Where ___**are you calling**___
(example)
from?

B: I _____ from the car. I _____
(1) *(2)*
my cell phone.

A: _____ home now?
(3)

B: No, I'm not. I'm driving to the airport.

A: Why _____ to the airport?
(4)

B: I'm going to pick up a client.

A: I can't hear you. There's so much noise.

B: Airplanes _____ overhead. They're very low.
(5)

A: I can't hear you. Talk louder please.

B: I _____ as loud as I can. I _____
(6) *(7)*
to the airport to pick up a client. I'm late. Her plane _____
(8)
now, and I'm stuck in traffic³. I'm getting nervous. Cars aren't moving.

A: Why _____ moving?
(9)

B: There's an accident on the highway.

A: I worry about you. _____?
(10)

B: Of course I'm wearing my seat belt.

³When you are stuck in traffic, you can't move because other cars aren't moving.

(continued)

A: That's good.

B: What _____ now?
  (11)

A: I _____ the computer. I _____
  (12)   (13)
for information about cars on the Internet.

B: What _____ doing?
  (14)

A: The kids? I can't hear you.

B: Yes, the kids.

A: Meg _____ TV. Pam _____ her
  (15)   (16)
homework.

B: Why _____ Meg doing her homework?
  (17)

A: She doesn't have any homework today.

B: _____ dinner for the kids?
  (18)

A: No, I'm not making dinner. I _____ for you to come
  (19)
home and make dinner.

B: Please don't wait for me. Oh. Traffic is finally moving. Talk to you later.

Observations in the School Cafeteria

Before You Read

1. When you observe the students at this school, do you see any strange behaviors?

2. Is your behavior in this school different from your behavior when you are with your family or people from your native culture?

Read the following entry from Dan's journal. Pay special attention to verbs—simple present and present continuous.

March 8

I'**m sitting** in the school cafeteria now. I'**m writing** in my journal. I **want** to know about American customs, so I'**m observing** the behavior of other students. I **see** many strange behaviors and customs around me.

I'**m looking** at a young couple at the next table. The young man and woman **are touching, holding** hands, and even **kissing**. It **looks** strange because people never **kiss** in public back home. At another table, a young man and woman **are sitting** with a baby. The man **is feeding** the baby. Men never **feed** their babies in our country. Why **isn't** the woman **feeding** the baby? Students in our country **are** usually single, not married with children.

Two women **are putting** on makeup. I **think** this **is** bad public behavior. These women **are wearing** shorts. In our country, women never **wear** shorts.

A group of students **is listening** to the radio. The music **is** very loud. Their music **is bothering** other people, but they don't care. I'**m sitting** far from them, but I **hear** their music.

A young man **is resting** his feet on another chair. His friend **is eating** a hamburger with his hands. Why **isn't** he **using** a fork and knife?

These kinds of behaviors **look** bad to me. I'**m trying** to understand them, but I'**m having** a hard time. I still **think** many of these actions are impolite.

6.5 Present Continuous and Simple Present

Form

SIMPLE PRESENT	PRESENT CONTINUOUS
Dan sometimes **wears** a suit.	He **is wearing** jeans now.
He **doesn't** usually **wear** shorts.	He **isn't wearing** a belt.
Does he ever **wear** a hat?	**Is** he **wearing** a T-shirt?
Yes, he **does**.	No, he **isn't**.
When **does** he **wear** a hat?	What **is** he **wearing**?
Who **wears** a hat?	Who **is wearing** a T-shirt?

(continued)

Uses

EXAMPLES	EXPLANATION
a. Dan **writes** in his journal once a week. b. People **eat** hamburgers with their hands. c. The college cafeteria **has** inexpensive food.	We use the *simple present tense* to talk about: a. a habitual activity b. a custom c. a general truth or fact
a. Dan **is writing** in his journal now. b. He **is learning** more and more about life in the U.S.	We use the *present continuous tense* for: a. an action that is in progress at this moment b. a longer action that is in progress at this general time
Compare: Dan's family **lives** in another country. Dan **is living** in a dorm this semester.	When we use *live* in the simple present, we mean that this is a person's home. In the present continuous, it shows a temporary, short-term residence.
Compare: What **does** she **do** for a living? She's a nurse. What **is** she **doing**? She's waiting for the bus.	*What does she do?* asks about a profession or job. *What is she doing?* asks about a present activity.

EXERCISE **12** Two students meet in the cafeteria and discuss American customs and the customs of their native countries. Fill in the blanks with the correct form of the verb in parentheses ( ). Practice the simple present and the present continuous.

CD 1, TR 31

A: Hi. What _____*are you doing*_____ here?
(example: you/do)

B: I _____ lunch. I always _____
(1 eat)   *(2 eat)*

lunch at this time. But I _____ behaviors and
(3 also/observe)

customs in this country.

A: What do you mean?

B: Well, look at that man over there. He _____ an
(4 wear)

earring. It looks so strange. Only women _____
(5 wear)

earrings in my country.

A: It *is* strange. And look at that woman. She _____

(6 *wear*)

three earrings in one ear.

B: And she _____ running shoes with a dress. In my

(7 *wear*)

country, people only _____ running shoes for sports

(8 *use*)

activities.

A: Look at that student over there. He _____ a colored

(9 *use*)

pen to mark his textbook. In my country, we never _____

(10 *write*)

in our textbooks because they _____ to the college,

(11 *belong*)

not to the students.

B: Many college activities are different here. For example, my English

teacher usually _____ at the desk in class. In my

(12 *sit*)

country, the teacher always _____ in class. And the

(13 *stand*)

students always _____ when the teacher

(14 *stand up*)

_____ the room.

(15 *enter*)

A: And college students always _____ English or

(16 *study*)

another foreign language. Here, nobody knows another language.

My American roommate _____ five courses this

(17 *take*)

semester, but no foreign language.

B: By the way, how many classes _____ this semester?

(18 *you/take*)

A: Four. In my country, I usually _____ eight courses a

(19 *take*)

semester, but my adviser here says I can only take four.

B: I have to go now. My girlfriend _____ for me at the

(20 *wait*)

library.

6.6 Nonaction Verbs

Some verbs are nonaction verbs. Nonaction verbs describe a state or condition, not an action.

EXAMPLES	EXPLANATION
The music is bothering Dan, but the other students **don't care**. Dan **needs** a quiet place to write now. He **doesn't understand** the behavior of some students.	We do not usually use the present continuous tense with nonaction verbs. We use the *simple present tense*, even if we are talking about now.

Some Nonaction Verbs:			
like	need	think (that)	see
love	prefer	care (about)	hear
hate	know	understand	seem
want	believe	remember	cost
			own

Compare action and nonaction verbs.

ACTION (USES THE PRESENT CONTINUOUS TENSE)	NONACTION (USES THE SIMPLE PRESENT TENSE)
The music **is bothering** Dan. Dan **is learning** about American customs. He **is looking** at two people kissing. He **is writing** about the students. He **is drinking** tea. Some students **are listening** to the music. Dan **is looking** at students in the cafeteria.	He **prefers** soft music. He **cares** about good behavior. This behavior **seems** strange to him. He **wants** to understand American customs. He **likes** tea very much. Dan **hears** the music. He **sees** some strange behaviors.

Language Note:
In the above sentences, *listen* and *look* are voluntary. They are action verbs. *Hear* and *see* are involuntary. They are nonaction verbs.

EXERCISE 13 **Fill in the blanks with the simple present or the present continuous tense of the verb in parentheses ( ).**

EXAMPLES   I ___understand___ the explanation now.
         (understand)

         I ___am writing___ now.
         (write)

1. I _____ English this semester.
      (study)

2. We _____ the textbook now.
      (use)

3. We _____ a lot of practice with verb tenses.
      (need)

4. We _____ action and nonaction verbs.
(compare)

5. I _____ every grammar rule.
(not/remember)

6. I _____ the board.
(see)

7. I _____ at the clock now. I _____
(not/look)   (look)

at my book.

8. I _____ my dictionary now.
(not/need)

9. We _____ a composition now.
(not/write)

10. We _____ the students in the next room.
(not/hear)

11. We _____ about nonaction verbs.
(learn)

12. We _____ a lot of grammar.
(know)

6.7 *Think*, *Have*, and the Sense Perception Verbs

Think, have, and the sense perception verbs can be action or nonaction verbs.

EXAMPLES	EXPLANATION
Action: Dan **is thinking** about his mother's cooking. **Nonaction:** He **thinks** it is wrong to kiss in public.	When we think <u>about</u> something, *think* is an action verb. When we *think* <u>that</u> something is true, *think* is a nonaction verb. We are giving an opinion about something.
Action: He **is having** lunch in the cafeteria. **Action:** He **is having** new experiences in the U.S. **Nonaction:** He **has** free time now. **Nonaction:** He **has** new American friends. **Nonaction:** His best friend **has** the flu now.	When *have* means to experience something or to eat or drink something, it is an action verb. When *have* shows possession, relationship, or illness, it is a nonaction verb.
Action: He **is looking** at a woman wearing shorts. **Nonaction:** This behavior **looks** bad to him. **Action:** He is **smelling** the coffee. **Nonaction:** The coffee **smells** delicious.	The sense perception verbs (*look, taste, feel, smell, sound*) can be action or nonaction verbs. When the sense perception verbs describe a state, they are nonaction verbs. When they describe an action, they are action verbs.

EXERCISE 14 **Fill in the blanks with the simple present or the present continuous tense of the verb in parentheses ( ).**

EXAMPLES I _____*am thinking*_____ about my family.
   (think)

I _____*think*_____ that life in the U.S. is not perfect.
   (think)

1. She _____ the flowers.
   (smell)

2. The flowers _____ beautiful.
   (smell)

3. She _____ about her boyfriend.
   (think)

4. She _____ that her boyfriend is wonderful.
   (think)

5. I _____ a good time in the U.S.
   (have)

6. I _____ a lot of new friends.
   (have)

7. I _____ a lot of free time.
   (not/have)

8. My friend _____ a cold today and she can't go out,
   (have)

so I _____ lunch alone now.
   (have)

EXERCISE 15 **Fill in the blanks with the simple present or the present continuous of the verb in parentheses ( ). Use the simple present for regular activity and with nonaction verbs.**

EXAMPLES Dan _____*wants*_____ to understand American behavior.
   (want)

He _____*is looking*_____ at some Americans in the cafeteria now.
   (look)

1. Dan _____ in his journal now.
   (write)

2. He _____ in the school cafeteria now.
   (sit)

3. He _____ a couple with a baby.
   (see)

4. He often _____ to the cafeteria between classes.
   (go)

5. He _____ in his journal once a week.
   (write)

6. He _____ that his family _____ to
   (think)   (want)

know about American customs.

7. He _____ at a young man and woman. They _____ hands.
(look)
(hold)

8. This behavior _____ bad in his country.
(look)

9. He _____ about American customs now.
(think)

10. Some women _____ shorts now.
(wear)

11. Women in Dan's country never _____ shorts.
(wear)

12. American customs _____ strange to him.
(seem)

EXERCISE 16 **Read each sentence. Write the negative form of the underlined words. Use the words in parentheses ( ).**

EXAMPLES

Dan is looking at Americans. (people from his country)
He isn't looking at people from his country.

He knows about customs from his country. (American customs)
He doesn't know about American customs.

1. The father is feeding the baby. (the mother)

_____

2. Dan's sitting in the cafeteria. (in class)

_____

3. He understands customs from his country. (American customs)

_____

4. Some men and women kiss in public. (men and women in his country)

_____

5. Americans use their hands to eat a hamburger. (to eat spaghetti)

_____

6. The man is wearing an earring. (a bracelet)

_____

7. Americans seem strange to him. (to me)

_____

(continued)

8. American men <u>like</u> to take care of babies. (Dan)

_____

9. American women often <u>wear</u> shorts in the summer. (women in Dan's country)

_____

EXERCISE 🔲 17 **Read each sentence. Then write a** _yes/no_ **question about the words in parentheses ( ). Write a short answer.**

EXAMPLES Women sometimes wear earrings. (men/ever)
Do men ever wear earrings? Yes, they do.

The women are wearing shorts. (the men)
Are the men wearing shorts? No, they aren't.

1. Dan is writing. (his homework)

_____

2. He's watching people. (American people)

_____

3. He understands his own customs. (American customs)

_____

4. American men wear shorts in the summer. (American women)

_____

5. The man is eating. (a hot dog)

_____

EXERCISE 🔲 18 **Read each statement. Then write a** _wh-_ **question about the words in parentheses ( ). An answer is not necessary.**

EXAMPLES A young man is resting his feet on a chair. (why)
Why is he resting his feet on a chair?

Dan lives in the U.S. (where/his family)
Where does his family live?

1. Dan is writing a letter. (to whom) OR (who . . . to)

_____

2. Dan wants to know about American customs. (why)

_____

3. Two women are putting on makeup. (where)

_____

4. American men and women touch and hold hands in public. (why)

_____

5. Dan writes to his family. (how often)

_____

6. The man isn't using a fork. (why/not)

_____

7. Women don't wear shorts in some countries. (why/not)

_____

8. Americans often wear jeans. (why)

_____

9. "Custom" means tradition or habit. (what/"behavior")

_____

EXERCISE 19 **This is a phone conversation between Dave (D) and his mother (M). Fill in the blanks with the correct form of the words in parentheses ( ) to complete the conversation.**

CD 1, TR 32

D: Hello?

M: Hi, Dave. It's Mom.

D: Hi, Mom. How _____**are you doing**_____?
     (example: you/do)

M: We _____ fine. And you?
        _(1 be)_

   How _____ college in the U.S.?
       (2 you/like)

D: Great. I _____ it a lot.
         (3 like)

   I _____ a lot of fun.
     (4 have)

M: Fun? _____?
          (5 why/you/not/study)

D: I _am_ studying. But I _____ new people from all over
                              (6 meet)

   the world. I _____ about getting an earring.
                (7 think)

M: What? Earrings are for women.

D: But, Mom, all the guys _____ it these days.
                              _(8 do)_

(continued)

M: I _____(9 not/care)_____. You _____(10 not/need)_____ an earring.

You just _____(11 need)_____ to study. _____(12 you/get)_____

good grades?

D: You _____(13 know)_____ I'm a good student. Of course

I _____(14 get)_____ good grades.

M: _____(15 you/practice)_____ your guitar these days?

D: Yes, I am. But I _____(16 not/have)_____ as much time as before.

I _____(17 take)_____ five classes this semester.

M: Only five? Students here _____(18 usually/take)_____ eight classes.

D: The system is different here. Freshmen only take four or five classes.

M: What _____(19 freshman/mean)_____?

D: A freshman is a student in the first year of college.

M: How's the food? _____(20 you/get)_____ enough to eat?

D: Yes, I am. In fact, I _____(21 gain)_____ weight. But I

_____(22 not/like)_____ the food here.

M: Why _____(23 not/like)_____ the food?

D: It's too greasy. And it _____(24 not/taste)_____ like food back home.

I really _____(25 miss)_____ your food.

M: I _____(26 make)_____ your favorite dish now.

D: Really? I _____(27 get)_____ hungry just thinking about it.

M: You and Dad _____(28 always/think)_____ that my food is the best.

D: Where's Dad?

M: He _____(29 work)_____ in the garden now. He's planting a new tree.

D: Thanks for sending me the sweater. I _____(30 wear)_____ it now.

M: _____ enough warm clothes?
   (31 you/have)

D: For now, I do. But it _____ to get cold these days.
   (32 start)

   And the days _____ shorter. Fall is beautiful here.
   (33 get)

   The trees _____ color. I _____
   (34 change)   *(35 look)*

   out my window now and I _____ a beautiful maple
   (36 see)

   tree with red leaves. But I _____ the climate back
   (37 prefer)

   home. It's warm all year. Here it's really cold in December and January.

M: I _____ a new sweater for you now. Your sister Ruby
   (38 make)

   _____ you a scarf.
   (39 make)

D: Thanks, Mom. Where's Ruby? _____ to talk to me now?
   (40 she/want)

M: I _____ so. She _____ a movie
   (41 not/think)   *(42 watch)*

   with her friends.

D: _____ good grades this semester?
   (43 she/get)

M: She _____ too much time with her friends these days.
   (44 spend)

D: Well, she's 16. Friends are really important when you're 16.

M: I'm worried about her.

D: Don't worry so much, Mom.

M: Of course I worry. I'm a mother. Dad _____ in now.
   (45 come)

   He _____ to talk to you now.
   (46 want)

D: OK, Mom. Bye.

Summary of Lesson 6

Uses of Tenses

Simple Present Tense	
General truths	Americans **speak** English. Oranges **grow** in Florida.
Regular activity, habit	I always **speak** English in class. I sometimes **eat** in the cafeteria. I **visit** my parents every Friday.
Customs	Americans **shake** hands. Japanese people **bow**.
Place of origin	Miguel **comes** from El Salvador. Marek **comes** from Poland.
With nonaction verbs	She **has** a new car. I **like** the U.S. You **look** great today.

Present Continuous (with action verbs only)	
Now	We **are reviewing** now. I **am looking** at page 180 now.
A long action in progress at this general time	Dan **is learning** about American customs. He **is studying** English.
A descriptive state	She **is wearing** shorts. He **is sitting** near the door. The teacher **is standing**.

Editing Advice

1. Include *be* with a continuous tense.

    is
He ^ working now.

2. Use the correct word order in a question.

    are you
Where ~~you're~~ going?

    don't you
Why ~~you don't~~ like New York?

3. Don't use the present continuous with a nonaction verb.

    has
She ~~is having~~ her own computer.

4. Use the *-s* form when the subject is *he*, *she*, or *it*.

    has   *s*
He ~~have~~ a new car. He like ^ to drive.

5. Don't use *be* with a simple present-tense verb.

    I
~~I'm~~ need a new computer.

6. Use *do* or *does* in a simple present-tense question.

    does   *live*
Where ~~lives~~ your mother? ^

7. Don't use the *-s* form after *does*.

Where does he take~~s~~ the bus?

Review the Editing Advice for the simple present tense on pages 65–67.

Editing Quiz

Some of the shaded words and phrases have mistakes. Find the mistakes and correct them. If the shaded words are correct, write C.

    are you C
A: What ~~you're~~ doing now?
    (example) *(example)*

B: I writing in my journal.
    (1)

A: Why you doing that?
(2)

B: It's an assignment for my English class.

A: What are you have to do?
(3)

B: We're needing to write about our observations.
(4)

A: I'm thinking that's a great idea. This way you're learning about
(5)   (6)

American life.

B: I'm having trouble with my spelling.
(7)

A: Maybe I can help you.

B: How spell "earring"?
(8)

A: E-A-R-R-I-N-G.

B: Thanks.

A: Why are you write about earrings?
(9)

B: Look at that woman. She wearing three earrings in one ear. I'm thinking
(10)   (11)

about doing that.

A: Where do they pierce ears?
(12)

B: There's a place on Main Street.

Lesson 6 Test/Review

PART 1 This is a conversation between two students, Alicia (A) and Teresa (T), who meet in the school library. Fill in the blanks with the simple present or the present continuous form of the verb in parentheses ( ).

T: Hi, Alicia.

A: Hi, Teresa. What _____*are you doing*_____ here?
(example: you/do)

T: I _____ for a book on American geography. What
(1 look)

about you?

A: I _____ a book. _____ to go for
     (2 return)   *(3 you/want)*

a cup of coffee?

T: I can't. I _____ for my friend.
          (4 wait)

We _____ on a geography project together, and
     (5 work)

we _____ to finish it by next week.
     (6 need)

A: _____ your geography class?
      (7 you/like)

T: Yes. I especially _____ the teacher, Bob. He's a
                    (8 like)

handsome young man. He's very casual. He always

_____ jeans and a T-shirt to class. He
     (9 wear)

_____ an earring in one ear.
     (10 have)

A: That _____ very strange to me.
          (11 seem)

I _____ that teachers in the U.S. are very informal.
     (12 think)

How _____ the class? By lecturing?
      (13 Bob/teach)

T: No. We _____ in small groups, and he
            (14 usually/work)

_____ us by walking around the classroom.
     (15 help)

A: _____ hard tests?
      (16 he/give)

T: No. He _____ in tests.
            (17 not/believe)

A: Why _____ in tests?
           (18 he/not/believe)

T: He _____ that students get too nervous during a test.
        (19 think)

He _____ it's better to work on projects. This week
     (20 say)

we _____ on city maps.
     (21 work)

A: That _____ interesting.
          (22 sound)

T: Why _____ me so many questions about my teacher?
           (23 you/ask)

A: I _____ about taking a geography course next semester.
     (24 think)

(continued)

T: Bob's very popular. Be sure to register early because his classes

always _____ up quickly. Oh. I _____
(25 fill)   (26 see)

my friend now. She _____ toward us. I have to go now.
(27 walk)

A: Good luck on your project.

T: Thanks. Bye.

PART 2 **Fill in the blanks with the negative form of the underlined word.**

EXAMPLE   Teresa <u>is</u> in the library. She _____isn't_____ at home.

1. Alicia <u>wants</u> to go for a cup of coffee. Teresa _____ to

   go for a cup of coffee.

2. Teresa <u>is looking</u> for a book. Alicia _____ for a book.

3. They <u>are talking</u> about school. They _____ about the

   news.

4. They <u>have</u> time to talk now. They _____ time for a cup

   of coffee.

5. Students in the geography class <u>work</u> in small groups.

   They _____ alone.

6. Alicia's teacher <u>gives</u> tests. Teresa's teacher _____ tests.

7. Teresa <u>is waiting</u> for a friend. Alicia _____ for a friend.

8. The teacher <u>seems</u> strange to Alicia. He _____ strange

   to Teresa.

9. Alicia <u>is returning</u> a book. Teresa _____ a book.

PART 3 **Read each sentence. Then write a *yes/no* question about the words in parentheses ( ). Write a short answer based on Part 1.**

EXAMPLE   Teresa is looking for a book. (a geography book)

   Is she looking for a geography book? Yes, she is.

1. Bob likes projects. (tests)

_____

2. Alicia has time now. (Teresa)

_____

3. They are talking about their classes. (their teachers)

_____

4. Bob wears jeans to class. (ever/a suit)

_____

5. Alicia wants to go for coffee. (Teresa)

_____

6. American teachers seem strange to Alicia. (to Teresa)

_____

7. Teresa is working on a geography project. (Alicia)

_____

PART 4 **Read each sentence. Then write a question with the words in parentheses ( ). An answer is not necessary.**

EXAMPLE Bob is popular. (Why)
Why is he popular?
_____

1. Bob sounds interesting. (Why)

_____

2. Bob doesn't like tests. (Why)

_____

3. Teresa and her friend are working on a project. (What kind of project)

_____

4. Teresa studies in the library. (How often)

_____

5. Teresa is looking for a book. (What kind)

_____

6. Teresa is waiting for her friend. (Why)

_____

7. Her classmates aren't writing in a journal. (Why)

_____

Expansion

❶ Think of a place (cafeteria, airport, train station, bus, playground, church, opera, movie theater, laundry, office at this school, kindergarten classroom, restaurant, department store, etc.). Pretend you are at this place. Write three or four sentences to tell what people in this place are doing. Other students will guess where you are.

EXAMPLE People are walking fast.
They're carrying suitcases.
They're standing in long lines.
They're holding passports.
Guess: Are you at the airport?

❷ Pretend you are calling from your cell phone. You are telling your family where you are. Fill in the blanks to tell what you and other people are doing. Then find a partner and see how many of your sentences match your partner's sentences.

a. I'm at the supermarket. I'm _____.
Do you need anything while I'm here?

b. I'm in my car. I'm _____.

c. I'm in the school library. I'm _____.
People _____ me to be quiet because
I'm _____ to you on my cell phone.

d. I'm in a taxi. I'm on my way home. I'm _____
you to let you know that _____.

e. I'm at the bus stop. I _____.

f. I'm at a shoe store. I _____.

g. I'm at the playground with the kids. The kids _____.

h. I'm at the movies. I can't talk now because the movie
_____.

i. I'm in the bedroom. I have to talk softly because my roommate
_____.

j. I'm in class now. I can't talk. The teacher _____.

Talk

About It Discuss behaviors that are strange to you. What American behaviors are not polite in your native culture?

Write

About It Go to the school cafeteria, student union, or other crowded place. Sit there for a while and observe. Write down some of the things you see. Report back to the class.

Observations in the Library

I'm in the public library now. I see two girls together.

They're talking and looking at books about dinosaurs.

They have a lot of books on the table. I think they're

doing a project together . . .

 For more practice using grammar in context, please visit our Web site.

Grammar
Future Tenses—*Will* and *Be Going To*

Comparison of Tenses

Context
Weddings

Planning for a Wedding

1. In your native culture, what kinds of gifts do people give to a bride and groom?

2. Are weddings expensive in your native culture?

CD 1, TR 33

Read the following magazine article. Pay special attention to future-tense verbs.

Karyn and Steve are engaged now and are planning their wedding. They need a lot of time to plan. They**'re going to graduate** from college next year, and the wedding **will take place** a year and a half after they graduate from college. They **will need** time to choose a photographer, invitations, a place for the reception,[1] a wedding dress, flowers, rings, a wedding cake, entertainment, and more. The wedding **is going to be** very expensive. In addition to paying for the wedding and reception, they **will need to rent** a limousine[2] and **pay** for a rehearsal dinner and a honeymoon. They **are going to invite** about 250 people, including many friends and relatives from out of town. They **are going to pay** for the hotel rooms for their grandparents, aunts, and uncles. It **is going to take** a lot of time and energy to plan for the wedding.

Before their wedding, they **will register** for gifts. They **will go** to stores and **select** the gifts they want to receive. When guests go to the stores, they **will choose** a gift from this list. This way, Karyn and Steve **are going to receive** exactly what they want. They **won't receive** duplicate presents. About six or seven weeks before the wedding, they **will send** out their invitations. After they return from their honeymoon in Hawaii, they **are going to send** thank-you cards to all the guests.

Who**'s going to pay** for all this? After they graduate, they **will work** and **save** money for their dream wedding. But their parents **are going to help** too. Like many young couples, they **will have** credit card debt for years after the wedding. This is in addition to college debt.

Did You Know?

Over two million couples get married in America each year. About half of these couples will get divorced. For many couples getting married today, their wedding debt will last longer than their marriage.

[1]A *reception* is a party after a wedding.
[2]A *limousine* is a fancy car, often longer than a normal car. A hired driver drives the car.

Average Wedding Cost in the U.S. (2007) = $28,800
Some Typical Costs
Wedding dress = $900
Invitations = $500
Flowers = $1,000
Reception = $13,000
Engagement ring = $3,215

7.1 Future with *Will*

EXAMPLES	EXPLANATION
Subject / *Will* / **Verb** / **Complement** They **will** **rent** a limousine. There **will** **be** a reception. The bride **will** **wear** a white dress.	We use *will* + the base form for the future tense. *Will* doesn't have an -s form.
They'll register for gifts. **She'll** buy a white dress. **He'll** rent a tuxedo. **It'll** take them a long time to plan for the wedding.	We can make a contraction with the subject pronoun and *will*. I will = I'll It will = It'll You will = You'll We will = We'll He will = He'll They will = They'll She will = She'll
They **will not receive** duplicate presents. They **won't pay** for everything. Their parents will help them.	Put *not* after *will* to form the negative. The contraction for *will not* is *won't*.
I will **always** love you. I will **never** leave you. We will **probably** give money as a gift.	You can put an adverb (*always, never, probably, even*) between *will* and the main verb.

EXERCISE **1** **Fill in the blanks with an appropriate verb in the future tense. Practice *will*. Answers may vary.**

EXAMPLE   Karyn and Steve's wedding _____*will be*_____ in a church.

1. They _____ 250 guests.

2. The wedding _____ expensive.

3. They _____ to Hawaii on their honeymoon.

4. They _____ debt for many years after the wedding.

5. Guests _____ presents that the bride
   and groom want.

6. The bride and groom _____ a limousine.

7. Their parents _____ them pay for the wedding.

7.2 Future with *Be Going To*

EXAMPLES	EXPLANATION
Subject **Be** **Going To** **Verb** **Complement** I **am** **going to** **buy** a gift. You **are** **going to** **attend** the wedding. They **are** **going to** **send** invitations. The bride **is** **going to** **wear** a white dress.	Use *is/am/are* + *going to* + the base form for the future tense.
They **are not going to graduate** this year. The bride **is not going to use** her sister's dress.	To make a negative statement, put *not* after *is/am/are*.
They **are going to go** on a honeymoon. OR They **are going** on a honeymoon.	When the main verb is *to go*, we often delete it.
They **are** *probably* **going to open** their gifts at home. They **are** *always* **going to remember** their wedding day.	We can put an adverb (*always, never, probably, even*) between *is, am, are* and *going*.

Language Note:
We can make contractions.
   The **bride's** going to wear a white dress.
   She **isn't** going to wear her sister's dress.
   We're not going to bring our present to the wedding.

Pronunciation Notes:
1. In informal speech, *going to* before another verb often sounds like "gonna." We don't write "gonna."
2. We pronounce "gonna" only if a verb follows *to*. We don't pronounce "gonna" in the following sentence: They are going to Hawaii.
Listen to your teacher pronounce the sentences in the above boxes.

EXERCISE 2 Fill in the blanks with an appropriate verb in the future tense. Practice *be going to*. Answers may vary.

EXAMPLE They _____ *are going to send* _____ invitations to the guests.

1. Musicians _____ at the wedding.

2. A professional photographer _____ pictures.

3. There _____ a lot of people at the wedding.

4. The bride _____ a white dress.

5. The wedding _____ a lot of money.

6. The wedding _____ in a church.

7. The wedding cake _____ very expensive.

7.3 Choosing *Will* or *Be Going To*

In many cases, you can use either *will* or *be going to*. But in a few cases, one is preferred over the other.

EXAMPLES	EXPLANATION
I think the newlyweds **will be** very happy together. I think the newlyweds **are going to be** very happy together.	For a prediction, we can use either *will* or *be going to*.
The wedding **will be** in a church. The wedding **is going to be** in a church. They **will send** out 250 invitations. They **are going to send** out 250 invitations.	For a simple fact about the future, we can use either *will* or *be going to*.
A: What **are you going to get** for a wedding gift? B: Maybe I**'ll give** them a check. Or maybe I**'ll buy** something.	Speaker B is considering her options at the time of the conversation. She chooses *will*. She did not think about the gift before.
A: What **are you going to get** them? B: I**'m going to get** them dishes. A: How many guests **is** your cousin **going to invite** to the wedding? B: He**'s going to invite** 100 guests.	Speaker B is talking about a decision or plan made before this conversation. She chooses *be going to*. "I'm **going** to get them dishes." = "I'm **planning** to get them dishes."
A: I don't have enough money for the gift. B: I**'ll lend** you some money.	Speaker B is making an offer to help. She's making this decision at the time of the conversation. She chooses *will*.
A: Can I borrow $50? B: Sure. A: I**'ll pay** you back tomorrow.	Speaker A is making a promise. He chooses *will*.

EXERCISE 3   **ABOUT YOU** Tell if you have plans to do these things or not. Practice *be going to.*

EXAMPLE   meet a friend after class
I'm (not) going to meet a friend after class.

1. get something to eat after class
2. watch TV tonight
3. eat dinner at home tonight
4. go to the library this week
5. go shopping for groceries this week
6. stay home this weekend
7. take a vacation this year
8. move (to a different apartment) this year
9. buy a car this year

EXERCISE 4   **ABOUT YOU** Predict if these things are going to happen or not in this class. Practice *be going to.*

EXAMPLE   we/finish this lesson today
We are going to finish this lesson today.

1. the teacher/give a test soon
2. the test/be hard
3. most students/pass the test
4. I/pass the test
5. the teacher/give everyone an A
6. my English/improve
7. we/finish this book by the end of the semester
8. the next test/cover the future tense
9. we/have a party at the end of the semester

EXERCISE 5   Fill in the blanks with the future tense of the verb in parentheses ( ). Practice *be going to.* Answers may vary.

EXAMPLE   The wedding costs a lot of money. Our parents ___are going to pay___ for the wedding.
                                                                              (pay)

1. Guests will give us gifts. Some people _____ us money.
                                                    (give)

2. We need a wedding cake. We _____ it at the best bakery.
                                        (buy)

3. We have to send out 250 invitations. We _____ them
                                                    (send)

out about two months before the wedding.

4. I have to choose a dress. I _____ a lot of money.
    (spend)

5. After the wedding, we _____ thank-you cards to all the
    (send)

 guests.

6. My grandparents are coming from another state. They

 _____ in a hotel. We _____ for their
    (stay)   *(pay)*

 hotel room.

EXERCISE 6 Use *will* or *be going to* to make predictions about the future of families (either in the U.S. or in your native country). Begin with *I think* or *I don't think*.

EXAMPLE divorce/increase
I don't think the divorce rate will increase in the U.S.

OR

I don't think the divorce rate is going to increase in the U.S. I think it's going to go down.

1. people/get married at an older age

2. the cost of weddings/go down

3. people/have more children

4. grown children/depend on their parents

5. grown children/take care of their parents

6. people/live longer

7. people/save more money

EXERCISE 7 Some friends of yours are going to have a birthday soon, and you want to buy them a present or do something special for them. What will you buy or do for these people?

EXAMPLE Maria's birthday is in the winter.
I'll buy her a sweater. OR   I'll take her skiing.

1. Bill loves to go fishing.

2. Tina loves to eat in restaurants.

3. Carl needs a new digital camera.

4. Jim has a new MP3 player.

5. Lisa loves the beach in the summer.

6. Tom loves movies.

EXERCISE 8   **A man is proposing marriage to a woman. He is making promises. Fill in the blanks with *will* + verb to complete these statements.**

EXAMPLE   I _____*will be*_____ a good husband to you.

1. I love you very much. I (always) _____ you.

2. I want to make you happy. I _____ everything I can to make you happy.

3. I don't have a lot of money, but I _____ hard and try to save money.

4. We _____ children, and I _____ a good father to them.

5. We _____ old together.

6. We _____ best friends and take care of each other.

7. You are the only woman for me. I (not) _____ at another woman.

EXERCISE 9   **The bride (B) has a lot to do before the wedding. She's getting nervous. Her sister (S) is offering to help. Use *will* + an appropriate verb. Answers may vary.**

EXAMPLE   **B:** I have to address a lot of invitations.

   S: *Give me a pen. I'll help you* _____.

1. **B:** I have to pick up stamps.

   S: I'm going to the post office. _____.

2. **B:** I have to make a reservation for Grandma and Grandpa at a hotel.

   S: _____.

3. **B:** I have to write a check for the flowers, and I'm low on money now.

   S: Don't worry. _____.
   You can pay me back next week.

4. **B:** Now the phone is ringing. I don't know what to do.

   S: Relax. _____.

5. **B:** I'm hungry. There's nothing in the house to eat.

   S: Let's go out to eat.

   B: I don't have money to eat out.

   S: That's OK. _____.

6. **B:** We need music for the wedding. I have the names of three bands. I don't know which is the best one.

   S: _____. I'll let you know which one has the best price. By the way, where's Steve? Why isn't he doing some of this?

Is the Honeymoon Over?

Before
You Read

1. Do married people usually agree on how to spend money?

2. In your country, do parents help their children after they get married?

CD 1, TR 34

After the wedding, the bride and groom usually go on a honeymoon. They take a trip together. Karyn (K) and Steve (S) are talking about their honeymoon plans. Pay special attention to questions with the future tense.

S: I have an idea for our honeymoon. How about a week in Hawaii?

K: I hear Hawaii's very expensive. **How much will it cost** us?

S: Well, the flight is about $700 per person.

K: That's not bad. How about the hotel?

S: About $3,000 for a week.

K: **Why is it going to cost** so much money?

S: It's one of the best hotels in Hawaii. And it's December, so it's high season.

K: **How will we pay** for this?

S: Our parents are going to give us a lot of money. And we're going to get a lot of money as gifts, I'm sure.

K: **Are we going to spend** all our gift money on our honeymoon? That means we're going to start our marriage with very little money. **Aren't we going to save** for a house?

S: Don't worry. When we get back, I'm going to start my new job.

K: I think it's a bad idea to start married life with so much debt.

S: You worry about money too much.

K: And you don't worry enough. **Am I going to be** the only one who thinks about saving? Maybe we should see a marriage counselor before we get married. I think the honeymoon is going to be over before it begins!

7.4 Questions with *Be Going To*

Compare affirmative statements and questions.

Wh- Word	Be	Subject	Be	Going To + Base Form	Complement	Short Answer
		They	are	going to spend	a lot of money.	
	Are	they		going to spend	more than $3,000?	Yes, they are.
How much	are	they		going to spend	for the honeymoon?	
		Who	is	going to spend	the money?	

Compare negative statements and questions.

Wh- Word	Be + n't	Subject	Be + not	Going To + Base Form	Complement
		They	aren't	going to save	money.
	Aren't	they		going to save	for a home?
Why	aren't	they		going to save	money?

EXERCISE 10 **ABOUT YOU** Ask another student a *yes/no* question with *are you going to* about a time later today. Then ask a *wh-* question with the words in parentheses ( ) whenever possible.

EXAMPLE listen to the radio (when)

A: Are you going to listen to the radio tonight?
B: Yes, I am.
A: When are you going to listen to the radio?
B: After dinner.

1. watch TV (what show)

2. listen to music (where)

3. read the newspaper (what newspaper)

4. go shopping (why)

5. take a shower (when)

6. eat dinner (with whom) OR (who . . . with)

7. call someone (whom) OR (who)

8. check your e-mail (when)

9. do your homework (when)

EXERCISE 11 **ABOUT YOU** Ask another student a *yes/no* question with *be going to* and the words given. Then ask a *wh-* question with the words in parentheses ( ) whenever possible.

EXAMPLE take another English course after this one (which course)

A: Are you going to take another English course after this one?
B: Yes, I am.
A: Which course are you going to take?
B: I'm going to take level 4.

1. stay in this city (why)

2. study something new (what)

3. look for a job (when)

4. get an A in this course (what grade)

5. buy a computer (why) (what kind)

6. visit other American cities (which cities)

7. transfer to another school (why) (which school)

7.5 Questions with *Will*

Compare affirmative statements and questions.

Wh- Word	*Will*	Subject	*Will*	Base Form	Complement	Short Answer
		The wedding	**will**	cost	a lot of money.	
	Will	it		cost	more than $10,000?	Yes, it will.
How much	**will**	it		cost?		
		Who	**will**	pay?		

Compare negative statements and questions.

Wh- Word	*Won't*	Subject	*Won't*	Base Form	Complement
		The flight	**won't**	cost	a lot of money.
	Won't	the flight		cost	more than $1,000?
Why	**won't**	the flight		cost	more than $1,000?

EXERCISE **12** **Fill in the blanks with the correct form of the verb in ( ). Use *will* for the future.**

CD 1, TR 35

A: When's your cousin's wedding?

B: It's tomorrow. I have to go to the store to check the wedding registry tonight.

A: I <u>'ll go</u> with you.
(example: be)

B: But look at the time. It's late. The store _____ closed
(1 be)

by the time we arrive. What _____?
(2 I/do)

A: You can probably find the registry online.

B: I don't know how to do that.

A: I _____ you.
(3 help)

B: But the gift _____ by tomorrow.
(4 not/arrive)

A: It doesn't have to arrive before the wedding. The bride and groom

_____ their presents after they return from their honeymoon.
(5 probably/open)

B: Or maybe I can just give them a check.

A: That's a good idea. Newlyweds always need money. What time

_____?
(6 the wedding/start)

B: The invitation says it _____ at 5:30 PM, but
(7 start)

usually weddings don't start exactly on time.

A: Where _____?
(8 the wedding/be)

B: It'll be in a hotel.

A: What _____ to the wedding?
(9 you/wear)

B: I don't know. I _____ my blue suit. Oh. I just
(10 probably/wear)

remembered that my blue suit is dirty. I _____ time
(11 not/have)

to take it to the cleaners. I _____ wear my gray suit.
(12 have to)

A: How many people _____ the wedding?
(13 attend)

B: About 200 people _____ the wedding.
(14 attend)

A: What kind of food _____ at the reception?
(15 they/serve)

B: There _____ a choice of chicken or fish.
(16 be)

A: How long _____?
(17 the wedding/last)

B: The ceremony _____ about a half hour. Then
(18 probably/last)

there's a dinner. People _____ for hours after
(19 probably/stay)

the dinner to dance.

A: _____ for their honeymoon immediately?
(20 the bride and groom/leave)

B: Probably not. They _____ tired after the
(21 be)

wedding. They _____ the next day.
(22 probably/leave)

A: Do you think the bride and groom _____ happy together?
(23 be)

B: Yes, I think they _____ very happy. They love each
(24 be)

other very much.

EXERCISE 13   **Fill in the blanks with *will* or *be going to* plus the verb in parentheses ( ). Use contractions. In some cases, more than one answer is possible.**

CD 1, TR 36

A: What color are you going to choose for your wedding?

B: Hmmm. Maybe I 'll choose _____ light blue or maybe green. I still
(example: choose)

can't decide.

A: Who are you going to have as your bridesmaids?

B: I _____ my sister and my best friend.
(1 have)

A: Where are you going to get your cake?

B: We _____ the cake at Alton's Bakery.
(2 get)

They _____ it to the wedding.
(3 deliver)

A: Where are you going to go on your honeymoon?

B: I don't really know. Maybe we _____ to Hawaii or maybe
(4 go)

we _____ to Puerto Rico.
(5 go)

A: Do you have your dress already?

B: Yes. I _____ my sister's dress.
(6 use)

A: When are you going to send out your invitations?

B: We're finishing writing the addresses now. We _____
(7 send)

them out next week. We're so busy. There are so many things to do.

A: I _____ you.
(8 help)

(continued)

B: Thanks. I could use help. Could you go to the post office for me and get me 200 stamps? I _____ you back tomorrow.
(9 pay)

A: No problem. How will you decorate your new home?

B: I don't know yet. We _____ that decision later.
(10 make)

EXERCISE 14 **In this conversation, fill in the blanks using the words in parentheses ( ). Choose *will* or *be going to* for the future tenses. In some cases, both answers are possible.**

CD 1, TR 37

A: I'm so excited. My sister ___*is going to get*___ married next year.
(example: get)

B: Why are *you* so excited?

A: I'm going to be a bridesmaid.

B: How many bridesmaids _____?
(1 she/have)

A: Two. Her best friend and I are going to be the bridesmaids.

B: What kind of dresses _____ ?
(2 you/wear)

A: We _____ blue dresses.
(3 wear)

B: _____ in your church?
(4 the wedding/be)

A: No, it isn't. It's going to be outdoors, in a garden. After that, there _____ a dinner at a restaurant.
(5 be)

B: Why _____ until next year to get married?
(6 they/wait)

A: They're both in college now, and they want to get married after they finish college.

B: Where _____ after they get married?
(7 live)

A: Probably here for a while. But then they _____ for jobs in the Boston area.
(8 look)

B: How many people _____ to the wedding?
(9 invite)

A: It _____ a big wedding because we have a large
(10 be)
family, and so does her fiancé³, Joe. They _____
(11 invite)
about 400 people.

B: Wow! The wedding _____ expensive.
(12 be)
Who _____ for it?
(13 pay)

³A woman's *fiancé* is the man she is going to marry. A man's *fiancée* is the woman he is going to marry.

A: Our parents and Joe's parents _____. They
(14 pay)

_____ the cost 50/50. A lot of relatives
(15 split)

and friends _____ here from out of town.
(16 come)

B: Where _____?
(17 they/stay)

A: In hotels.

B: It _____ expensive for the guests too. They
(18 be)

_____ pay for their flights, hotels, and a wedding gift.
(19 have to)

A: I know. But they want to come. Of course, some people

_____ because it _____ too
(20 not come)   (21 be)

expensive for them.

7.6 Future Tense + Time/*If* Clause[4]

TIME OR *IF* CLAUSE (SIMPLE PRESENT TENSE)	MAIN CLAUSE (FUTURE TENSE)	EXPLANATION
After they **graduate**, Before they **get** married,	they **are going to work**. they **are going to send** out invitations.	The sentences on the left have two clauses, a time or *if* clause and a main clause.
When they **return** from the honeymoon, If their grandparents **come** from out of town,	they **will send** thank-you cards. they **will pay** for their hotel.	We use the *future tense* only in the main clause; we use the *simple present tense* in the time/*if* clause.

MAIN CLAUSE (FUTURE TENSE)	TIME OR *IF* CLAUSE (SIMPLE PRESENT TENSE)	EXPLANATION
They **are going to work** Their grandparents **will stay** in a hotel	after they **graduate**. if they **come**.	We can put the main clause before the time/*if* clause.

Punctuation Note: If the time/*if* clause comes before the main clause, we use a comma to separate the two parts of the sentence. If the main clause comes first, we don't use a comma.

Compare:
   If I get an invitation, I'll go to the wedding.
   I'll go to the wedding if I get an invitation.

Usage Note:
There is a proverb that means "I will decide when I need to decide." The proverb is:
   I'll cross that bridge when I come to it.

[4]A *clause* is a group of words that has a subject and a verb. Some sentences have more than one clause.

EXERCISE 15 **Fill in the blanks with the correct form of the verb in parentheses ( ).**

EXAMPLE Before they __get__ married, they __are going to send__ invitations.
(get)   (send)

1. If their grandparents _____ to the wedding, they
(come)

   _____ in a hotel.
   (stay)

2. Karyn and Steve _____ a photo album when they
(make)

   _____ from their honeymoon.
   (return)

3. They _____ into their new home when they
(move)

   _____ from their honeymoon.
   (return)

4. When they _____ back from the honeymoon, they
(get)

   _____ their gifts.
   (open)

5. They _____ their money before they _____
(save)   (have)

   children.

6. Their grandparents _____ home after the
(go)

   wedding _____ over.
   (be)

EXERCISE 16 **ABOUT YOU** **Complete each statement.**

EXAMPLES When this class is over, __I'll go home.__

When this class is over, __I'm going to get something to eat.__

1. When this semester is over, _____

2. When this class is over, _____

3. When I get home today, _____

4. When I graduate (or finish my courses at this school), _____

   _____

5. When I return to my country / become a citizen, _____

6. When I retire, _____

7. When I speak English better, _____

EXERCISE 17 **ABOUT YOU** Complete each statement.

EXAMPLES If I drink too much coffee, _____ I won't sleep tonight.

If I drink too much coffee, _____ I'm going to feel nervous.

1. If I practice English, _____

2. If I don't study, _____

3. If I don't pay my rent, _____

4. If I pass this course, _____

5. If we have a test next week, _____

6. If the teacher is absent tomorrow, _____

7. If I find a good job, _____

EXERCISE 18 **A young Korean woman and her fiancé, Kim, are planning to get married. Her friend is asking her questions about her plans. Fill in the blanks to complete this conversation.**

CD 1, TR 38

A: I'm getting married!

B: That's wonderful! Congratulations. __Are you going to have__ a big
(example: have)

wedding?

A: No, we're going to have a small wedding. We _____
(1 invite)

about 50 people.

B: Where _____?
_(2 be)_

A: It'll be at St. Peter's Church. We _____ a reception
(3 have)

at a Korean restaurant after the wedding.

B: _____ a wedding dress?
(4 buy)

A: No, I _____ my sister's dress for the wedding.
(5 use)

Then, for the reception, I _____ a traditional
(6 wear)

Korean dress.

B: Where _____ after you get married?
(7 live)

A: For a few years, we _____ with Kim's parents.
(8 live)

When Kim _____ college and _____
(9 finish) _(10 get)_

a job, we _____ our own apartment.
(11 get)

B: You're going to live with your in-laws? I can't believe it.

(continued)

A: In my country, it's common. My in-laws are very nice. I'm sure it

_____ a problem. We _____
      (12 not/be)   *(13 not/have)*

children right away.

B: _____ here for the wedding?
     (14 come)

A: No, my parents aren't going to come. But a month after the wedding,

we _____ a trip to Korea, and Kim can meet my
          (15 take)

parents there.

B: When _____ married?
        (16 get)

A: On May 15. I hope you'll be able to attend. We _____
                                                          (17 send)

you an invitation.

B: I _____ glad to attend.
   (18 be)

A traditional Korean bride

Jason and Katie—Starting a Married Life

Before You Read

1. Do you think life is hard for newlyweds? In what way?

2. In your community, do parents help their children after they get married?

CD 1, TR 39

Jason and Katie are newlyweds. Read Katie's journal page. Pay special attention to verb tenses: simple present, present continuous, and future.

April 27

The wedding **is** over, the honeymoon was great, we opened our gifts, and our life as a married couple **is beginning**. We **are learning** that we **have** many responsibilities as a married couple.

I **work** as a nurse full-time. Everyone **thinks** I work in a hospital, but I **don't**. I **go** to people's homes and **help** them there. Jason **isn't working** now. He's still **attending** college. He's in his last year. He's **studying** to be a lawyer. After classes every day, he **studies** at home or **goes** to the law library at his college. He's **going to graduate** next June. When he **graduates**, he **will have** to take a special exam for lawyers. If he **passes** it, he'll **get** a good job and **make** good money. But when he **starts** to work, he'll **have** to pay back student loans. For now, we're both **living** on my salary.

We're **saving** money little by little. We're **planning** to buy a house in a suburb some day. We're also **thinking** about having two children in the future. But we **want** to be financially stable before we **have** children. Our parents sometimes **offer** to help us, but we **don't want** to depend on them. Because Jason **is** so busy with his studies and I'm so busy with my job, we rarely **go** out. Staying at home **helps** us save money.

7.7 Comparison of Tenses

Uses

EXAMPLES	EXPLANATION
a. Katie **works** as a nurse. Jason **studies** law. Lawyers **make** a lot of money in the U.S. b. Grown children **don't like** to depend on their parents. c. Jason **goes** to the library almost every day. d. Jason and Katie **have** a lot of responsibilities now. e. When Jason **graduates**, he will look for a job.	Use the **simple present tense**: a. with facts b. with customs c. with habits and regular activities d. with nonaction verbs e. in a time clause or an *if* clause when talking about the future
a. I **am reviewing** verb tenses now. b. Jason and Katie **are saving** money to buy a house. They **are planning** to move to a suburb.	Use the **present continuous tense**: a. with an action in progress now, at this moment b. with a long-term action that is in progress; it may not be happening at this exact moment
a. Katie thinks Jason **will be** a good lawyer. b. The law exam **will be** in March. c. "I**'ll always** love you, Katie," says Jason. d. "I**'ll help** you in the kitchen," says Katie. e. What will you do next year? I**'ll** cross that bridge when I come to it.	Use *will* for the **future**: a. with predictions b. with facts c. with promises d. with an offer to help e. when you don't have a previous plan; when you decide what to do at the time of speaking
a. I think they **are going to have** a wonderful life. b. For many years, they **are going to receive** bills for student loans. c. Jason **is going to look** for a job next year.	Use *be going to* for the **future**: a. with predictions b. with facts c. with plans

Forms

SIMPLE PRESENT TENSE	PRESENT CONTINUOUS TENSE
Jason **studies** in the library.	They **are saving** money to buy a house.
He **doesn't study** at home.	They **aren't saving** to buy a new car.
Does he **study** every day?	**Are** they **saving** for a vacation?
Yes, he **does**.	No, they **aren't**.
When **does** he **study**?	How **are** they **saving** money?
Why **doesn't** he **study** at home?	Why **aren't** they **saving** to buy a car?
Who **studies** at home?	Who **is saving** money?

FUTURE WITH *WILL*	FUTURE WITH *BE GOING TO*
Jason **will graduate** next year.	They **are going to buy** a house.
He **won't graduate** this year.	They **aren't going to buy** a new car.
Will he **graduate** in January?	**Are** they **going to buy** a house in the city?
No, he **won't**.	No, they **aren't**.
When **will** he **graduate**?	Where **are** they **going to buy** a house?
Why **won't** he **graduate** in January?	Why **aren't** they **going to buy** a house there?
Who **will graduate** in January?	Who **is going to buy** a house?

EXERCISE 19 Fill in the blanks with the correct tense and form of the verb in parentheses ( ).

EXAMPLE Jason __is going to graduate__ next year.
(graduate)

1. He _____ a good job when he _____.
   (have)   (graduate)

2. He _____ in the library.
   (often/study)

3. Jason and Katie _____ out.
   (rarely/go)

4. They _____ their money now.
   (save)

5. They _____ about buying a house.
   (think)

6. They _____ it's better to live in a suburb.
   (think)

EXERCISE 20 Fill in the blanks with the negative form of the underlined verb.

EXAMPLE They <u>are</u> young. They __aren't__ old.

1. They <u>have</u> an apartment now. They _____ a house.

2. They <u>want</u> children, but they _____ children right now.

3. Katie <u>is working</u>. Jason _____ now. He's going to school.

(continued)

4. They <u>depend</u> on each other. They _____ on their parents.

5. Jason <u>will graduate</u> in June. He _____ in January.

EXERCISE **21** **Read each statement. Then write a *yes/no* question with the words in parentheses ( ). Write a short answer. Refer to Katie's journal entry on page 207.**

EXAMPLE Katie works as a nurse. (in a hospital).
Does she work in a hospital? No, she doesn't.

1. Jason is a student. (Katie)

_____

2. Jason is attending college now. (Katie)

_____

3. Jason will have a job. (a good job)

_____

4. They are thinking about buying a house. (about having children)

_____

5. They are going to have children. (five children)

_____

EXERCISE 22 **Read each statement. Then write a *wh-* question using the words in parentheses ( ). An answer is not necessary.**

EXAMPLE   Katie works as a nurse. (Where)
Where does she work as a nurse?

1. They are saving their money. (why)

2. They don't want to depend on their parents. (why)

3. Jason will make good money. (when)

4. Jason wants to be a lawyer. (why)

5. Katie isn't going to work when her children are small. (why)

6. Jason will pay back his student loans. (when)

7. They don't go out very much. (why)

8. Jason is attending college. (what college)

9. He is going to graduate. (when)

10. Jason isn't earning money now. (who)

11. Someone wants to help them. (who)

12. They are learning about responsibilities. (how)

Summary of Lesson 7

1. Future patterns with *will*:

AFFIRMATIVE:	He **will buy** a car.
NEGATIVE:	He **won't buy** a used car.
YES/NO QUESTION:	**Will** he **buy** a new car?
SHORT ANSWER:	Yes, he **will.**
WH- QUESTION:	When **will** he **buy** a car?
NEGATIVE QUESTION:	Why **won't** he **buy** a used car?
SUBJECT QUESTION:	Who **will buy** a car?

2. Future patterns with *be going to*:

AFFIRMATIVE:	He **is going to buy** a car.
NEGATIVE:	He **isn't going to buy** a used car.
YES/NO QUESTION:	**Is** he **going to buy** a new car?
SHORT ANSWER:	Yes, he **is.**
WH- QUESTION:	When **is** he **going to buy** a car?
NEGATIVE QUESTION:	Why **isn't** he **going to buy** a used car?
SUBJECT QUESTION:	Who **is going to buy** a car?

3. Uses of *be going to* and *will*:

USE	WILL	BE GOING TO
Prediction	You **will become** rich and famous.	You **are going to become** rich and famous.
Fact	The sun **will set** at 6:32 PM tonight.	The sun **is going to set** at 6:32 PM tonight.
Plan		I'**m going to buy** a new car next month.
Promise	I **will help** you tomorrow.	
Offer to help	**A:** I can't open the door. **B:** I'**ll open** it for you.	
No previous plan	**A:** I need to go to the store. **B:** I'**ll go** with you.	

4. Review and compare the four tenses on pages 208–209.

Editing Advice

1. In a future with *will*, don't add *be* before the main verb.

   I will ~~be~~ go.

2. Use *be* in a future sentence that has no other verb.

   He will ˄ angry.
   be

   There will ˄ a party soon.
   be

3. Don't combine *will* and *be going to*.

   He ~~will~~ going to leave.   OR   *He will leave.*
   is

4. Don't use the present tense for a future action.

   I'm going home now. I ˄ see you later.
   'll

5. Don't use the future tense after a time word or *if*.

   When they ~~will~~ go home, they will watch TV.

6. Use a form of *be* with *going to*.

   He ˄ going to help me.
   is

7. Use *to* after *going*.

   I'm going ˄ study on Saturday.
   to

8. Use the correct word order for questions.

   Why ~~you aren't~~ going to eat lunch?
   aren't you

Editing Quiz

Some of the shaded words and phrases have mistakes. Find the mistakes and correct them. If the shaded words are correct, write C.

To: MomHelen@e*mail.com

Subject: New job!

Dear Mom,

_____**am**_____   **C**

Next week I ~~will~~ going to start a new job. I'm so excited. My pay will be
(example)   *(example)*

higher. I going to make $10,000 a year more than I do now. Isn't that
(1)

great? And I will having a company car. When I'll get the car, I'm going send
(2)   *(3)*   *(4)*

you a picture of it.

When you will come and visit me? Soon, I hope. I send you money for a
(5)   *(6)*

ticket. If I'll have time, I'll take you to visit many places. But that depends
(7)   *(8)*

on my job. Anyway, it will nice to see you again.
(9)

I write you more later.
(10)

Love,
Anne

Lesson 7 Test/Review

PART 1 **Fill in the blanks with a form of *be + going to* or with *will*. In some cases, both answers are possible.**

EXAMPLES I believe the next president ___**will** OR **is going to**___ be a woman.

You can't move your piano alone. I __'ll_____ help you do it.

1. We _____ eat in a new restaurant tomorrow. Do you

want to go with us?

2. My friend is planning her wedding. She _____ invite

150 guests to her wedding.

3. I _____ clean my room tomorrow.

4. If you come to work late every day, you _____ lose your job.

5. You don't know anything about computers? Come to my house. I _____ teach you.

6. The teacher _____ give a test next Friday.

7. Next week we _____ begin Lesson 8.

8. Mother: Please call me when you arrive.

Daughter: Don't worry, Mom. I _____ call you as soon as I arrive.

9. We're planning a picnic, but I think it _____ rain tomorrow.

PART 2 **Fill in the blanks with the negative form of the underlined word.**

EXAMPLE She <u>will get</u> married in a church. She _____*won't get*_____ married at home.

1. She <u>is going to invite</u> all her relatives. She _____ all her friends.

2. He <u>will wear</u> a tuxedo. He _____ a suit.

3. I <u>am going to buy</u> a gift. I _____ dishes.

4. I'<u>ll help</u> the bride, but I _____ her today.

5. You <u>are going to meet</u> my parents. You _____ my brothers.

PART 3   **Read each statement. Then write a *yes/no* question about the words in parentheses ( ). Write a short answer.**

EXAMPLE   She will write a letter. (a postcard) (no)
Will she write a postcard? No, she won't.

1. They will send a gift. (money) (no)

   _____

2. You're going to invite your friends. (relatives) (yes)

   _____

3. They are going to receive gifts. (open the gifts) (yes)

   _____

4. They will need things for their kitchen. (for their bathroom) (yes)

   _____

5. There will be a party after the wedding. (music at the party) (yes)

   _____

PART 4   **Read each statement. Then write a question with the words in parentheses ( ). No answer is necessary.**

EXAMPLES   I'm going to buy something. (What)
What are you going to buy?

1. They'll use the money. (How)

   _____

2. I'm going to send a gift. (What kind of gift)

   _____

3. They'll thank us. (When)

   _____

4. They're going to get married. (Where)

   _____

5. They aren't going to open the gifts at the wedding. (Why)

   _____

6. There will be a lot of people at the wedding. (How many people)

   _____

7. Some people will give money. (Who)

   _____

Test on Comparison of Tenses

PART **1**   Read the following e-mail. Fill in the blanks with the simple present, the present continuous, or the future tense.

To: judyp@metoyou.net

Subject: Hello!

Dear Judy,

Please excuse me for not writing sooner. I rarely _____**have**_____ (example: have)

time to sit and write an e-mail. My husband _____ on (1 work)

his car now, and the baby _____. So now (2 sleep)

I _____ a few free moments. (3 have)

I _____ a student now. I _____ to (4 be)   (5 go)

Kennedy College twice a week. The school _____ a few (6 be)

blocks from my house. I usually _____ to school, but (7 walk)

sometimes I _____. My mother usually (8 drive)

_____ the baby when I'm in school. This semester (9 watch)

I _____ English and math. Next semester (10 study)

I _____ a computer course. I _____ (11 take)   (12 think)

knowledge about computers _____ me find a good job. (13 help)

When the semester _____ over, we (14 be)

_____ to Canada for vacation. (15 go)

We _____ my husband's sister. She _____ (16 visit)   (17 live)

in Montreal. We _____ Christmas with her family this year. (18 spend)

When we _____ to Montreal, I _____ (19 get)   (20 send)

you a postcard.

Please write and tell me what is happening in your life.

Love,
Barbara

PART 2 Fill in the blanks with the negative form of the underlined verb.

EXAMPLE Barbara's a student. She _____isn't_____ a teacher.

1. She's writing an e-mail now. She _____ a composition.
2. Her mother sometimes takes care of her baby. Her father _____ care of her baby.
3. They're going to visit her husband's sister. They _____ her mother.
4. She goes to Kennedy College. She _____ to Truman College.
5. Barbara and her husband live in the U.S. They _____ in Canada.
6. Her family will go to Montreal. They _____ to Toronto.

PART 3 Read each statement. Then write a *yes/no* question with the words in parentheses ( ). Write a short answer, based on the e-mail.

EXAMPLE Barbara's studying English. (math)
Is she studying math? Yes, she is. _____

1. The baby's sleeping. (her husband)

   _____

2. She sometimes drives to school. (ever/walk to school)

   _____

3. She's going to take a computer course next semester. (a math class)

   _____

4. She'll go to Canada. (Montreal)

   _____

5. She's going to send Judy a postcard. (a letter)

   _____

6. She sometimes writes e-mails. (write an e-mail/now)

   _____

7. Her sister-in-law lives in Canada. (in Toronto)

   _____

PART 4 **Read each statement. Then write a *wh-* question with the words in parentheses ( ). Write an answer, based on the e-mail.**

EXAMPLE   Barbara goes to college. (Where)

A: _Where does she go to college?_

B: _She goes to Kennedy College._

1. Her baby's sleeping. (What/her husband/do)

    A: _____

    B: _____

2. She's taking two courses this semester. (What courses)

    A: _____

    B: _____

3. Someone watches her baby. (Who)

    A: _____

    B: _____

4. She's going to take a course next semester. (What course)

    A: _____

    B: _____

5. They'll go on vacation for Christmas. (Where)

    A: _____

    B: _____

6. Her husband's sister lives in another city. (Where/she)

    A: _____

    B: _____

7. She doesn't usually drive to school. (Why)

    A: _____

    B: _____

Expansion

❶ Check (✓) the activities that you plan to do soon. Find a partner. Ask your partner for information about the items he or she checked off. Report something interesting to the class about your partner's plans.

EXAMPLE   _✓_ move

When are you going to move?
Why are you going to move?
Are your friends going to help you?
Are you going to rent a truck?
Where are you going to move to?

a. ____ get married

b. ____ go back to my country

c. ____ spend a lot of money

d. ____ send a package

e. ____ buy something (a computer, a DVD player, a TV, etc.)

f. ____ go to a party

g. ____ have a job interview

h. ____ transfer to another college

i. ____ become a citizen

j. ____ eat in a restaurant

❷ Role-play the following characters. Practice the future tense.

a. A fortune-teller and a young woman. The woman wants to know her future.

b. A man proposing marriage to a woman. The man is making promises.

c. A teenager and his/her parents. The teenager wants to go to a party on Saturday night.

d. A politician and a voter. The politician wants votes.

e. A landlord and a person who wants to rent an apartment. The person wants to know what the landlord will do to fix up the apartment.

❸ **What are your concerns and plans for the future? Write one or two sentences (statements or questions) for each of the categories in the box below. Then find a partner. Discuss your concerns and plans with your partner.**

Job/Career	
Money	
Learning English	
Home	
Family and children	
Health	
Fun and recreation	
Other	

EXAMPLE   Job/Career: I'll get my degree in two years. Where will I find a job?

❹ **Imagine that you are going to buy a gift for someone in the following circumstances. What gift would you buy? Find a partner and compare your list of gifts to your partner's list.**

a. a friend in the hospital after surgery _____

b. a couple with a new baby _____

c. a cousin graduating from high school _____

d. a friend getting married for the second time _____

e. a friend moving into a new apartment _____

f. a family that invites you to dinner at their house _____

Talk

About It

❶ In a small group or with the entire class, talk about gift-giving customs in your native culture. What kinds of gifts do people give for weddings? How much money do they spend? Do newlyweds open presents at the wedding? Do they send thank-you cards? What kind of gifts do people give for other occasions?

❷ Once a couple marries, both people often work. Sometimes only the man or only the woman works. In your native culture, does a woman ever support a man financially? Discuss.

Write

About It

Use one of the topics in the chart on page 221 (job, money, learning English, etc.). Write a short composition about your plans or concerns for the future.

After I Graduate

I'm going to graduate next May. I'm worried about finding a job. Will I find a job in my profession? Will I have to move to another city? I don't want to move. But if I don't find a job here, I'll move to San Antonio because my brother lives there . . .

For more practice using grammar in context, please visit our Web site.

Grammar
The Simple Past Tense

Context
Flying

The Wright Brothers—Men with a Vision

Before
You Read

1. Do you like to travel by airplane? Why or why not?

2. What are the names of some famous inventors?

CD 2, TR 01

Read the following textbook article. Pay special attention to simple-past-tense verbs.

Wilbur Wright, 1867–1912;
Orville Wright, 1871–1948

Over 100 years ago, people only **dreamed** about flying. The Wright brothers, Wilbur and Orville, **were** dreamers who **changed** the world.

Wilbur Wright **was** born in 1867 and Orville **was** born in 1871. In 1878, they **received** a paper flying toy from their father. They **played** with kites and **started** to think about the possibility of flight.

When they were older, they **started** a bicycle business. They **used** the bicycle shop to design their airplanes. They **studied** three aspects of flying: lift, control, and power. In 1899, they **constructed** their first flying machine—a kite made of wood, wire, and cloth. It **had** no pilot. Because of wind, it was difficult to control. They **continued** to study aerodynamics.[1] Finally Wilbur **designed** a small machine with a gasoline engine. Wilbur **tried** to fly the machine, but it **crashed**. They **fixed** it and **flew** it for the first time on December 17, 1903, with Orville as the pilot. The airplane **remained** in the air for twelve seconds. It **traveled** a distance of 120 feet. This historic flight **changed** the world. However, only four newspapers in the U.S. **reported** this historic moment.

The Wright brothers **offered** their invention to the U.S. government, but the government **rejected**[2] their offer at first. The government **didn't believe** that these men **invented** a flying machine. Finally, President Theodore Roosevelt **investigated** their claims and **offered** the inventors a contract to build airplanes for the U.S. Army.

December 17, 2003, **marked** 100 years of flight. There **was** a six-day celebration at Kitty Hawk, North Carolina, the location of the first flight. A crowd of 35,000 people **gathered** to see a replica[3] of the first plane fly. The cost to re-create the plane **was** $1.2 million. However, it **rained** hard that day and the plane **failed** to get off the ground.

You can now see the Wright brothers' original airplane in the Air and Space Museum in Washington, D.C.

---

[1]*Aerodynamics* is the branch of mechanics that deals with the motion of air and its effect on things.
[2]*Reject* means not accept.
[3]A *replica* is a copy of an original.

8.1 The Simple Past Tense of Regular Verbs

EXAMPLES	EXPLANATION
The Wright brothers **started** a bicycle business. They **dreamed** about flying. They **designed** an airplane. The president **offered** them a contract.	To form the simple past tense of regular verbs, we add -ed to the base form. **Base Form** **Past Form** start start**ed** dream dream**ed** design design**ed** offer offer**ed** The past form is the same for all persons.
The Wright brothers **wanted** to *fly*. They **continued** to *study* aerodynamics.	The verb after *to* does **not** use the past form.
The Wright brothers **invented** the airplane over 100 years **ago**. We **celebrated** the 100th anniversary of flight a few years **ago**.	We often use *ago* in sentences about the past. *Ago* means *before now*.

EXERCISE **1** Read more about the Wright brothers. Underline the past tense verbs in the following sentences.

EXAMPLE   The Wright brothers <u>lived</u> in Dayton, Ohio.

1. Their father worked as a Christian minister.
2. The boys learned mechanical things quickly.
3. They loved bicycles.
4. They opened the Wright Cycle Company repair shop, where they repaired bicycles.
5. They started to produce their own bicycle models.
6. The first airplane weighed over 600 pounds.
7. They succeeded in flying the first airplane in 1903.
8. Wilbur died nine years later, of typhoid.[4]
9. Orville lived to be 76 years old.

---

[4]*Typhoid* is a serious infection causing a fever and often death.

8.2 Spelling of the Past Tense of Regular Verbs

RULE	BASE FORM	PAST FORM
Add -ed to most regular verbs.	start rain	start**ed** rain**ed**
When the base form ends in e, add -d only.	die live	die**d** live**d**
When the base form ends in a consonant + y, change y to i and add -ed.	carry study	carr**ied** stud**ied**
When the base form ends in a vowel + y, add -ed. Do not change the y.	stay enjoy	stay**ed** enjoy**ed**
When a one-syllable verb ends in a consonant-vowel-consonant, double the final consonant and add -ed.	stop hug	stop**ped** hug**ged**
Do not double a final w or x.	show fix	show**ed** fix**ed**
When a two-syllable verb ends in a consonant-vowel-consonant, double the final consonant and add -ed only if the last syllable is stressed.	occúr permít	occur**red** permit**ted**
When the last syllable of a two-syllable verb is not stressed, do not double the final consonant.	ópen óffer	open**ed** offer**ed**

EXERCISE **2** Write the past tense of these regular verbs. (Accent marks show you where a word is stressed.)

EXAMPLES learn __learned__   clap __clapped__

love __loved__   lísten __listened__

1. play _____   **11.** enjoy _____

2. study _____   **12.** drag _____

3. decide _____   **13.** drop _____

4. want _____   **14.** start _____

5. like _____   **15.** follow _____

6. show _____   **16.** prefér _____

7. look _____   **17.** like _____

8. stop _____   **18.** mix _____

9. háppen _____   **19.** admít _____

10. carry _____   **20.** propél _____

8.3 Pronunciation of -ed Past Forms

PRONUNCIATION	RULE	EXAMPLES	
/t/	Pronounce /t/ after voiceless sounds: /p, k, f, s, š, č/	jump—jumped cook—cooked cough—coughed	kiss—kissed wash—washed watch—watched
/d/	Pronounce /d/ after voiced sounds: /b, g, v, đ, z, ž, ǰ, m, n, ŋ, l, r/ and all vowel sounds.	rub—rubbed drag—dragged love—loved bathe—bathed use—used massage—massaged charge—charged	name—named learn—learned bang—banged call—called care—cared free—freed
/əd/	Pronounce /əd/ after /d/ or /t/ sounds.	wait—waited hate—hated want—wanted	add—added decide—decided

EXERCISE 3 Go back to Exercise 2 and pronounce the base form and past form of each verb.

EXERCISE 4 Fill in the blanks with the past tense of the verb in parentheses ( ). Use the correct spelling.

EXAMPLE The Wright brothers _____received_____ a flying toy from their father.
(receive)

1. They _____ with kites.
(play)

2. They _____ about flying.
(dream)

3. They _____ everything they could about flying.
(study)

4. They _____ a bicycle business.
(start)

5. They _____ the bicycle shop to design airplanes.
(use)

6. They _____ to fly their first plane in 1899.
(try)

7. Their first plane _____.
(crash)

8. They _____ it.
(fix)

9. In 1903, their plane _____ in the air for 12 seconds.
(stay)

10. They _____ their invention to the U.S. government.
(offer)

11. The government _____ to offer them a contract.
(decide)

(continued)

12. Wilbur Wright _____ in 1912.
　　　　　　　　　　　　　(die)

13. Orville Wright _____ for many more years.
　　　　　　　　　　　　　(live)

14. Their invention _____ the world.
　　　　　　　　　　　　　(change)

Charles Lindbergh and Amelia Earhart

Before
You Read

1. When was the first time you traveled by airplane?

2. Do you recognize the people in the photos below?

CD 2, TR 02

Read the following textbook article. Pay special attention to the past-tense forms of *be*.

Charles Lindbergh,
1902–1974

At the beginning of the twentieth century, flight **was** new. It **was** not for everyone. It **was** only for the brave and adventurous. Two adventurers **were** Charles Lindbergh and Amelia Earhart.

Charles Lindbergh loved to fly. He **was** born in 1902, one year before the Wright brothers' historic flight. In 1927, a man offered a $25,000 reward for the first person to fly from New York to Paris nonstop. Lindbergh **was** a pilot for the United States Mail Service at that time. He wanted to win the prize.

He became famous because he **was** the first person to fly alone across the Atlantic Ocean. His plane **was** in the air for 33 hours. The distance of the flight **was** 3,600 miles. There **were** thousands of people in New York to welcome him home. He **was** an American hero. He **was** only 25 years old.

Another famous American aviator[5] **was** Amelia Earhart. She **was** the first woman to fly across the Atlantic Ocean alone. She **was** 34 years old. Americans **were** in love with Earhart. In 1937, however, she **was** on a flight around the world when her plane disappeared somewhere in the Pacific Ocean. No one really knows what happened to Earhart.

Amelia Earhart,
1897–1937

[5]*Aviator* means pilot.

8.4 Past Tense of *Be*

The verb *be* has two forms in the past: *was* and *were*.

EXAMPLES			EXPLANATION
Subject I Charles He Amelia She The airplane It	*Was* **was**	**Complement** interested in the story. a pilot. brave. a pilot too. popular. new in 1903. in the air for 12 seconds.	*I* *He* *She* } *was* *It* singular subject
Subject We You Amelia and Charles They	*Were* **were**	**Complement** interested in the story. in class yesterday. brave. adventurous.	*We* *You* } *were* *They* plural subject
There There	*Was* **was**	**Singular Subject** a celebration in 2003.	*There* + *was* + singular noun
There There	*Were* **were**	**Plural Subject** thousands of people.	*There* + *were* + plural noun
Charles Lindbergh **was not** the first person to fly. We **were not** at the 2003 celebration.			To make a negative statement, put *not* after *was* or *were*.
I **wasn't** here yesterday. You **weren't** in class yesterday.			The contraction for *was not* is *wasn't*. The contraction for *were not* is *weren't*.

EXERCISE 5 Fill in the blanks with *was* or *were*.

EXAMPLE Lindbergh and Earhart ___was___ very famous.

1. The Wright brothers _____ the inventors of the airplane.

2. The first airplane _____ in the air for 12 seconds.

3. Lindbergh and Earhart _____ aviators.

4. There _____ thousands of people in New York to welcome Lindbergh home.

5. Earhart _____ the first woman to fly across the Atlantic Ocean.

6. I _____ interested in the story about Earhart and Lindbergh.

7. _____ you surprised that a woman was a famous aviator?

8. Lindbergh _____ in Paris.

9. We _____ happy to read about flight.

10. There _____ a celebration of 100 years of flight in 2003.

11. There _____ thousands of people at the celebration.

8.5 Uses of *Be*

EXAMPLES	EXPLANATION
Lindbergh **was** an aviator.	Classification of the subject
Lindbergh **was** brave.	Description of the subject
Lindbergh **was** in Paris.	Location of the subject
Earhart **was** from Kansas.	Place of origin of the subject
She **was** born in 1897.	With *born*
There **were** thousands of people in New York to welcome Lindbergh.	With *there*
Lindbergh **was** 25 years old in 1927.	With age

EXERCISE **6** **Read each statement. Then write a negative statement with the words in parentheses ( ).**

EXAMPLE The Wright brothers were inventors. (Earhart and Lindbergh)
Earhart and Lindbergh weren't inventors.

1. The train was common transportation in the early 1900s. (the airplane)

_____

2. Earhart was from Kansas. (Lindbergh)

_____

3. Lindbergh's last flight was successful. (Earhart's last flight)

_____

4. Lindbergh's plane was in the air for many hours. (the Wright brothers' first plane)

_____

5. The Wright brothers were inventors. (Earhart)

_____

6. There were a lot of trains 100 years ago. (planes)

_____

7. Lindbergh was born in the twentieth century. (the Wright brothers)

_____

8. The 1903 flight at Kitty Hawk was successful. (the 2003 flight)

_____

8.6 Questions with *Was/Were*

EXAMPLES	EXPLANATION
Was the first flight long? 　　No, it **wasn't**. **Was** the first flight successful? 　　Yes, it **was**. **Were** the Wright brothers inventors? 　　Yes, they **were**.	*Yes/No* Questions 　　*Was/were* + subject . . . ? **Short answers** 　　Yes, + subject + *was/were*. 　　No, + subject + *wasn't/weren't*.
Were there a lot of people at the 100-year celebration? 　　Yes, there **were**. **Was** there a lot of rain that day? 　　Yes, there **was**.	*There* Questions 　　*Was/were* + there . . . ? **Short Answers** 　　Yes, there *was/were*. 　　No, there *wasn't/weren't*.
How long **was** the first flight? Where **was** the first flight?	*Wh-* Questions 　　*Wh-* word + *was/were* + subject . . . ?
Why **wasn't** Amelia successful? Why **weren't** you there?	**Negative Questions** 　　*Why* + *wasn't/weren't* + subject . . . ?
Who **was** with Earhart when she disappeared? How many people **were** in the airplane?	**Subject Questions** 　　*Who* + *was* . . . ? 　　*How many* . . . + *were* . . . ?

Compare affirmative statements and questions.

Wh- Word	*Was/Were*	Subject	*Was/Were*	Complement	Short Answer
When		Amelia	**was**	born before 1903.	
	Was	she		born in the U.S.?	Yes, she was.
	was	she		born?	In 1897.
		Charles and Amelia	**were**	famous.	
	Were	they		inventors?	No, they weren't.
		Someone	**was**	with Amelia.	
		Who	**was**	with Amelia?	A copilot.
		Many people	**were**	at the celebration.	
		How many people	**were**	at the celebration?	Thousands.

Compare negative statements and questions.

Wh- Word	*Wasn't/Weren't*	Subject	*Wasn't/Weren't*	Complement
		Air travel	**wasn't**	safe 100 years ago.
Why	**wasn't**	it		safe?
		The Wright brothers	**weren't**	afraid of flying.
Why	**weren't**	they		afraid?

EXERCISE 7 **Read each statement. Then write a *yes/no* question with the words in parentheses ( ). Give a short answer.**

EXAMPLE The Wright brothers were inventors. (Lindbergh)
<u>Was Lindbergh an inventor? No, he wasn't.</u>

1. The airplane was an important invention. (the telephone)

_____

2. Thomas Edison was an inventor. (the Wright brothers)

_____

3. Amelia Earhart was American. (Lindbergh)

_____

4. Travel by plane is common now. (100 years ago)

_____

5. There were telephones 100 years ago. (airplanes)

_____

6. You are in class today. (yesterday)

_____

7. I was interested in the story about the aviators. (you)

_____

8. I wasn't born in the U.S. (you)

_____

EXERCISE 8 **ABOUT YOU** **Interview a classmate who is from another country.**

1. Where were you born?
2. Were you happy or sad when you left your country?
3. Who was with you on your trip?
4. Were you happy or sad when you arrived?
5. What was your first impression of your new home?
6. Were you tired when you arrived?
7. Who was at the airport to meet you?
8. How was the weather on the day you arrived?

EXERCISE 9 Read each statement. Then write a *wh-* question with the words in parentheses ( ). Answer the question.

EXAMPLE   Lindbergh was very famous. (why)

A: _Why was Lindbergh famous?_

B: _He was one of the first aviators._

1. Lindbergh was a hero. (why)

    A: _____

    B: _____

2. Lindbergh was American. (what nationality/Earhart)

    A: _____

    B: _____

3. Earhart was 34 years old when she crossed the ocean. (how old/Lindbergh)

    A: _____

    B: _____

4. Lindbergh was a famous aviator. (who/the Wright brothers)

    A: _____

    B: _____

5. Lindbergh was born in 1902. (when/Earhart)

    A: _____

    B: _____

6. The Wright brothers were famous. (why)

    A: _____

    B: _____

7. The flight at Kitty Hawk in 2003 wasn't successful. (why)

    A: _____

    B: _____

EXERCISE 10 Fill in the blanks with the correct past-tense form of *be*. Add any other necessary words.

CD 2, TR 03

A: I tried to call you last weekend. I ____was____ worried about you.
                                          (example)

B: I _____ home. I _____ out of town.
      (1 not)   *(2)*

A: Where _____?
                (3)

B: In Washington, D.C.

A: _____ alone?
        (4)

(continued)

The Simple Past Tense   233

National Air and Space Museum

B: No, I _____. I was with my brother.

(5)

A: _____ expensive?

(6)

B: No. Our trip wasn't expensive at all.

A: Really? Why _____ expensive?

(7)

B: The flight from here to Washington _____ cheap.

(8)
And we stayed with some friends in their apartment.

They _____ very helpful. They showed us a lot of beautiful

(9)

places in Washington. But my favorite place was the Air and

Space Museum.

A: _____ a lot of people at the museum?

(10)

B: Yes, there were. It _____ very crowded. But it _____

(11)   (12)

wonderful to see the Wright brothers' airplane and the airplane that

Lindbergh used when he crossed the Atlantic. Also it _____

(13)

interesting to see the spacecraft of the astronauts. We _____

(14 not)

bored for one minute in that museum.

A: How long _____ your flight to Washington?

(15)

B: It _____ only 2 hours and 15 minutes from here. We don't think

(16)

about flying as anything special anymore. But just a little over

100 years ago, flight _____ just a dream of two brothers.

(17)

Can you believe it? There _____ only 66 years between the first

(18)

flight in 1903 and the trip to the moon in 1969!

A: That's amazing!

8.7 Simple Past Tense of Irregular Verbs—An Overview

EXAMPLES	EXPLANATION
I **came** to the U.S. by plane. My flight **took** six hours. I **felt** happy when I arrived.	Many verbs are irregular in the past tense. An irregular verb does not use the *-ed* ending.

Robert Goddard

Before You Read

1. Did you ever see the first moon landing in 1969?

2. Are you interested in astronauts and rockets?

CD 2, TR 04

Read the following textbook article. Pay special attention to past-tense verbs.

Did You Know?

The first woman in space was a Russian, Valentina Tereshkova, in 1963.

Robert Goddard with early rocket, 1926

Robert Goddard **was** born in 1882. When he **was** a child, he **became** interested in firecrackers and **thought** about the possibility of space travel. He later **became** a physics professor at a university. In his free time, he **built** rockets and **took** them to a field, but they **didn't fly**. When he **went** back to his university after his failed attempts, the other professors **laughed** at him.

In 1920, Goddard **wrote** an article about rocket travel. He **believed** that one day it would be possible to go to the moon. When *The New York Times* **saw** his article, a reporter **wrote** that Goddard **had** less knowledge about science than a high school student. Goddard **wanted** to prove that *The New York Times* **was** wrong.

In 1926, he **built** a ten-foot rocket, **put** it into an open car, and **drove** to his aunt's nearby farm. He **put** the rocket in a field and **lit** the fuse. Suddenly the rocket **went** into the sky. It **traveled** at 60 miles per hour (mph) to an altitude of 41 feet. Then it **fell**

Astronaut Buzz Aldrin of Apollo 11 on the moon, 1969

into the field. The flight **lasted** 2½ seconds, but Goddard **was** happy about his achievement. Over the years, his rockets **grew** to 18 feet and **flew** to 9,000 feet in the air. No one **made** fun of him after he was successful.

When Goddard **died** in 1945, his work **did not stop**. Scientists **continued** to build bigger and better rockets. In 1969, when the American rocket Apollo 11 **took** the first men to the moon, *The New York Times* **wrote**: *"The Times regrets[6] the error."*

---

[6]*Regret* means to be sorry for.

8.8 List of Irregular Past Tense Verbs[7]

VERBS WITH NO CHANGE		FINAL *d* CHANGES TO *t*	
bet—bet	hurt—hurt	bend—bent	send—sent
cost—cost	let—let	build—built	spend—spent
cut—cut	put—put	lend—lent	
fit—fit	quit—quit		
hit—hit	shut—shut		

VERBS WITH A VOWEL CHANGE			
feel—felt	lose—lost	bring—brought	fight—fought
keep—kept	mean—meant[8]	buy—bought	teach—taught
leave—left	sleep—slept	catch—caught	think—thought
break—broke	steal—stole	begin—began	sing—sang
choose—chose	speak—spoke	drink—drank	sink—sank
freeze—froze	wake—woke	ring—rang	swim—swam
dig—dug	spin—spun	drive—drove	shine—shone
hang—hung	win—won	ride—rode	write—wrote
blow—blew	grow—grew	bleed—bled	meet—met
draw—drew	know—knew	feed—fed	read—read[9]
fly—flew	throw—threw	lead—led	
sell—sold	tell—told	find—found	wind—wound
shake—shook	mistake—mistook	lay—laid	pay—paid
take—took		say—said[10]	
tear—tore	wear—wore	bite—bit	hide—hid
		light—lit	
become—became	eat—ate	fall—fell	hold—held
come—came			
give—gave	lie—lay	run—ran	see—saw
forgive—forgave		sit—sat	
forget—forgot	get—got	stand—stood	
shoot—shot		understand—understood	

MISCELLANEOUS CHANGES			
be—was/were	go—went	hear—heard	
do—did	have—had	make—made	

[7]For an alphabetical list of irregular verbs, see Appendix D.
[8]There is a change in the vowel sound. *Meant* rhymes with *sent*.
[9]The past form of *read* is pronounced like the color *red*.
[10]*Said* rhymes with *bed*.

EXERCISE 11 Read the following facts about the history of rockets. Underline the verbs. Write *R* for a regular verb. Write *I* for an irregular verb.

EXAMPLE Goddard <u>published</u> a paper on rockets in 1920. **R**

1. Goddard built and flew rockets from 1926 to 1939.
2. Germany used the first rockets in World War II in 1944.
3. The Russians launched their first satellite, Sputnik 1, in 1957.
4. The Americans sent up their first satellite, Explorer 1, in 1958.
5. Yuri Gagarin, a Russian, became the first person in space in 1961.
6. Alan Shepard, an American, went into space in 1961.
7. The United States put the first men on the moon in 1969.
8. A spacecraft on Mars transmitted color photos to Earth in 2004.

EXERCISE 12 Fill in the blanks with the past tense of one of the words from the box below.

fly	think	drive	be	fall
write	put	become ✔	see	

EXAMPLE Goddard __became__ interested in rockets when he was a child.

1. He _____ a professor of physics.
2. People _____ that space travel was impossible.
3. Goddard _____ his first rocket in a car and _____ to his aunt's farm.
4. The rocket _____ for 2½ seconds and then it _____ to the ground.
5. Goddard never _____ the first moon landing.
6. *The New York Times* _____ about their mistake 49 years later.

EXERCISE 13 Fill in the blanks with the past tense of the verb in parentheses ( ).

EXAMPLE The Wright brothers' father __gave__ them a flying toy.
(give)

1. They _____ a dream of flying.
   (have)
2. They _____ interested in flying after seeing a flying toy.
   (become)
3. They _____ many books on flight.
   (read)

(continued)

4. They _____ bicycles.
  (sell)

5. They _____ the first airplane.
  (build)

6. At first they _____ problems with wind.
  (have)

7. They _____ some changes to the airplane.
  (make)

8. They _____ for the first time in 1903.
  (fly)

9. Only a few people _____ the first flight.
  (see)

10. President Theodore Roosevelt _____ about their airplane.
  (hear)

11. The airplane was an important invention because it _____
  (bring)

  people from different places closer together.

12. Thousands of people _____ to North Carolina for the 100th
  (go)

  anniversary of flight.

8.9 Negative Forms of Past Tense Verbs

Compare affirmative (A) and negative (N) statements with past-tense verbs.

EXAMPLES	EXPLANATION
A. Lindbergh **returned** from his last flight. **N.** Earhart **didn't return** from her last flight.	For the negative past tense, we use *didn't* + the base form for ALL verbs, regular and irregular.
A. The Wright brothers **flew** in their airplane. **N.** Goddard **didn't fly** in his rocket.	**Compare:** returned—didn't return flew—didn't fly
A. Goddard **built** rockets. **N.** He **didn't build** airplanes.	built—didn't build put—didn't put
A. The Russians **put** a woman in space in 1963. **N.** The Americans **didn't put** a woman in space until 1983.	**Remember:** *Put* and a few other past-tense verbs are the same as the base form.

EXERCISE 14 **Fill in the blanks with the negative form of the underlined words.**

EXAMPLE   Goddard <u>believed</u> in space flight. Other people _____*didn't believe*_____ in space flight at that time.

1. The Wright brothers <u>dreamed</u> about flying. They _____ about rockets.

2. They <u>sold</u> bicycles. They _____ cars.

3. Their 1903 airplane <u>had</u> a pilot. Their first airplane _____ a pilot.

4. The Wright brothers <u>wanted</u> to show their airplane to the U.S. government. The government _____ to see it at first.

5. The Wright brothers <u>built</u> the first airplane. They _____ the first rocket.

6. Goddard <u>thought</u> his ideas were important. His colleagues _____ his ideas were important.

7. He <u>wanted</u> to build rockets. He _____ to build airplanes.

8. In 1920, a newspaper <u>wrote</u> that he was foolish. The newspaper _____ about the possibility of rocket travel.

9. In 1926 his rocket <u>flew</u>. Before that time, his rockets _____.

10. The first rocket <u>stayed</u> in the air for 2½ seconds. It _____ in the air for a long time.

11. Goddard <u>saw</u> his rockets fly. He _____ rockets go to the moon.

12. In 1957, the Russians <u>put</u> the first man in space. The Americans _____ the first man in space.

13. In 1969, the first Americans <u>walked</u> on the moon. Russians _____ on the moon.

14. A rocket <u>went</u> to the moon in 1969. A rocket _____ to the moon during Goddard's lifetime.

EXERCISE 15 **ABOUT YOU** If you came to the U.S. from another country, fill in the blanks with the affirmative or negative form of the verb in parentheses to tell about the time before you came to the U.S. Add some specific information to tell more about each item.

EXAMPLES   I ___studied___ English before I came to the U.S. **I studied with a**
            (study)
            private teacher for three months.

                                          OR

            I ___didn't study___ English before I came to the U.S. **I didn't have**
            (study)
            enough time.

1. I _____ my money for dollars before I came to
      (exchange)

   the U.S.

2. I _____ a passport.
      (get)

3. I _____ for a visa.
      (apply)

4. I _____ English.
      (study)

5. I _____ my furniture.
      (sell)

6. I _____ goodbye to my friends.
      (say)

7. I _____ an English dictionary.
      (buy)

8. I _____ a clear idea about life in the U.S.
      (have)

9. I _____ afraid about my future.
      (be)

10. I _____ to another country first.
      (go)

11. I _____ English well.
      (understand)

12. I _____ a lot about American life.
      (know)

EXERCISE 16 **ABOUT YOU** If you come from another city or country, tell if these things happened or didn't happen after you moved to this city. Add some specific information to tell more about each item.

EXAMPLE   find an apartment

I found an apartment two weeks after I arrived in this city.

OR

I didn't find an apartment right away. I lived with my cousins for two months.

1. find a job
2. register for English classes
3. rent an apartment
4. buy a car
5. get a Social Security card
6. go to the bank
7. visit a museum
8. see a relative
9. buy clothes
10. get a driver's license

EXERCISE 17 **ABOUT YOU** Tell if you did or didn't do these things in the past week. Add some specific information to tell more about each item.

EXAMPLE   go to the movies

I went to the movies last weekend with my brother. We saw a great movie.

OR

I didn't go to the movies this week. I didn't have time.

1. use the Internet
2. write a letter
3. go to the library
4. do laundry
5. buy groceries
6. use a phone card
7. buy a magazine
8. work hard
9. look for a job
10. rent a DVD
11. send e-mail
12. read a newspaper

Hero Pilot

Before You Read

1. Do you think that plane travel is safe?

2. Do you know of any heroes?

CD 2, TR 05 **Read the following conversation. Pay special attention to past-tense questions.**

A: Last night there was a great program about heroes on TV. **Did you see** it?

B: No, I didn't. **Was it** good?

A: Yes. There was a part about a pilot, Chesley Sullenberger, or "Sully" for short. He was a real hero.

B: What did he do?

Chesley Sullenberger, pilot of Flight 1549

A: His airplane had to make an emergency landing a few minutes after takeoff. Sully saved the lives of more than 150 passengers.

B: That's amazing! But **how many people died?**

A: No one died. That's why everyone says he's a hero.

B: Why did he make an emergency landing?

A: Because his plane lost power.

B: How did it lose power?

A: A flock[11] of birds flew into the engine.

B: You say he was close to the airport. **Didn't he try** to go back?

A: No, he didn't. He didn't have time.

B: So **where did he land?**

A: He made a perfect landing on the Hudson River, next to New York City.

B: Did the passengers fall into the water?

A: No. The passengers waited on the wings for rescue.

B: I'm sure they were scared. **When did this happen?**

A: In January 2009. It was a week before the inauguration of President Obama. Obama invited him and his crew to attend the inauguration.

[11]A *flock* of birds is a group of birds that fly together.

8.10 Questions with Past-Tense Verbs

Compare affirmative statements and questions.

Wh- Word	Did	Subject	Verb	Complement	Short Answer
		The pilot	**landed**	the plane.	
	Did	he	**land**	at an airport?	No, he didn't.
Where	**did**	he	**land?**		On the Hudson River.
		The plane	**lost**	power.	
	Did	the plane	**lose**	an engine?	Yes, it did.
How	**did**	it	**lose**	an engine?	Birds flew into the engine.

Language Notes:

1. To form a *yes/no* question, use:
   Did + subject + base form + complement
2. To form a short answer, use:
   Yes, + subject pronoun + *did*.
   No, + subject pronoun + *didn't*.
3. To form a *wh-* question, use:
   Wh- word + *did* + subject + base form + complement

Compare negative statements and questions.

Wh- word	Didn't	Subject	Verb	Complement
		The pilot	**didn't go**	to the airport.
	Didn't	he	**go**	back?
Why	**didn't**	he	**go**	back to the airport?

EXERCISE 18 **Read the questions and answer with a short answer.**

EXAMPLE Did you read about the pilot? ___Yes, I did.___

1. Did the pilot return to the airport? _____
2. Did he make the right decision? _____
3. Did any of the passengers die? _____
4. Did the plane go into the river? _____
5. Was the pilot brave? _____

EXERCISE 19 **ABOUT YOU** Use these questions to ask another student about the time when he or she lived in his or her native country.

1. Did you study English in your country?
2. Did you live in a big city?
3. Did you live with your parents?
4. Did you know a lot about the U.S.?
5. Did you finish high school?
6. Did you own a car?
7. Did you have a job?
8. Did you think about your future?
9. Were you happy?

EXERCISE 20 Read each statement. Write a *yes/no* question about the words in parentheses ( ). Write a short answer.

EXAMPLE   The Wright brothers had a dream. (Goddard) (yes)
Did Goddard have a dream? Yes, he did.

1. Wilbur Wright died in 1912. (his brother) (no)

_____

2. The Wright brothers built an airplane. (Goddard) (no)

_____

3. Earhart loved to fly. (Lindbergh) (yes)

_____

4. Lindbergh crossed the ocean. (Earhart) (yes)

_____

5. Lindbergh worked for the U.S. Mail Service. (Earhart) (no)

_____

6. Lindbergh became famous. (Earhart) (yes)

_____

7. Earhart disappeared. (Lindbergh) (no)

_____

8. Lindbergh was born in the twentieth century. (Earhart) (no)

_____

9. Lindbergh won money for his flight. (the Wright brothers) (no)

_____

10. People didn't believe the Wright brothers at first. (Goddard) (no)

_____

11. The Wright brothers dreamed about flight. (Goddard) (yes)

_____

12. Sully made an emergency landing. (a safe landing) (yes)

_____

13. Birds flew into one engine. (both engines) (no)

_____

14. Sully was safe. (the passengers) (yes)

_____

EXERCISE **21** **Fill in the blanks with the correct words.**

EXAMPLE What kind of engine _did the first airplane have?_____?
The first airplane had a gasoline engine.

1. Where _____?
The Wright brothers built their plane in their bicycle shop.

2. Why _____?
The first plane crashed because of the wind.

3. Why _____ the
first flight in 1903?
Many newspapers didn't report it because no one believed it.

4. Where _____?
Lindbergh worked for the U.S. Mail Service.

5. Why _____?
He crossed the ocean to win the prize money.

6. How much money _____?
He won $25,000.

7. How old _____ when he crossed the ocean?
Lindbergh was 25 years old when he crossed the ocean.

8. Where _____?
Earhart was born in Kansas.

9. Where _____?
She disappeared in the Pacific Ocean.

(continued)

10. Why _____?
Nobody knows why Earhart didn't return.

11. When _____?
The first man walked on the moon in 1969.

12. Why _____ the first moon landing?
Goddard didn't see the first moon landing because he died in 1945.

13. Why _____?
Sully was a hero because he saved lives.

14. How many _____?
He saved 150 lives.

15. Why _____?
He didn't return to the airport because he didn't have time.

EXERCISE 22 **Read each statement. Then write a question with the words in parentheses ( ). Answer with a complete sentence. (The answers are at the bottom of page 247.)**

EXAMPLE The Wright brothers were born in the nineteenth century. (Where)
Where were they born?

They were born in Ohio.

1. The Wright brothers were born in the nineteenth century.
(When/Lindbergh)

_____

_____

2. Their father gave them a toy. (What kind of toy)

_____

_____

3. They had a shop. (What kind of shop)

_____

_____

4. They designed airplanes. (Where)

_____

_____

5. They flew their first plane in North Carolina. (When)

_____

_____

6. The first plane stayed in the air for a few seconds. (How many seconds)

_____

_____

7. The U.S. government didn't want to see the airplane at first. (Why)

_____

_____

8. The Wright brothers invented the airplane. (What/Goddard)

_____

_____

9. Goddard took his rocket to his aunt's farm. (Why)

_____

_____

10. People laughed at Goddard. (Why)

_____

_____

11. Sully landed his plane. (Where)

_____

_____

12. Sully received an invitation from the president. (When)

_____

_____

13. The president thanked him. (Where)

_____

_____

ANSWERS TO EXERCISE 22:

(1) 1902, (2) a flying toy, (3) a bicycle shop, (4) in their bicycle shop, (5) in 1903, (6) 12 seconds, (7) they didn't believe it, (8) the rocket, (9) to see if it would fly, (10) they didn't believe him (they thought he was a fool), (11) on the Hudson River in New York City, (12) in January 2009, (13) at the inauguration

EXERCISE **23** **ABOUT YOU** Check (✓) all statements that are true for you. Then read aloud one statement that you checked. Another student will ask a question with the words in parentheses ( ). Answer the question.

EXAMPLES   __✓__ I did my homework. (where)
   A: I did my homework.
   B: Where did you do your homework?
   A: I did my homework in the library.

   __✓__ I got married. (when)
   A: I got married.
   B: When did you get married?
   A: I got married six years ago.

   1. _____ I graduated from high school. (when)

   2. _____ I studied biology. (when)

   3. _____ I bought an English dictionary. (where)

   4. _____ I left my country. (when)

   5. _____ I came to the U.S. (why)

   6. _____ I brought my clothes to the U.S. (what else)

   7. _____ I rented an apartment. (where)

   8. _____ I started to study English. (when)

   9. _____ I chose this college/school. (why)

   10. _____ I found my apartment. (when)

   11. _____ I needed to learn English. (when)

   12. _____ I got a driver's license. (when)

EXERCISE **24** **ABOUT YOU** Check (✓) which of these things you did when you were a child. Make an affirmative or negative statement about one of these items. Another student will ask a question about your statement.

EXAMPLE   _____ I attended public school.
   A: I didn't attend public school.
   B: Why didn't you attend public school?
   A: My parents wanted to give me a religious education.

   1. _____ I participated in a sport.   **7.** _____ I had a pet.

   2. _____ I enjoyed school.   **8.** _____ I lived on a farm.

   3. _____ I got good grades in school.   **9.** _____ I played soccer.

   4. _____ I got an allowance.[12]   **10.** _____ I studied English.

   5. _____ I lived with my grandparents. **11.** _____ I had a bike.

   6. _____ I took music lessons.   **12.** _____ I thought about my future.

[12]An *allowance* is money children get from their parents, usually once a week.

8.11 Questions About the Subject

EXAMPLES			EXPLANATION
Subject	**Verb**	**Complement**	When we ask a question about the subject, we use the past-tense form, not the base form. We don't use *did* in the question.
Someone	saved	the passengers.	
Who	saved	the passengers?	
			Compare:
Something	happened	to Sully's plane.	Where **did** the pilot **land** the airplane?
What	happened	to Sully's plane?	Who **landed** the airplane?
A president	invited	Sully.	When **did** the accident **happen**?
Which president	invited	Sully?	What **happened**?

EXERCISE 25 Choose the correct words to answer these questions about the subject. (The answers are at the bottom of the page.)

EXAMPLE Who invented the airplane?
(the Wright brothers)/ Goddard / Lindbergh)

1. Which country sent the first rocket into space?

   (*the U.S.* / *China* / *Russia*)

2. Who walked on the moon in 1969?

   (*an American* / *a Russian* / *a Canadian*)

3. Who sent up the first rocket?

   (*the Wright brothers* / *Goddard* / *Lindbergh*)

4. Who disappeared in 1937?

   (*Earhart* / *Goddard* / *Lindbergh*)

5. Who won money for flying across the Atlantic Ocean?

   (*Earhart* / *Lindbergh* / *Goddard*)

6. Which president showed interest in the Wright brothers' airplane?

   (*T. Roosevelt* / *Lincoln* / *Wilson*)

7. Which newspaper said that Goddard was a fool?

   (*Chicago Tribune* / *The Washington Post* / *The New York Times*)

8. How many people died in Sully's emergency landing?

   (*150* / *10* / *no one*)

ANSWERS TO EXERCISE 25:

(1) Russia, (2) an American, (3) Goddard, (4) Earhart, (5) Lindbergh, (6) T. Roosevelt, (7) *The New York Times*, (8) no one

EXERCISE 26   **ABOUT YOU**   **Read one of the *who* questions below. Someone will volunteer an answer. Then ask the person who answered "I did" a related question.**

EXAMPLE   **A:** Who went to the bank last week?

B: I did.

A: Why did you go to the bank?

B: I went there to buy a money order.

1. Who brought a dictionary to class today?
2. Who drank coffee this morning?
3. Who wrote a composition last night?
4. Who watched TV this morning?
5. Who came to the U.S. alone?
6. Who made an international phone call last night?
7. Who studied English before coming to the U.S.?
8. Who bought a newspaper today?

EXERCISE 27   **Fill in the blanks in this conversation between two students about their past.**

A: I _____was born_____ in Mexico. I _____
   (example: born)   *(1 come)*

to the U.S. ten years ago. Where _____ born?
                                        (2 be)

B: In El Salvador. But my family _____ to Guatemala
                                            (3 move)

when I _____ ten years old.
           (4 be)

A: Why _____ to Guatemala?
            (5 move)

B: In 1998, we _____ our home.
                        (6 lose)

A: What _____?
                (7 happen)

B: A major earthquake _____ (8 hit) my town. Luckily, my family was fine, but the earthquake _____ (9 destroy) our home and much of our town. We _____ (10 go) to live with cousins in Guatemala.

A: How long _____ (11 stay) in Guatemala?

B: I stayed there for about three years. Then I _____ (12 come) to the U.S.

A: What about your family? _____ (13 come) to the U.S. with you?

B: No. They _____ (14 wait) until I _____ (15 find) a job and _____ (16 save) my money. Then I _____ (17 bring) them here later.

A: My parents _____ (18 not/come) with me either. But my older brother did. I _____ (19 start) to go to school as soon as I _____ (20 arrive).

B: Who _____ (21 support) you while you were in school?

A: My brother _____ (22).

B: I _____ (23 not/go) to school right away because I _____ (24 have) to work. Then I _____ (25 get) a grant and _____ (26 start) to go to City College.

A: Why _____ (27 choose) City College?

B: I chose it because it has a good ESL program.

A: Me too.

Summary of Lesson 8

The Simple Past Tense

1. *Be*

Was	Were
I He She It } was in Paris.	We You They } were in Paris.
There was a problem.	There were many problems.

	Was	Were
AFFIRMATIVE	He **was** in Poland.	They **were** in France.
NEGATIVE	He **wasn't** in Russia.	They **weren't** in England.
YES/NO QUESTION	**Was** he in Hungary?	**Were** they in Paris?
SHORT ANSWER	No, he **wasn't**.	No, they **weren't**.
WH- QUESTION	Where **was** he?	When **were** they in France?
NEGATIVE QUESTION	Why **wasn't** he in Russia?	Why **weren't** they in Paris?
SUBJECT QUESTION	Who **was** in Russia?	How many people **were** in France?

2. Other Verbs

	REGULAR VERB (*WORK*)	IRREGULAR VERB (*BUY*)
AFFIRMATIVE	She **worked** on Saturday.	They **bought** a car.
NEGATIVE	She **didn't work** on Sunday.	They **didn't buy** a motorcycle.
YES/NO QUESTION	**Did** she **work** in the morning?	**Did** they **buy** an American car?
SHORT ANSWER	Yes, she **did**.	No, they **didn't**.
WH- QUESTION	Where **did** she **work**?	What kind of car **did** they **buy**?
NEGATIVE QUESTION	Why **didn't** she **work** on Sunday?	Why **didn't** they **buy** an American car?
SUBJECT QUESTION	Who **worked** on Sunday?	How many people **bought** an American car?

Editing Advice

1. Use the base form, not the past form, after *to*.

   buy
   I wanted to ~~bought~~ a new car.

2. Review the spelling rules for adding *-ed*, and use correct spelling.

   studied
   I ~~studyed~~ for the last test.

   dropped
   He ~~droped~~ his pencil.

3. Use the base form after *did* or *didn't*.

   know
   She didn't ~~knew~~ the answer.

   come
   Did your father ~~came~~ to the U.S.?

4. Use the correct word order in a question.

   your mother go
   Where did ~~go your mother~~?

   did your sister buy
   What ~~bought your sister~~?

5. Use *be* with *born*. (Don't add *-ed* to *born*.) Don't use *be* with *died*.

   was born
   Her grandmother ~~borned~~ in Russia.

   She ~~was~~ died in the U.S.

   was
   Where ~~did~~ your grandfather born?

   did
   Where ~~was~~ your grandfather died?

6. Check your list of verbs for irregular verbs.

   brought
   I ~~bringed~~ my photos to the U.S.

   saw
   I ~~seen~~ the accident yesterday.

7. Use *be* with age.

   was
   My grandfather ~~had~~ 88 years old when he died.

8. Don't confuse *was* and *were*.

   were
   Where ~~was~~ you yesterday?

9. Don't use *did* in a question about the subject.

took
Who ~~did take~~ my pencil?

10. Don't use *was* before *happened*.

What ~~was~~ happened to the airplane?

Editing Quiz

Some of the shaded words and phrases have mistakes. Find the mistakes and correct them. If the shaded words are correct, write C.

had   C

A: Last week we ~~have~~ an interesting homework assignment. We had to
(example)   *(example)*

wrote about a famous person.
(1)

B: Who you wrote about?
(2)

A: I wrote about Yuri Gagarin.

B: Who's that?

A: He was the first person in space.
(3)

B: He was an American?
(4)

A: No, he was Russian.
(5)

B: When he went into space?
(6)

A: In 1961.

B: Did he went alone?
(7)

A: Yes. But he wasn't the first living thing in space. There was fruit flies
(8)   *(9)*

and dogs in space before him. And later there were chimpanzees and
(10)

even turtles in space.

B: Is Gagarin still alive?

A: No. He was died in 1968.
(11)

B: When did he born?
(12)

A: He born in 1934. He had only 34 years old when he died. He never see
   (13)   (14)   (15)   (16)

the moon landing. That was happened in 1969, one year before he died.
                              (17)   (18)

B: Who did walk on the moon first? I forgetted his name.
       (19)   (20)

A: That was Neil Armstrong.

B: How did Gagarin died?
                        (21)

A: He were in a plane crash.
       (22)

B: That's so sad.

A: Yes, it is. They named a town in Russia after him.
                          (23)

Lesson 8 Test/Review

PART 1 **Write the past tense of each verb.**

EXAMPLES   live ___*lived*___   feel ___*felt*___

1. eat _____
2. see _____
3. get _____
4. sit _____
5. hit _____
6. make _____
7. take _____
8. find _____
9. say _____
10. read _____

11. drink _____
12. build _____
13. stop _____
14. leave _____
15. buy _____
16. think _____
17. run _____
18. carry _____
19. sell _____
20. stand _____

PART 2 **Fill in the blanks with the negative form of the underlined verb.**

EXAMPLE   Lindbergh <u>worked</u> for the U.S. Mail Service. Earhart

___*didn't work*___ for the U.S. Mail Service.

1. There <u>were</u> trains in 1900. There _____ any airplanes.

2. The Wright brothers <u>flew</u> a plane in 1903. They _____ a plane in 1899.

3. Charles Lindbergh <u>was</u> an aviator. He _____ a president.

4. The Wright brothers <u>invented</u> the airplane. They _____ the telephone.

5. Wilbur Wright <u>died</u> of typhoid fever. He _____ in a plane crash.

6. Lindbergh <u>went</u> to Paris. Earhart _____ to Paris.

7. Lindbergh <u>came</u> back from his flight. Earhart _____ back from her last flight.

8. Goddard <u>was born</u> in the nineteenth century. He _____ in the twentieth century.

9. Goddard <u>built</u> a rocket. He _____ an airplane.

10. Sully <u>lost</u> one engine. He _____ both engines.

PART 3 **Read each statement. Write a *yes/no* question about the words in parentheses ( ). Write a short answer.**

EXAMPLE Lindbergh crossed the ocean. (Earhart) (yes)
<u>**Did Earhart cross the ocean? Yes, she did.**</u>

1. Wilbur Wright became famous. (Orville Wright) (yes)

_____

2. Lindbergh was an aviator. (Goddard) (no)

_____

3. Lindbergh flew across the Atlantic Ocean. (Earhart) (yes)

_____

4. Lindbergh was born in the U.S. (Goddard) (yes)

_____

5. Goddard wrote about rockets. (the Wright brothers) (no)

_____

6. The Russians sent a man into space. (the Americans) (yes)

_____

7. Goddard died in 1945. (Wilbur Wright) (no)

_____

8. The U.S. put men on the moon in 1969. (Russia) (no)

_____

9. People laughed at Goddard's ideas in 1920. (in 1969) (no)

_____

10. Sully landed the airplane in the river. (safely) (yes)

_____

PART 4 **Write a _wh-_ question about the words in parentheses ( ). An answer is not necessary.**

EXAMPLE The Wright brothers became famous for their first airplane. (why/Lindbergh)

_**Why did Lindbergh become famous?**_____

1. Earhart was born in 1897. (when/Lindbergh)

_____

2. Lindbergh crossed the ocean in 1927. (when/Earhart)

_____

3. Lindbergh got money for his flight. (how much)

_____

4. Earhart wanted to fly around the world. (why)

_____

5. Many people saw Lindbergh in Paris. (how many people)

_____

6. Goddard's colleagues didn't believe his ideas. (why)

_____

7. Wilbur Wright died in 1912. (when/Orville Wright)

_____

8. A president examined Goddard's ideas. (which president)

_____

9. Sully lost an engine. (how)

_____

10. Someone made an emergency landing. (who)

_____

Expansion

Classroom Activities

1 In a small group or with the entire class, interview a student who recently immigrated to the U.S. Ask about his or her first experiences in the U.S.

EXAMPLES

Where did you live when you arrived?
Who picked you up from the airport?
Who helped you in the first few weeks?
What was your first impression of the U.S.?

2 Find a partner from another country to interview. Ask questions about the circumstances that brought him or her to the U.S. and the conditions of his or her life after he or she arrived. Write your conversation. Use Exercise 26 as your model.

EXAMPLE

A: When did you leave your country?
B: I left Ethiopia five years ago.
A: Did you come directly to the U.S.?
B: No. First I went to Sudan.
A: Why did you leave Ethiopia?

3 Finish these statements five different ways. Then find a partner and compare your sentences to your partner's sentences. Did you have any sentences in common?

EXAMPLE

When I was a child, _I didn't like to do my homework._

When I was a child, _my parents sent me to camp every summer._

When I was a child, _my nickname was "Curly."_

a. When I was a child, _____

When I was a child, _____

When I was a child, _____

When I was a child, _____

When I was a child, _____

b. Before I came to the U.S., _____

Before I came to the U.S., _____

Before I came to the U.S., _____

Before I came to the U.S., _____

Before I came to the U.S., _____

Talk

About It

1 Do you think space exploration is important? Why or why not?

2 Do you think there is life on another planet?

3 Would you want to take a trip to the moon or to another planet? Why or why not?

Write

About It

1 Write about your personal hero. You can write about a family member, friend, teacher, coworker, or someone you read about. Tell why you admire this person.

2 Write a paragraph about a famous person that you admire. Tell what this person did.

EXAMPLE

Abraham Lincoln

I really admire Abraham Lincoln. He was the 16th president of the U.S. He wanted every person to be free. At that time, there were slaves in the U.S. Lincoln wanted to end slavery . . .

For more practice using grammar in context, please visit our Web site.

Grammar
Infinitives

Modals

Imperatives

Context
Smart Shopping

9.1 Infinitives—An Overview

EXAMPLES	EXPLANATION
I want **to go** shopping. I need **to buy** a new DVD player. It's important **to compare** prices. It's not hard **to be** a good shopper.	An infinitive is *to* + the base form: *to go, to buy, to compare, to be*

Getting the Best Price

Before
You Read

1. Do you like to shop for new things such as TVs, DVD players, computers, and microwave ovens?

2. Do you try to compare prices in different stores before you buy an expensive item?

CD 2, TR 06

Read the following magazine article. Pay special attention to infinitives.

Are you planning **to buy** a new TV, digital camera, or DVD player? Of course you want **to get** the best price. Sometimes you see an item you like at one store and then go to another store **to compare** prices. If you find the same item at a higher price, you probably think it is necessary  **to go** back to the first store **to get** the lower price. But it usually isn't. You can simply tell the salesperson in the second store that you saw the item at a better price somewhere else. Usually the salesperson will try **to match**[1] the other store's price. However, you need **to prove** that you can buy it cheaper elsewhere.[2] The proof can be an advertisement from the newspaper. If you don't have an ad, the salesperson can call the other store **to check** the price. The salesperson doesn't want you **to leave** the store without buying anything. He wants his store **to make** money. Some salespeople are happy to call the other store **to check** the price.

What happens if you buy something and a few days later see it cheaper at another store? Some stores will give you the difference in price for a limited period of time (such as 30 days). It's important **to keep** the receipt **to show** when you bought the item and how much you paid.

Every shopper wants **to save** money.

[1]To *match* a price means to give you an equal price.
[2]*Elsewhere* means somewhere else, another place.

9.2 Verbs Followed by an Infinitive

We often use an infinitive after certain verbs.

EXAMPLES				EXPLANATION
Subject	**Verb**	**Infinitive**	**Complement**	We use an infinitive after these verbs:
I	plan	**to buy**	a camera.	begin hope prefer
We	want	**to get**	the best price.	continue like promise
You	need	**to be**	a smart shopper.	decide love start
She	likes	**to save**	money.	expect need try
				forget plan want
They	want	**to buy**	a DVD player.	An infinitive never has an ending. It never shows tense. Only the first verb has an ending or shows tense.
We	wanted	**to buy**	a new TV.	
He	is planning	**to buy**	a microwave oven.	*Wrong*: He wanted to *bought* a new TV.

Pronunciation Notes:

1. In informal speech, *want to* is pronounced "wanna." Listen to your teacher pronounce these sentences:

     I *want to* buy a DVD.
     Do you *want to* go shopping with me?
2. In other infinitives, we often pronounce *to* like "ta" (after a consonant sound), "da" (after a vowel sound), or "a" (after a "d" sound). Listen to your teacher pronounce these sentences:

     Do you like to watch movies at home? ("ta")
     I plan to buy a new DVD player. ("ta")
     Try to get the best price. ("da")
     We decided to buy a digital camera. ("a")
     I need to compare prices. ("a")

EXERCISE **1** Fill in the blanks with an infinitive. Answers may vary.

EXAMPLE   I want ___to buy___ a new TV.

1. I like _____ money.
2. I decided _____ about $500.
3. I want _____ the best price.
4. I forgot _____ the Internet before going to the stores.
5. I need _____ a smart shopper.
6. Some people prefer _____ online.

EXERCISE **2** **ABOUT YOU** Make a sentence about yourself with the words given. Use an appropriate tense. You may find a partner and compare your sentences to your partner's sentences.

EXAMPLES   like/eat
I like to eat pizza.

learn/speak
I learned to speak German when I was a child.

try/find
I'm trying to find a bigger apartment.

1. love/go
2. like/play
3. need/have
4. expect/get
5. want/go
6. plan/buy
7. need/understand
8. not need/have
9. try/learn

EXERCISE **3** **ABOUT YOU** Ask a question with the words given in the present tense. Another student will answer.

EXAMPLE   like/shop

A: Do you like to shop?
B: Yes, I do. OR No, I don't.

1. try/compare prices
2. plan/buy something new
3. like/shop alone
4. like/shop online
5. like/use coupons
6. try/get the best price

EXERCISE 4 **ABOUT YOU** Ask a question with "Do you want to . . . ?" or "Do you plan to . . . ?" and the words given. Another student will answer. Then ask a *wh-* question with the words in parentheses ( ) whenever possible.

EXAMPLE   buy a car (why)

A: Do you plan to buy a car?
B: Yes, I do.
A: Why do you want to buy a car?
B: I don't like public transportation.

1. take a computer course next semester (why)

2. move (why) (when)

3. leave this country (why) (when)

4. get a job/get another job (what kind of job)

5. become an American citizen (why)

6. transfer to a different school (why)

7. take another English course next semester (which course)

8. learn another language (which language)

9. review the last lesson (why)

9.3 *It* + *Be* + Adjective + Infinitive

We often use an infinitive with sentences beginning with an impersonal *it*.

EXAMPLES				EXPLANATION
It	*Be* (+ *not*)	**Adjective**	**Infinitive Phrase**	An infinitive can follow these adjectives:
It	is	important	**to save** your receipt.	
It	is	easy	**to shop**.	dangerous hard good
It	isn't	necessary	**to go** back to the first store.	possible difficult expensive
				impossible easy boring
				important necessary nice

EXERCISE 5 Complete each statement.

EXAMPLE It's expensive to own __a big car.__

1. It's important to learn _____
2. It's hard to pronounce _____
3. It's hard to lift _____
4. It's necessary to own _____
5. It's easy to learn _____
6. It's hard to learn _____
7. It isn't necessary to know _____

EXERCISE 6 Complete each statement with an infinitive phrase.

EXAMPLE It's easy __to ride a bike.__

1. It's boring _____
2. It's impossible _____
3. It's possible _____
4. It's necessary _____
5. It's dangerous _____
6. It's hard _____
7. It isn't good _____
8. It isn't necessary _____

EXERCISE 7 Answer the following questions. (You may work with a partner and ask and answer with your partner.)

1. Is it important to be bilingual?
2. Is it important to know English in your native country?
3. Is it possible to find a job in the U.S. without knowing any English?
4. Is it easy to learn English grammar?
5. Is it dangerous to text while driving?
6. Is it necessary to have a computer?

9.4 *Be* + Adjective + Infinitive

We often use an infinitive after certain adjectives.

EXAMPLES				EXPLANATION
Subject	***Be***	**Adjective**	**Infinitive Phrase**	We can use an infinitive after these adjectives:
I	am	ready	**to buy** a camera.	happy afraid lucky
The salesman	is	glad	**to help** you.	sad prepared proud
He	is	prepared	**to make** a sale.	glad ready pleased

EXERCISE 8 **ABOUT YOU** Fill in the blanks.

EXAMPLE   I'm ready _to do the exercise._

1. I'm lucky _____

2. I'm proud _____

3. I'm happy _____

4. I'm sometimes afraid _____

5. I'm not afraid _____

6. I'm not prepared _____

7. I was sad _____

EXERCISE 9 **ABOUT YOU** Answer the following questions.

1. Are you happy to be in this country?

2. Are you afraid to make a mistake when you speak English?

3. Were you sad to leave your country?

4. Are you prepared to have a test on this lesson?

5. Are you happy to be a student at this school?

6. Are you afraid to walk alone at night?

9.5 Using an Infinitive to Show Purpose

EXAMPLES	EXPLANATION
I went to a store **to buy** a digital camera. I went to a second store **to compare** prices. The saleswoman called the first store **to check** the price.	We use an infinitive to show the purpose of an action. Do not use *for* to show purpose. *Wrong*: I went to a store *for buy* a digital camera.
I use a digital camera **to** e-mail photos to my friends. I use a digital camera **in order to** e-mail photos to my friends.	*To* for purpose is the short form of *in order to*.

EXERCISE 10 Fill in the blanks to show purpose.

EXAMPLE   I bought a phone card to __call my friends.__

1. I use my dictionary to _____

2. He went to an appliance store in order to _____
_____

3. She worked overtime in order to _____
_____

4. I bought the Sunday newspaper to _____

5. You need to show your driver's license to _____
_____

6. Some people join a health club in order to _____
_____

7. On a computer, you use the mouse to _____

8. When you return an item to a store, take your receipt in order to _____
_____

9. Shoppers use coupons in order to _____

10. Many people shop online to _____

EXERCISE 11 Fill in the blanks to complete this conversation. Answers may vary.

CD 2, TR 07

A: Do you want to see my new digital camera?

B: Wow. It's so small. Does it take good pictures?

A: Absolutely. I use this camera _____ **to take** _____ all my pictures.
        (example)

B: Was it expensive?

A: Not really. I went online _____ (1) prices. Then I went to several stores in this city _____ (2) the best price.

B: Do you take a lot of pictures?

A: Oh, yes. And I e-mail them to my family back home.

B: Do you ever make prints of your pictures?

A: Yes. I buy high-quality glossy paper _____ (3) prints for my family album.

B: Is it hard to use the camera?

A: At first I had to read the manual carefully _____ (4) how to take good pictures and transfer them to my computer. But now it's easy. I'll take a picture of you. Smile.

B: Let me see it. My eyes are closed in the picture. Take another picture of me.

A: OK. This one's better. But I don't like the background. It's too dark. I can use a photo-editing program _____ (5) the color.

B: Can you use the program _____ (6) me more handsome?

Getting A Customer's Attention

Before You Read

1. Do you try free samples of food in supermarkets?
2. Do you ever go to the movies early in the day to get a cheaper ticket?

CD 2, TR 08

Read the following magazine article. Pay special attention to objects before an infinitive.

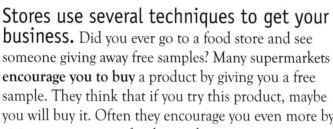

Stores use several techniques to get your business. Did you ever go to a food store and see someone giving away free samples? Many supermarkets **encourage you to buy** a product by giving you a free sample. They think that if you try this product, maybe you will buy it. Often they encourage you even more by giving you a coupon for the product.

Sometimes a store will advertise "two for the price of one." This is a marketing technique to get your interest. After you come into the store for the sale item, the manager **wants you to do** the rest of your shopping there too.

Movie theaters will lower their price in the early hours. This is because most people don't think of going to a movie early in the day. Both you and the movie theater benefit when you take advantage of the reduced price. You help fill the theater and get a cheap ticket in return.

Another way to get customer attention is with good service. Sometimes as you're leaving a store, a salesperson may ask you, "Do you **want me to take** this out to your car for you?" There is no extra charge for such service.

With so much competition between businesses, owners and managers have to use all kinds of techniques to get our attention and **encourage us to shop** at their store and return often.

9.6 Object Before an Infinitive

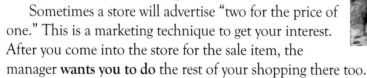

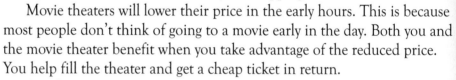

EXAMPLES	EXPLANATION
They **like you to try** the free samples. Do you **want me to carry** this out to your car for you? They **want us to do** all our shopping in one store. I **expect salespeople to be** courteous. I **expect them to be** helpful, too.	After *like, want, need, expect,* and *encourage,* we can use a noun or object pronoun (*me, you, him, her, it, us, them*) + an infinitive.

EXERCISE 12 **Circle the correct words in parentheses ( ) to complete each conversation.**

CD 2, TR 09

Conversation 1

Salesman: Do you want (**me** / I) (to help / help) you
find something?

Mother: Yes. We could use your help. Our daughter
wants (we / us) (bought / to buy) her a new

cell phone. We don't know which plan to buy.

Salesman: How many minutes a month does she talk on the phone?

Mother: She never stops talking on the phone. I want

(her to use / that she use) it just for emergencies, but she chats with

her friends all the time.

Salesman: Here's a plan I want (you to consider / that you consider).

It has unlimited calls at night and on weekends.

Mother: You don't understand. We want (her / she) to use the phone

less, not more.

Conversation 2

Man: I'm going to buy a digital camera on Saturday. I need

(that you / you to) come with me.

Friend: Why? How do you want (that I / me to) help you?

Man: You already have a digital camera, so you can give me advice.

Conversation 3

Husband: Oh, look. There's free food over there. Do you want

(me to get / that I get) you a little hot dog?

(continued)

Wife: No. They just want (*us* / *we*) to spend our money on things
(2)

we don't need.

Conversation 4

Grocery Clerk: Excuse me, miss. You have a lot of bags. Do you want

(*me* / *I*) (*to help* / *helping*) you take them to your car?
(1)   (2)

Shopper: Thanks. My husband's in the car. I wanted (*him* / *he*)
(3)

(*to help* / *helped*) me, but he hates shopping. He prefers
(4)

to wait in the car. Besides, he has a bad back, and I

don't want (*that he* / *him to*) lift anything. We're having a
(5)

dinner party on Saturday and we invited 20 guests, but I . . .

Grocery Clerk: Uh, excuse me. I hear my boss calling me. He needs

me now (*to give* / *giving*) him some help.
(6)

EXERCISE 13 Two brothers are talking. Fill in the blanks with the first verb, an object pronoun, and the second verb.

A: Mom and Dad say I spend too much money. They _**expect me to save**_
(example: expect/save)

my money for the future. I _____ me alone.
(1 want/leave)

B: You do? I thought you _____ you a car.
(2 wanted/buy)

A: Well, I do. You know how much I hate to take the bus. I

_____ to them for me. Tell them I need a car.
(3 want/talk)

B: I'm not going to do that. They are trying to _____
(4 encourage/be)

more responsible.

A: I *am* responsible.

B: No, you're not. Remember when you told Mom you wanted a

new MP3 player? You _____ it for you.
(5 expected/buy)

And remember when you lost your cell phone? You told Dad because

you _____ you a new one.
(6 wanted/buy)

A: Well, I'm still in school and I don't have much money.

B: Mom and Dad _____ and start to take

(7 expect/graduate)

responsibility for yourself. You buy too much stuff.

A: No, I don't. By the way, did I tell you I broke my camera?

9.7 Overview of Modals

LIST OF MODALS	FACTS ABOUT MODALS

can
 	
could
 	
should
 	
will
 	
would
 	
may
 	
might
 	
must
	1. Modals are different from other verbs because they don't have an *-s, -ed,* or *-ing* ending.
	    He **can** compare prices. (not: He *cans*)
	2. Modals are different from other verbs because we don't use an infinitive after a modal.[3] We use the base form.
	    COMPARE:
	    He **wants to buy** a digital camera.
	    He **might buy** a digital camera.
	3. To form the negative, put *not* after the modal.
	    You **should not** throw away the receipt.
	    Hurry! These prices **may not** last.
	4. Some verbs are like modals in meaning: *have to, be able to.*
	    You **must** return the item within 30 days. = You **have to** return the item within 30 days.
	    He **can't** get a credit card. = He **is not able to** get a credit card.

Compare affirmative statements and questions.

Wh- Word	Modal	Subject	Modal	Base Form	Complement	Short Answer
		You	**should**	**buy**	a new TV.	
	Should	you		**buy**	a DVD player?	No, you shouldn't.
What	**should**	you		**buy?**		
		Who	**should**	**buy**	a new TV?	
		She	**can**	compare	prices.	
	Can	she		compare	prices online?	Yes, she can.
How	**can**	she		compare	prices online?	
		Who	**can**	compare	prices?	

Compare negative statements and questions.

Wh- Word	Modal	Subject	Modal	Base Form	Complement
		He	**shouldn't**	**buy**	an expensive camera.
Why	**shouldn't**	he		**buy**	an expensive camera?

[3]Exception: *ought to. Ought to means should.*

Smart Shopping: Coupons, Rain Checks, and Rebates

Before You Read

1. Do you see coupons in magazines and newspapers? Do you use them?

2. Do you see signs that say "rebate" on store products? Do you see signs that say "Buy one, get one free"?

MANUFACTURER'S COUPON	DO NOT DOUBLE	EXPIRES 12/15/2011

Save 50¢
Tony T's
Homemade Pizza Sauce

CONSUMER: Limit one coupon per purchase.
RETAILER: Please redeem for face value as specified. Any other use constitutes fraud.
Cash value: 1/100 cent.

4677000072

GTG Good Time Grocery — **Rain Check** — No. 7942

Date _____ Item size _____
Item _____ Discount _____
Item quantity _____ Item Price _____ Expiration _____

Good toward similar item of equal or lesser value

Authorization _____

CD 2, TR 10

Read the following magazine article. Pay special attention to modals and related expressions.

Do you ever receive coupons in the mail?

Manufacturers often send coupons to shoppers. They want people to try their products. If you always use the same toothpaste and the manufacturer gives you a coupon for a different toothpaste, you **might** try the new brand.[4] Coupons have an expiration date. You **should** pay attention to this date because you **cannot** use the coupon after this date.

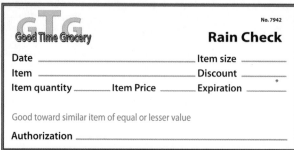

Rebate Form
Name
Address
City/State   Zip   Phone
Product name: _____
Size/Weight: _____
Price: _____
Store where purchased: _____
Date of purchase: _____
Proof of purchase attached: **yes / no**

Stores have weekly specials. But there is usually a limit. If you see a sign that says, "Eggs, $1.69 a dozen. Limit 2," this means you **can** buy only two dozen at this price. If you see a sign that says, "3 for $1.00," you **don't have to** buy three items to get the special price. If you buy only one, you **will** pay 34¢.

What **should** you do if a store has a special but you **can't** find this item on the shelf? If this item is sold out, you **can** go to the customer service desk and ask for a rain check. A rain check allows you to buy this item at the sale price even after the sale is over. A rain check usually has an expiration date. You **must** buy this item by the expiration date if you want to receive the sale price.

If you see a sign that says "rebate," this means that you **can** get money back from the manufacturer. You **have to** mail the proof of purchase and the cash register receipt to the manufacturer to prove that you bought this product. Also you **have to** fill out a small form. The manufacturer **will** return some money to you. It **may** take six to eight weeks to receive this money.

These sales techniques help manufacturers get your attention, but they also help you save money.

[4]The *brand* is the company name.

9.8 Can

EXAMPLES	EXPLANATION
I **can** find many ways to save money. I **can** explain how to use a rebate.	Ability
If you use coupons, you **can** save money. If the item is sold out, you **can** get a rain check.	Possibility
The sign says, "Eggs $1.69 a dozen. Limit 2." You **can** buy only two cartons of eggs at the special price. You **can** return an item within 30 days.	Permission
I **can't afford to** eat in a restaurant every day. **Can** you **afford** to buy steaks?	*Can afford to* means have enough money to buy something.
You **cannot** buy more than the limited quantity. You **can't** use a coupon after the expiration date.	The negative of *can* is *cannot*. The contraction is *can't*.

Pronunciation Notes:

1. In affirmative statements, we usually pronounce *can* /kən/. In negative statements, we pronounce *can't* /kænt/. Sometimes it is hard to hear the final **t**, so we must pay attention to the vowel sound and the stress to hear the difference between *can* and *can't*. Listen to your teacher pronounce these sentences:

   I *can* gó. /kən/
   I *cán't* go. /kænt/

2. In a short answer, we pronounce *can* /kæn/.

   Can you help me later?
   Yes, I *can*. /kæn/

EXERCISE 14   These sentences are true about an American supermarket. Check (✓) which ones are true about a supermarket in another country.

1. ____ You can use coupons.

2. ____ You can sometimes buy two items for the price of one.

3. ____ You can cash a check.

4. ____ You can buy stamps.

5. ____ You can get a rain check.

6. ____ You can pay by check or credit card.

7. ____ You can't bargain⁵ for the price.

8. ____ You can return an item if you're not satisfied. You can get your money back.

---

⁵To *bargain* for a price means to make an offer lower than the price the seller is asking.

(continued)

9. ____ You can get free bags (paper or plastic).

10. ____ You can use a shopping cart. Small children can sit in the cart.

11. ____ If you have a small number of items, you can go to a special lane.

12. ____ You can shop 24 hours a day (in some supermarkets).

EXERCISE 15　　**ABOUT YOU** Fill in the blanks with *can* or *can't* to tell about your abilities.

EXAMPLE　　I ____*can*____ drive a car.

I ____*can't*____ fly a plane.

1. I _____ read without glasses.

2. I _____ speak Spanish.

3. I _____ drive a car.

4. I _____ play tennis.

5. I _____ sing well.

6. I _____ change a tire.

7. I _____ save money.

8. I _____ read the newspaper without a dictionary.

EXERCISE 16　　**ABOUT YOU** Ask a question about a classmate's abilities with the word(s) given. Another student will answer.

EXAMPLE　　speak Spanish

A: Can you speak Spanish?
B: Yes, I can.　OR　No, I can't.

1. write with your left hand

2. type without looking at the keyboard

3. run fast

4. play chess

5. ski

6. play the piano

7. speak French

8. bake a cake

9. play the guitar

10. sew

EXERCISE 17　　**ABOUT YOU** Write down one thing that you can do well. Share your answer with a partner or with the entire class.

_____

9.9 Should

EXAMPLES	EXPLANATION
You **should** use coupons to save money. What **should** I do if the item is sold out? You **should** compare prices before you buy.	We use *should* to give or ask for advice.
You **should not** waste your money. You **shouldn't** buy things you don't need.	The negative of *should* is *should not*. The contraction is *shouldn't*. We use the negative to give advice or a warning.

EXERCISE 18 If someone from another country is going to live in the U.S., what advice would you give him or her about shopping? Work with a partner to write six sentences of advice.

EXAMPLE   You should always look at the expiration date on a food product.

You should shop for summer clothes in July and August. Summer

clothes are cheapest at that time.

1. _____
2. _____
3. _____
4. _____
5. _____
6. _____

EXERCISE 19 Write a sentence to give advice in each of the following situations. Answers will vary.

EXAMPLE   The price of strawberries is high this week.

Maybe we shouldn't buy them this week.

1. I love this coffee. It's half price this week.

   _____

2. I have a rain check for eggs. It expires tomorrow.

   _____

3. I spent too much money on groceries last week.

   _____

4. My supermarket gives you 10¢ for every bag you bring back.

   _____

(continued)

Infinitives; Modals; Imperatives   277

5. I have ice cream in my bag, and it's a warm day today.

_____

6. My kids always want me to buy them sweets.

_____

7. I get coupons in the mail, but I always throw them away.

_____

EXERCISE **20** A wife (W) and husband (H) are at the supermarket. Fill in the blanks with *should* + a verb to complete the conversation. Answers may vary.

CD 2, TR 11

W: _____Should we buy_____ ice cream? It's on sale.
 (example)

H: It's so hot today. And we have to stop at the dentist before we go home.

We _____ it today. It'll melt.
 (1)

H: Look. Our favorite coffee is half price this week. _____
 (2)

a bag?

W: We _____ a lot.
 (3)

H: How about candy for the kids? They always ask us for candy.

W: That's not a good idea. They _____ so much
 (4)

candy. It's not good for them. Where's our shopping list? We

_____ our list and not buy things we don't need.
 (5)

We _____ careful how we spend our money.
 (6)

H: You're right. Cheese is on our list. (*Husband picks up cheese.*)

W: You _____ at the expiration date. This cheese has
 (7)

tomorrow's date. We _____ fresher cheese. You
 (8)

almost never come shopping with me. You _____
 (9)

with me more often. You can learn to be a better shopper.

H: You're right. Look. The sign says, "Bring your own bags. Get 10¢ for

each bag." Next time we _____ our own bags. You see?
 (10)

I'm learning.

W: Great. _____ with a credit card or use cash?
 (11)

H: I've got enough cash on me. Let's use cash.

EXERCISE 21 Check (✓) if you agree or disagree about what schoolchildren should or shouldn't do. Discuss your answers with the whole class or in a small group.

	I agree.	I disagree.
1. Children should go to a teacher when they have a family problem.		
2. They shouldn't play video games.		
3. They should select their own TV programs.		
4. They shouldn't trust all adults.		
5. They should always tell the truth.		
6. They should be responsible for taking care of younger sisters and brothers.		
7. They should select their own friends.		
8. They should always obey their parents and teachers.		
9. They should learn to use a computer.		
10. They should study a foreign language.		
11. They should help their parents with small jobs in the house.		
12. They should learn about money when they're young.		

EXERCISE 22 Read each statement. Then ask a question with the word(s) in parentheses ( ). Another student will answer.

EXAMPLE The students should do the homework. (why)

A: Why should they do the homework?
B: It helps them understand the lesson.

1. The students should study the lessons. (why)
2. The teacher should take attendance. (when)
3. The students should bring their textbooks to class. (what else)
4. I should study modals. (why)
5. We should register for classes early. (why)
6. The teacher should speak clearly. (why)
7. The students shouldn't talk during a test. (why)
8. We shouldn't do the homework in class. (where)
9. The teacher should announce a test ahead of time. (why)

9.10 *Must*

EXAMPLES	EXPLANATION
To get a rebate, you **must** send the proof of purchase. You **must** include your receipt.	We use *must* to talk about rules and laws. *Must* has a very official, formal tone.
It's late. I **must** get to the store before it closes. We're almost out of milk!	We can use *must* for personal necessity. It shows a sense of urgency.
You **must not** use the handicapped parking space if you don't have permission. The store **mustn't** sell a product after its expiration date.	For the negative, use *must not*. The contraction is *mustn't*. *Must not* and *cannot* are very close in meaning. You *must not* park in the handicapped space = You *cannot* park in the handicapped space.

EXERCISE 23 Here are some rules in a supermarket. Fill in the blanks with *must* or *must not.*

1. Employees in the deli department _____ wear gloves.

2. Employees _____ touch food with their bare hands.

3. When employees use the washroom, they _____ wash their hands before returning to work.

4. The store _____ sell food after the expiration date.

5. Customers _____ take shopping carts out of the parking lot.

EXERCISE 24 Name something. Discuss your answers.

EXAMPLE Name something you must have if you want to drive.
You must have a license.

1. Name something you must do or have if you want to leave the country.

2. Name something you must not carry onto an airplane.

3. Name something you must not do in the classroom.

4. Name something you must not do during a test.

5. Name something you must not do or have in your apartment.

6. Name something you must do or have to enter an American university.

7. Name something you must do when you drive a car.

9.11 Have To

	EXAMPLES	EXPLANATION
AFFIRMATIVE	I don't have enough milk. I **have to** go shopping. If you want to return an item, you **have to** show a receipt.	*Have to* is similar in meaning to *must*. *Have to* is less formal. We use it for personal obligations.
NEGATIVE	A: The DVD player was cheaper in the first store. Let's go back there. B: You **don't have to** go back there. Just tell the salesperson, and she'll probably give you the same price. A: Can we sample those cookies? B: Sure. If we don't like them, we **don't have to** buy them.	*Don't have to* means it's not necessary. You have a choice.

EXERCISE 25 **ABOUT YOU** Tell if you *have to* or *don't have to* do these things at this school. (Remember: *don't have to* means it's not necessary.)

EXAMPLES study before a test
I have to study before a test.

study in the library
I don't have to study in the library. I can study at home.

1. wear a suit to school
2. come to class on time
3. stand up to ask a question in class
4. do homework
5. notify the teacher if I'm going to be absent
6. call the teacher "professor"
7. raise my hand to answer
8. take a final exam
9. wear a uniform
10. buy my own textbooks

EXERCISE 26 Ask your teacher what he or she *has to* or *doesn't have to* do.

EXAMPLE work on Saturdays

A: Do you have to work on Saturdays?
B: Yes, I do. OR No, I don't.

1. take attendance
2. give students grades
3. call students by their last names
4. wear a suit
5. work in the summer
6. have a master's degree
7. work on Saturdays
8. come to school every day

EXERCISE **27** **ABOUT YOU** If you are from another country, write four sentences about students and teachers in your country. Tell what they *have to* or *don't have to* do. Use the ideas from the previous exercises. You may share your sentences with a small group or with the class.

EXAMPLE In my country, students have to wear a uniform.

1. _____
2. _____
3. _____
4. _____

EXERCISE **28** Tell what Judy *has to* or *doesn't have to* do in these situations. Answers may vary.

EXAMPLE Judy has a coupon for cereal. The expiration date is tomorrow.
She has to ___use it by tomorrow or she won't get the discount.___ .

1. The coupon for cereal says "Buy 2, get 50¢ off."
   She has to _____ in order to get the discount.
2. Judy has no milk in the house.
   She has to _____ more milk.
3. Eggs are on sale for $1.69, limit two cartons. She has three cartons of eggs.
   She has to _____ one of the cartons of eggs.
4. She has a rebate application. She has to fill out the application if she wants to get money back.
   She also has to _____ the proof-of-purchase symbol and the receipt to the manufacturer.
5. She wants to pay by check. The cashier asks for her driver's license.
   She has to _____.
6. She has 26 items in her shopping cart. She can't go to a lane that says "10 items or fewer."
   She has to _____ another lane.

9.12 *Must* and *Have To*

**In affirmative statements, *have to* and *must* are very similar in meaning.
In negative statements, *have to* and *must* are very different in meaning.**

	EXAMPLES	EXPLANATION
AFFIRMATIVE	If you wish to return an item, you **must** have a receipt. You **must** send the rebate coupon by October 1. You **have to** send the rebate coupon by October 1.	Use *must* or *have to* for rules. *Must* is more formal or more official, but we can use *have to* for rules too.
	I don't have any milk. I **have to** go to the store to buy some. I need to buy a lot of things. I **have to** use a shopping cart.	Use *have to* for personal obligations or necessities.
NEGATIVE	You **must not** park in the handicapped parking space. The store **must not** sell an item after the expiration date.	*Must not* shows that something is prohibited or against the law.
	The sign says, "3 for $1.00," but you **don't have to** buy three to get the sale price. You **don't have to** pay with cash. You can use a credit or debit card.	*Don't have to* shows that something is not necessary, that there is a choice.

EXERCISE 29   **Fill in the blanks with *must not* or *don't have to*.**

EXAMPLES   You   ___**must not**___   take a shopping cart out of the parking lot.

We   ___**don't have to**___   shop every day. We can shop once a week.

1. If you sample a product, you _____ buy it.

2. If you have just a few items, you _____ use a shopping cart. You can use a basket.

3. If you have a lot of items in your shopping cart, you

   _____ use the checkout that says "10 items or fewer."

4. You _____ park in the handicapped parking space if you don't have permission.

5. You _____ take your own bags to the supermarket. The cashier will give you bags for your groceries.

9.13 Might/May and Will

EXAMPLES	EXPLANATION
I have a coupon for a new toothpaste. I **might** buy it. I **may** like it. A rebate check **might** take six to eight weeks.	*May* and *might* have the same meaning. They show possibility. Compare *maybe* (adverb) with *may* or *might* (modal verbs): *Maybe* it *will* take eight weeks. It *may* take eight weeks. It *might* take eight weeks.
Those cookies taste great, but they **may not** be healthy for you. I **might not** have time to shop next week, so I'll buy enough for two weeks.	The negative of *may* is *may not*. The negative of *might* is *might not*. We do not make a contraction for *may not* and *might not*.
If the price is 3 for $1.00, you **will** pay 34¢ for one. If the sign says "Two for one," the store **will** give you one item for free.	*Will* shows certainty about the future.

EXERCISE **30** Tell what may or might happen in the following situations. Answers may vary.

EXAMPLE Meg needs to go shopping. She's not sure what her kids want.

They might _____ **want a new kind of** _____ cereal.

1. She's not sure if she should buy the small size or the large size of cereal. The large size may _____ cheaper.

2. If she sends in the rebate form today, she might _____ a check in about six weeks.

3. The store sold all the coffee that was on sale. The clerk said, "We might _____ more coffee tomorrow."

4. Bananas are so expensive this week. If she waits until next week, the price may _____.

5. The milk has an expiration date of June 27. Today is June 27. She's not going to buy the milk because it might _____.

6. She's not sure what brand of toothpaste she should buy. She might buy the one she usually buys, or she might _____.

EXERCISE **31** Tell what *may* or *might* happen in the following situations. If you think the result is certain, use *will*.

EXAMPLES If you don't put money in a parking meter, ___you might get a ticket.___

If you are absent from tests, ___you may not pass the course.___

If you don't pass the tests, ___you'll fail the course.___

1. If you drive too fast, _____

2. If you get a lot of tickets in one year, _____

3. If you don't water your plants, _____

4. If you don't take the final exam, _____

5. If you don't lock the door of your house, _____

_____

6. If you eat too much, _____

7. If you work hard and save your money, _____

_____

8. If the weather is nice this weekend, _____

9. If you park in the handicapped space without permission, _____

_____

9.14 Making Requests

EXAMPLES	EXPLANATION
Park over there. **Don't park** in the handicapped space. **Send** the rebate coupon soon. **Do not** wait.	We can use imperatives to make a request. The imperative is the base form of the verb. The subject is *you*, but we don't include *you* in the sentence. For a negative, put *don't* (or *do not*) before the verb.
May I see your driver's license? **Could** you give me change for a dollar?	We also use modals to make requests. Modals give the request a more polite tone.

The Customer Service Counter

1. Do you have a check-cashing card at a local supermarket?

2. Do you pay with cash when you shop in a supermarket?

CD 2, TR 12

Read the following conversation, first between two friends (A and B), and then between A and a customer service representative (C). Pay special attention to requests.

A: I need to cash a check.

B: Let's go to the customer service counter at Nick's. Someone told me they have a check-cashing service there.

A: Could you drive?

B: Why don't we walk? It's not far.

At the customer service counter:

C: Can I help you?

A: Yes. **I'd like** to cash a check.

C: Do you have a check-cashing card?

A: No, I don't.

C: Here's an application. Please **fill** it out.

A: I don't have a pen. **Could** I use your pen?

C: Here's a pen.

A: Thanks.

A few minutes later:

A: Here's my application.

C: May I see your driver's license?

A: Here it is. Did I fill out the application correctly?

C: No. Please **don't write** in the gray box. You made another mistake too. You wrote the day before the month. Please **write** the month before the day. For August 29, we write 8/29, not 29/8. **Why don't you fill out** another form? Here's a clean one.

A: Thanks.

(continued)

A few minutes later:

A: Here it is. **Could** you check to see if I filled it out right this time?

C: You forgot to sign your name. Please **sign** your name on the bottom line.

A: OK. **Could** you cash my check now?

C: I'm sorry, sir. We have to wait for approval. We'll send you your check-cashing card in the mail in a week to ten days. **Can** I help you with anything else?

A: Yes. **I'd like** to buy some stamps.

C: Here you are. Anything else?

A: No. That's it.

C: Have a nice day.

Nick's **Check Cashing Application**

9.15 Imperatives

Imperatives give instructions, warnings, and suggestions.

EXAMPLES	EXPLANATION
Please **sign** your name at the bottom. **Write** the month before the day. **Be** careful when you fill out the application. **Don't write** in the gray box.	We use the imperative form to give instructions.
Stand up. **Walk, don't run!**	We use the imperative to give a command.
Watch out! There's a car coming! **Don't move.** There's a bee on your nose!	We use the imperative to give a warning.
Always do your best. **Never give** up.	We use the imperative to give encouragement. We can put *always* and *never* before an imperative.
Have a nice day. **Make** yourself at home.	We use the imperative in certain conversational expressions.
Go away. **Leave** me alone.	We use the imperative in some angry, impolite expressions.
Let's get an application for check cashing. **Let's not** make any mistakes.	*Let's = let us.* We use *let's* + the base form to make a suggestion. The negative form is *let's not. Let's* includes the speaker.

EXERCISE 32 **Fill in the blanks with an appropriate imperative verb (affirmative or negative) to give instructions. Answers may vary.**

EXAMPLE _____*Go*_____ to the customer service desk for an application.

1. _____ out the application in pen.

2. _____ a pencil to fill out an application.

3. _____ all the information in clear letters.

4. If you have a middle name, _____ your middle initial.

5. _____ anything in the box in the lower right corner.

6. If you are not married, _____ out the second part about spouse information.

7. When you give your telephone number, always _____ your area code.

8. _____ your last name before your first name on this application.

9. _____ the application to a person at the customer service counter.

EXERCISE 33 Choose one of the activities from the following list. Use imperatives to give instructions on how to do the activity. (You may work with a partner.)

EXAMPLE get from school to your house

Take the number 53 bus north from the corner of Elm Street. Ask the driver for a transfer. Get off at Park Avenue. Cross the street and wait for a number 18 bus.

1. hang a picture
2. change a tire
3. fry an egg
4. prepare your favorite recipe
5. hem a skirt
6. write a check
7. make a deposit at the bank
8. tune a guitar
9. get a driver's license
10. use a washing machine
11. prepare for a job interview
12. get from school to your house
13. get money from a cash machine (automatic teller)
14. do a search on the Internet
15. send a text message

EXERCISE 34 Work with a partner. Write a list of command forms that the teacher often uses in class. Read your sentences to the class.

EXAMPLE *Open your books to page 10.*

Don't come late to class.

1. _____
2. _____
3. _____
4. _____
5. _____

EXERCISE 35 **Fill in the blanks with an appropriate verb to complete this conversation.**

A: I need to cash a check.

B: We need to get some groceries. Let's ___*go*___ to the
      (example)
      supermarket.

A: Do you want to drive there?

B: The supermarket is not so far. Let's _____.
                                            (1)

A: It looks like rain.

B: No problem. Let's _____ an umbrella.
                        (2)

A: Let's _____. It's late and the stores will close soon.
            (3)

B: Don't worry. This store is open 24 hours a day.

A: We're almost out of dog food. Let's _____ a
                                            (4)
      20-pound bag.

B: Let's not _____ then. I don't want to carry a
                (5)
      20-pound bag home. Let's _____ instead.
                                (6)

EXERCISE 36 **Work with a partner. Write a few suggestions for the teacher or other students in this class using *let's* or *let's not*. Read your suggestions to the class.**

EXAMPLES Let's review verb tenses.

Let's not speak our native languages in class.

1. _____

2. _____

3. _____

4. _____

5. _____

6. _____

9.16 Using Modals to Make Requests and Ask Permission

An imperative form may sound too strong in some situations. Modals can make a request sound more polite.

EXAMPLES	EXPLANATION
Would **Could** } you cash my check, please?	We use these modals in a question to make a request. These forms are more polite than "Cash my check."
May **Could** } I use your pen, please? **Can**	We use these modals in a question to ask permission. These forms are more polite than "Give me your pen."
I **would like** to cash a check. How **would** you **like** your change?	*Would like* has the same meaning as *want*. *Would like* is softer than *want*. The contraction of *would* after a pronoun is *'d*: I*'d* like to cash a check.
Why don't you fill out another form? **Why don't we** walk to the supermarket?	Use *why don't you . . . ?* and *why don't we . . . ?* to offer suggestions.
May **Can** } I help you?	Salespeople often use these questions to offer help to a customer.

EXERCISE **37** Read the following conversation between a salesperson (S) and a customer (C) in an electronics store. Change the underlined words to make the conversation more polite. Change the punctuation if necessary. Answers may vary.

> May I help you?

S: <u>What do you need?</u>
       (example)

C: <u>I want</u> to buy a new computer. <u>Show</u> me your latest models.
       (1)   *(2)*

S: <u>Do you want</u> to see the laptops or the desktops?
       (3)

C: <u>Show</u> me the desktops.
       (4)

S: This is one of our most popular desktops.

C: <u>Turn</u> it on.
       (5)

S: It *is* on. Just hit the space bar.

C: I don't know how much memory to buy.

S: How do you use your computer?

C: We like to play games and watch movies.

S: Then <u>buy</u> this computer, which has a lot of memory and speed.
(6)

C: <u>Tell</u> me the price.
(7)

S: We have a great deal on this one. It's $1,299. If you buy it this week, you can get a $200 rebate from the manufacturer.

C: <u>Let me take</u> it home and try it out.
(8)

S: No problem. If you're not happy with it, you can return it within 30 days and get your money back. <u>Do you want</u> to buy a service contract?
(9)

C: What's that?

S: If you have any problem with the computer for the next two years, we will replace it for free. The contract costs $129.99.

C: <u>Let me see</u> the service contract.
(10)

S: Here's a copy. Take this card to the customer service desk and someone will bring you your computer.

C: Thanks.

S: Have a nice day.

C: You too.

Summary of Lesson 9

1. **Imperatives**
   Sit down. **Don't** be late.

2. *Let's*
   Let's go to the movies. **Let's not** be late.

3. **Infinitive Patterns**
   He wants **to go**.
   It's necessary **to learn** English.
   I'm afraid **to stay**.
   I use coupons **to save** money.
   I want them **to help** me.

4. **Modals**

MODAL	EXAMPLES	EXPLANATION
can can't	He **can** speak English. An 18-year-old **can** vote. **Can** I borrow your pen? You **can't** park here. It's a bus stop. I **can't** help you now. I'm busy.	He has this ability. He has permission. I'm asking permission. It is not permitted. I am not able to.
should shouldn't	You **should** eat healthy food. You **shouldn't** drive if you're sleepy.	It's good advice. It's a bad idea.
may may not	**May** I borrow your pen? I **may** buy a new car. I **may not** be here tomorrow.	I'm asking permission. This is possible. This is possible.
might might not	It **might** rain tomorrow. We **might not** have our picnic.	This is possible. This is possible.
must must not	A driver **must** have a license. I'm late. I **must** hurry. You **must not** drive without a license.	This is a legal necessity. This is a personal necessity. This is against the law.
will will not	The manufacturer **will** send you a check. You **will not** receive the check right away.	This is in the future.
would would like	**Would** you help me move? I **would like** to use your pen.	I'm asking a favor. I want to use your pen.
could	**Could** you help me move?	I'm asking a favor.
have to not have to	She **has to** leave. She **doesn't have to** stay.	It's necessary. It's not necessary.

Editing Advice

1. Don't use *to* after a modal.

   I must ~~to~~ go.

2. Use *to* between verbs.

   They like ˄play.
   to

3. Always use the base form after a modal.

   He can swim~~s~~.

   She can't ~~driving~~ the car.
   drive

4. Use the base form in an infinitive.

   He wants to go~~es~~.

   I wanted to work~~ed~~.

5. We can introduce an infinitive with *it* + an adjective.

   ~~Is~~ important to get exercise.
   It's

6. Use the correct word order in a question.

   Why ~~you can't~~ stay?
   can't you

7. Use an infinitive after some adjectives.

   I'm happy ˄meet you.
   to

   It's necessary ˄have a job.
   to

8. Use *to*, not *for*, to show purpose.

   We went to the theater ~~for~~ see a play.
   to

9. Use the object pronoun and an infinitive after *want, expect, need*, etc.

   I want ~~he closes~~ the door.
   him to close

Editing Quiz

Some of the shaded words and phrases have mistakes. Find the mistakes and correct them. If the shaded words are correct, write *C*.

To: lovetodrive2@e*mail.com

Subject: Buying a GPS

Dear Son,

C

Recently I bought a flat-screen TV and I wanted to ~~got~~ *get* the best price. Now
(example)   *(example)*

you say that you want I help you choose a new GPS.
                  (1)

I want you be a good shopper. First, do the research. Is important compare
    (2)   *(3)*

prices at different stores, so buy the Sunday newspaper for look at ads.
                                                 (4)

You can to look for prices online too. Remember that if you buy online,
       (5)

you have pay for shipping too. Go to the stores and try use the product. It
     (6)   *(7)*

might look good online, but you need to see it and try it out.
   (8)   *(9)*

It's not always easy make a decision. But if you follow this advice, you
                 (10)

can be a smart shopper. Let me know if you need help with something else.
 (11)

I'm always happy help you. And dear, when you can help me move some
              (12)   *(13)*

furniture? I sometimes need you to help me too!
                   (14)

Love, Mom

Lesson 9 Test/Review

PART 1   Fill in the first blanks with *to* or nothing (X). Then write the negative form in the second blank.

EXAMPLES   I'm ready ____to____ study Lesson 10.

I _'m not ready to study_ Lesson 11.

You should ____X____ drive carefully.

You ___shouldn't drive___ fast.

1. I need _____ learn English. I _____ Polish.

2. You must _____ stop at a red light. You _____ on the highway.

3. The teacher expects _____ pass most of the students. She _____ all of the students.

4. We want _____ study grammar. We _____ literature.

5. The teacher has _____ give grades. He _____ an A to everyone.

6. We might _____ have time for some questions later. We _____ time for a discussion.

7. It's important _____ practice American pronunciation now. It _____ British pronunciation.

8. It's easy _____ learn one's native language. It _____ a foreign language.

9. Let's _____ speak English in class. _____ our native languages in class.

10. You must attend the meeting. Please _____ be here at six o'clock. _____ late.

PART 2

Change each sentence to a question.

EXAMPLES I'm afraid to drive.

Why _____ **are you afraid to drive?** _____

He can help you.

When _____ **can he help me?** _____

1. You should wear a seat belt.

Why _____

2. I want to buy some grapes.

Why _____

3. He must fill out the application.

When _____

4. She needs to drive to New York.

When _____

5. You can't park at a bus stop.

Why _____

6. It's necessary to eat vegetables.

Why _____

7. She has to buy a car.

Why _____

8. They'd like to see you.

When _____

PART **3** **This is a phone conversation between a woman (W) and her mechanic (M). Choose the correct words to fill in the blanks.**

W: This is Cindy Fine. I'm calling about my car.

M: I _____ **can't** _____ hear you. _____
       (example: can't / may not)   *(1 could / might)*

you speak louder, please?

W: This is Cindy Fine. Is my car ready yet?

M: We're working on it now. We're almost finished.

W: When _____ I pick it up?
       (2 would / can)

M: It will be ready by four o'clock.

W: How much will it cost?

M: $375.

W: I don't have that much money right now. _____
(3 Can / Might)
I pay by credit card?

M: Yes. You _____ use any major credit card.
(4 may / might)

Later, at the mechanic's shop:

M: Your car's ready, ma'am. The engine problem is fixed. But you

_____ replace your brakes. They're not so good.
(5 may / should)

W: _____ do it right away?
(6 Do I have to / May I)

M: No, you _____ do it immediately, but you
(7 must not / don't have to)

_____ do it within a month or two. If you don't do
(8 would / should)

it soon, you _____ have an accident.
(9 may / would)

W: How much will it cost to replace the brakes?

M: It _____ cost about $200.
(10 would / will)

W: I _____ like to make an appointment to take care
(11 will / would)

of the brakes next week. _____ I bring my car in
(12 Can / Will)

next Monday?

M: Yes, Monday is fine. You _____ bring it in early
(13 could / should)

because we get very busy later in the day.

W: OK. See you Monday morning.

PART 4 **Decide if the sentences have the same meaning or different meanings. Write _S_ for same, _D_ for different.**

EXAMPLES   Would you like to go to a movie? Do you want to go to a movie?   S

We will not go to New York. We should not go to New York.   D

1. You should go to the doctor. You can go to the doctor.
2. I may buy a new car. I must buy a new car.
3. Could you help me later? Would you help me later?
4. She must not drive her car. She doesn't have to drive her car.
5. She has to leave immediately. She must leave immediately.
6. We will have a test soon. We may have a test soon.
7. I can't go to the party. I might not go to the party.
8. You shouldn't buy a car. You don't have to buy a car.
9. May I use your phone? Could I use your phone?
10. He might not eat lunch. He may not eat lunch.
11. I should go to the doctor. I must go to the doctor.
12. I have to take my passport with me. I should take my passport with me.

PART 5 **Circle the correct word(s) to complete each sentence.**

1. If you sample a product in a supermarket, you (_don't have to / shouldn't_) buy it.
2. If you have just a few items, you (_shouldn't / don't have to_) use a shopping cart. You (_can / must_) use a small basket.
3. You (_must / should_) use coupons to save money.
4. You (_shouldn't / don't have to_) pay with cash. You can use a credit card.
5. Salesperson to customer: (_May / Would_) I help you?
6. You (_must / should_) make a list before going shopping.
7. You (_don't have to / must not_) take your own bags to the supermarket. Bags are free.
8. Try this new pizza. You (_should / might_) like it.
9. You (_can't / shouldn't_) use coupons after the expiration date.
10. You (_must not / don't have to_) park in a handicapped parking space. It's against the law.

Expansion

❶ Imagine that a friend of yours is getting married. You are giving him or her advice about marriage. Write some advice for this person. You may work with a partner or compare your advice to your partner's advice when you are finished.

It's important	It's not important
It's important to be honest.	It's not important to do everything together.

❷ Imagine that a friend of yours is going to travel to the U.S. You are giving him or her advice about the trip and life in the U.S. Write as many things as you can in each box. Then find a partner and compare your advice to your partner's advice.

It's necessary OR It's important OR You should	It's difficult OR You shouldn't
It's necessary to have a passport.	It's difficult to understand American English.

❸ Working in a small group, write a list to give information to a new student or to a foreign student. If you need more space, use your notebook.

should or shouldn't	You should bring your transcripts to this college.
must or have to	
don't have to	
might or might not	
can or can't	

❹ With a partner, write a few instructions for one of the following situations.

EXAMPLE   using a microwave oven
You shouldn't put anything metal in the microwave.
You can set the power level.
You should rotate the dish in the microwave. If you don't, the food might not cook evenly.

a. preparing for the TOEFL®[6]

b. taking a test in this class

c. preparing for the driver's test in this state

[6]The *TOEFL*® is the Test of English as a Foreign Language.

5 Bring in an application. (Bring two of the same application, if possible.) It can be an application for a job, driver's license, license plate, apartment rental, address change, check-cashing card, rebate, etc. Work with a partner. One person will give instructions. The other person will fill it out.

6 Bring in ads from different stores. You can bring in ads from supermarkets or any other store. See what is on sale this week. Find a partner and discuss the products and the prices. Compare prices at two different stores, if possible. What do these products usually cost in your native country? Do you have all of these products in your native country?

Talk About It

1 Talk about ways you can save money when you shop.

2 Do you prefer to shop alone or with a friend or relative? Explain why.

Write About It

1 Write about the differences between shopping in the U.S. and in another country.

2 Imagine that a new classmate just arrived from another country. Write a composition giving advice about shopping in the U.S.

> ### Shopping Advice
>
> I recently bought a flat-screen TV in the U.S.
> and would like to give advice about how to shop for
> electronics here. The Sunday newspaper often has
> flyers with the sale items for the week. You can
> compare prices before you go to the store . . .

 For more practice using grammar in context, please visit our Web site.

Grammar
Count and Noncount Nouns

Quantity Words

Context
Nutrition and Health

Nouns can be divided into two groups: count and noncount nouns.

EXAMPLES	EXPLANATION
I eat four **eggs** a week. I eat one **apple** a day. Do you like **grapes**?	Count nouns have a singular and plural form. egg—eggs grape—grapes apple—apples
I like **milk**. I drink **coffee** every day. Do you like **cheese**?	Noncount nouns have no plural form.

A Healthy Diet

Before
You Read

1. What kind of food do you like to eat? What kind of food do you dislike?

2. What are some popular dishes from your country or native culture?

CD 2, TR 13

Read the following magazine article. Pay special attention to count and noncount nouns.

It is important to eat well to maintain good **health**.

A healthy **diet** consists of a **variety** of **foods**.

You need **carbohydrates**. The best carbohydrates come from whole **grain bread**, **cereal**, and **pasta**. Brown **rice** is much healthier than white rice. **Sugar** is a carbohydrate too, but it has no real nutritional value.

Of course, you need **fruits** and **vegetables** too. But not all vegetables are equally good. **Potatoes** can raise the sugar in your **blood**, which can be a **problem** for people with diabetes. It is better to eat **carrots**, **broccoli**, **corn**, and **peas**.

You also need **protein**. Red **meat** is high in protein, but a diet with a lot of red meat can cause heart disease, diabetes, and cancer. Better **sources** of protein are **chicken**, **fish**, **beans**, **eggs**, and **nuts**. Some people worry that eggs contain too much **cholesterol**. (Cholesterol is a **substance** found in animal foods.) But recent studies show that eating one egg a **day** is not usually harmful and gives us other nutritional **benefits**.

Did You **Know?**

Americans spend $23.7 billion on vitamin and mineral supplements a year.

Many **people** think that all **fat** is bad. But this is not true. The fat in **nuts** (especially **walnuts**) and olive **oil** is very healthy. The fat in **butter** and **cheese** is not good.

It is not clear how much **milk** and other dairy **products** an **adult** needs. It is true that dairy products are a good source of **calcium**, but a calcium supplement can give you what you need without the fat and **calories** of milk.

The best way to stay healthy is to eat the right kinds of **food**. Food **packages** have information about **nutrition** and **calories**. You should read the package to avoid artificial **ingredients** and high levels of fat and sugar. It is also important to control your **weight** and to exercise every day.

10.2 Noncount Nouns

Noncount nouns fall into four different groups.

Group A: Nouns that have no distinct, separate parts. We look at the whole.

milk	air	meat
oil	pork	butter
water	cholesterol	poultry
coffee	paper	cheese
tea	soup	
yogurt	bread	

Group B: Nouns that have parts that are too small or insignificant to count.

rice	snow	hair
sugar	sand	grass
salt	corn	popcorn

Group C: Nouns that are classes or categories of things. The members of the category are not the same.

money (nickels, dimes, dollars)
food (vegetables, meat, spaghetti)
candy (chocolates, mints, candy bars)
furniture (chairs, tables, beds)
clothing (sweaters, pants, dresses)
mail (letters, packages, postcards)
fruit (cherries, apples, grapes)
makeup (lipstick, blush, eye shadow)
homework (compositions, exercises, reading)

(continued)

Group D: Nouns that are abstractions.

love	advice	happiness
life	knowledge	education
time	nutrition	experience
truth	intelligence	crime
beauty	unemployment	music
luck	patience	art
fun	noise	work
help	information	health

EXERCISE 1 **Fill in the blanks with a noncount noun. Answers will vary.**

EXAMPLE Brown _____*rice*_____ is healthier than white _____*rice*_____.

1. Babies need to drink a lot of _____, but adults don't.

2. Food from animals contains _____.

3. Children like to eat _____, but it's not good for their teeth.

4. Food packages have information about _____.

5. Some people put _____ in their coffee.

6. _____ is a good source of fat. _____ is not a good source of fat.

7. _____ contains caffeine. Don't drink it at night.

8. People with high blood pressure shouldn't put a lot of _____ on their food.

9. Soda and candy contain a lot of _____.

EXERCISE 2 Fill in the blanks with a noncount noun from the lists on pages 307–308. Answers may vary.

EXAMPLE Students at registration need _____information_____.

1. I get a lot of _____ every day in my mailbox.

2. In the winter, there is a lot of _____ in the northern parts of the U.S.

3. In the U.S., people eat _____ in a movie theater.

4. Students have to do _____ every day.

5. When you walk on the beach, you get _____ in your shoes.

6. Money doesn't buy _____.

7. Our parents often give us a lot of _____ about how to live our lives.

8. Some cities have a lot of _____. Many people are without jobs.

10.3 Count and Noncount Nouns

EXAMPLES	EXPLANATION
I eat a lot of **rice** and **beans**. 　rice = noncount noun 　beans = count noun	*Count and noncount* are grammatical terms, but they are not always logical. *Rice* is very small and is a noncount noun. *Beans* and *peas* are also very small, but they are count nouns.
a. He eats a lot of **fruit**. a. She bought a lot of **food** for the party. b. Oranges and lemons are **fruits** that contain vitamin C. b. **Foods** that contain a lot of cholesterol are not good for you.	a. Use *fruit* and *food* as noncount nouns when you mean fruit and food in general. b. Use *fruits* and *foods* as count nouns when you mean kinds of fruit or categories of food.
a. **Candy** is not good for your health. b. There are three **candies** on the table.	a. When you talk about candy in general, *candy* is noncount. b. When you consider individual pieces of candy, you can use the plural form.

Language Note:
Other words that have both a count and a noncount form are: *time, experience, life, trouble, noise, pie.*

Fill in the blanks with the singular or plural form of the word in parentheses ( ). Use the singular for noncount nouns. Use the plural for count nouns.

EXAMPLE   Add ____*peas*____ to the soup. Then put in some ____*salt*____.
                        (pea)   *(salt)*

1. Do you like to eat _____?
                                    (fruit)

2. Oranges, grapefruits, and lemons are _____ that have a lot
                                                          (fruit)
of vitamin C.

3. When children eat a lot of _____, they sometimes get sick.
                                            (candy)

4. Let's go shopping. There is no _____ in the house.
                                                (food)

5. Milk and eggs are _____ that contain cholesterol.
                                (food)

6. She's going to make _____ and _____ for dinner.
                                    (rice)   *(bean)*

10.4 Describing Quantities of Count and Noncount Nouns

EXAMPLES	EXPLANATION
She ate three **apples** today. He ate four **eggs** this week.	We can put a number before a count noun.
I ate two **slices of bread**. Please buy a **bottle of olive oil**. She drank three **glasses of milk**.	We cannot put a number before a noncount noun. We use a unit of measure, which we can count.

Ways we see noncount nouns:

BY CONTAINER	BY PORTION	BY MEASUREMENT[1]	BY SHAPE OR WHOLE PIECE	OTHER
a bottle of water a carton of milk a jar of pickles a bag of flour a can of soda (pop)[2] a bowl of soup a cup of coffee a glass of milk	a slice (piece) of bread a piece of meat a piece of cake a piece (sheet) of paper a slice of pizza a piece of candy a strip of bacon	a spoonful of sugar a scoop of ice cream a quart of oil a pound of meat a gallon of gasoline	a loaf of bread an ear of corn a piece of fruit a head of lettuce a candy bar a tube of toothpaste a bar of soap	a piece of mail a piece of furniture a piece of advice a piece of information a work of art

[1]For a list of conversions from the American system of measurement to the metric system, see Appendix G.
[2]Some Americans say "soda"; others say "pop."

EXERCISE **4** **Fill in the blanks with a logical quantity for each of these noncount nouns. Answers may vary.**

EXAMPLES She bought _____ *one pound of* _____ coffee.

She drank _____ *two cups of* _____ coffee.

1. She ate _____ meat.
2. She bought _____ meat.
3. She bought _____ bread.
4. She ate _____ bread.
5. She bought _____ rice.
6. She ate _____ rice.
7. She bought _____ sugar.
8. She put _____ sugar in her coffee.
9. She ate _____ soup.
10. She ate _____ corn.
11. She bought _____ gas for her car.
12. She put _____ motor oil into her car's engine.
13. She used _____ paper to do her homework.

10.5 A Lot Of, Much, Many

Use *many* for count nouns. Use *much* for noncount nouns. Use *a lot of* for both count and noncount nouns.

	COUNT (PLURAL)	NONCOUNT
Affirmative	He baked **many** cookies. He baked **a lot of** cookies.	He baked **a lot of** bread.
Negative	He didn't bake **many** cookies. He didn't bake a **lot of** cookies.	He didn't bake **much** bread. He didn't bake **a lot of** bread.
Question	Did he bake **many** cookies? Did he bake **a lot of** cookies? **How many** cookies did he bake?	Did he bake **much** bread? Did he bake **a lot of** bread? **How much** bread did he bake?

Language Notes:
1. *Much* is rarely used in affirmative statements. Use *a lot of* in affirmative statements.
2. When the noun is omitted (in the following case, *cookies*), use *a lot*, not *a lot of*.
    He baked a lot of cookies, but he didn't eat **a lot**.

EXERCISE **5**   **Fill in the blanks with** *much, many,* **or** *a lot of.* **In some cases, more than one answer is possible.**

EXAMPLES   She doesn't eat ___much___ pasta.

___Many___ American supermarkets are open 24 hours a day.

___A lot of___ sugar is not good for you.

1. In the summer in the U.S., there's _____ corn.
2. Children usually drink _____ milk.
3. _____ people have an unhealthy diet.
4. I drink coffee only about once a week. I don't drink _____ coffee.
5. There are _____ places that sell fast food.
6. It's important to drink _____ water.
7. How _____ glasses of water did you drink today?
8. How _____ fruit did you eat today?
9. How _____ cholesterol is there in one egg?
10. It isn't good to eat _____ candy.
11. We should eat _____ vegetables.

10.6 A Few, A Little

	EXAMPLES	EXPLANATION
Count	I bought **a few** bananas. She ate **several** cookies. She drank **a few** cups of tea.	Use *a few* and *several* with count nouns or with quantities that describe noncount nouns (*cup, bowl, piece,* etc.).
Noncount	He ate **a little** meat. He drank **a little** tea.	Use *a little* with noncount nouns.

EXERCISE **6**   **Fill in the blanks with** *a few, several,* **or** *a little.*

EXAMPLES   He has ___a few___ good friends.

He has ___a little___ time to help you.

1. Every day we study _____ grammar.
2. We do _____ exercises in class.
3. The teacher gives _____ homework every day.
4. We do _____ pages in the book each day.
5. _____ students always get an A on the tests.

M: No, you don't. Sometimes you have (*a lot of / too much*) homework,
(4)
but you turn on the TV as soon as you get home from school.

I'm going to make a rule: no TV until you finish your homework.

S: Oh, Mom. You have too (*much / many*) rules.
(5)

M: That's what parents are for: to guide their kids to make the right decisions.

There are (*a lot of / too many*) things to do besides watching TV. Why
(6)
don't you go outside and play? When I was your age, we played outside.

S: "*When I was your age*." Not again. You always say that.

M: Well, it's true. We had (*too much / a lot of*) fun outside, playing with
(7)
friends. I didn't have (*a lot of / too much*) toys when I was your age.
(8)
And I certainly didn't have video games or computer games. Also we

helped our parents (*a lot / too much*) after school. We cut the grass
(9)
and washed the dishes.

S: My friend Josh cuts the grass, throws out the garbage, and cleans the

basement once a month. His mom pays him (*too much / a lot of*)
(10)
money for doing it. Maybe if you pay me, I'll do it.

M: Not again. "*Josh does it. Josh has it. Why can't I?*" You always say that.

You're not Josh, and I'm not Josh's mother. I'm not going to pay you

for things you should do.

S: OK. Just tell me what to do, and I'll do it.

M: There are (*a lot of / too much*) leaves on the front lawn. Why don't
(11)
you start by putting them in garbage bags? And you can walk

Sparky. He's getting fat too. He eats (*too much / too many*) and
(12)
sleeps all day. Both of you need more exercise.

EXERCISE **15** **ABOUT YOU** **Fill in the blanks with *much* or *many*, and complete each statement.**

EXAMPLE If I drink too ____much____ coffee, __I won't be able to sleep tonight.__

1. If the teacher gives too _____ homework, _____

_____

2. If I take too _____ classes, _____

_____

3. If I eat too _____ candy, _____

_____

4. If I'm absent too _____ days, _____

_____

10.9 *Too Much/Too Many vs. Too*

EXAMPLES	EXPLANATION
I don't eat ice cream because it's **too** fattening. He needs to eat more. He's **too** thin.	Use *too* with adjectives and adverbs.
I don't eat ice cream because it has **too many** calories and **too much** fat.	Use *too much* and *too many* before nouns.

EXERCISE 16 **Fill in the blanks with *too*, *too much*, or *too many*.**

Situation A. Some students are complaining about the school cafeteria. They are giving reasons why they don't want to eat there.

EXAMPLE It's _____*too*_____ noisy.

1. The food is _____ greasy.

2. There are _____ students. I can't find a place to sit.

3. The lines are _____ long.

4. The food is _____ expensive.

5. There's _____ noise.

Situation B. Some students are complaining about their class and school.

1. The classroom is _____ small.

2. We spend _____ time reviewing old lessons.

3. We have to write _____ compositions.

4. The teacher gives _____ homework.

5. There are _____ tests.

EXERCISE 17 **ABOUT YOU** Write a few sentences to complain about something: your apartment, your roommate, this city, this college, and so on. Use *too*, *too much*, or *too many* in your sentences.

EXAMPLE My roommate spends too much time in the bathroom in the morning.
He's too messy.[3]

_____

_____

_____

EXERCISE 18 Fill in the blanks with *too*, *too much*, or *too many* if a problem is presented. Use *a lot of* if no problem is presented.

EXAMPLE Strawberries are _____ too _____ expensive this week. Let's not buy them.

1. There are _____ noncount nouns in English.

2. "Rice" is a noncount noun because the parts are _____ small to count.

3. If this class is _____ hard for you, you should go to a lower level.

4. Good students spend _____ time doing their homework.

5. If you spend _____ time watching TV, you won't have time for your homework.

6. It takes _____ time to learn English, but you can do it.

7. Oranges have _____ vitamin C.

8. If you are on a diet, don't eat potato chips. They have _____ calories and _____ fat.

9. Babies drink _____ milk.

10. If you drink _____ coffee, you won't sleep.

---

[3]A *messy* person does not put his or her things in order.

EXERCISE 19 A doctor (D) and patient (P) are talking. Fill in the blanks with an appropriate quantity word or unit of measurement to complete this conversation. In some cases, more than one answer is possible.

CD 2, TR 18

D: I'm looking at your lab results and I see that your cholesterol level

is very high. Also your blood pressure is _____**too**_____ high.

(example)

Do you use _____ salt on your food?

(1)

P: Yes, Doctor. I love salt. I eat _____ potato chips and

(2)

popcorn.

D: That's not good. You're overweight too. You need to lose 50 pounds.

What do you usually eat?

P: For breakfast I usually grab _____ coffee and a

(3)

doughnut. I don't have _____ time for lunch, so I eat

(4)

_____ cookies and drink _____

(5) *(6)*

soda while I'm working. I'm so busy that I have _____

(7)

time to cook at all. So for dinner, I usually stop at a fast-food place and

get a burger and fries.

D: That's a terrible diet! How _____ exercise do you get?

(8)

P: I never exercise. I don't have _____ time at all. I own

(9)

my own business and I have _____ work. Sometimes I

(10)

work 80 hours a week.

D: I'm going to give you an important _____ advice.

(11)

You're going to have to change your lifestyle.

P: I'm _____ old to change my habits.

(12)

D: You're only 45 years old. You're _____ young to die.

(13)

And if you don't change your habits, you're going to have a heart

attack. I'm going to give you a booklet about staying healthy. It has

_____ information that will teach you about diet

(14)

and exercise. Please read it and come back in six months.

Summary of Lesson 10

Words that we use before count and noncount nouns:

WORD	COUNT (SINGULAR) EXAMPLE: *BOOK*	COUNT (PLURAL) EXAMPLE: *BOOKS*	NONCOUNT EXAMPLE: *TEA*
the	X	X	X
a	X		
one	X		
two, three, etc.		X	
some (affirmatives)		X	X
any (negatives and questions)		X	X
no	X	X	X
a lot of		X	X
much (negatives and questions)			X
many		X	
a little			X
a few		X	
several		X	

Editing Advice

1. Don't put *a* or *an* before a noncount noun.

                    some
I want to give you ~~an~~ advice.

2. Noncount nouns are always singular.

                 a lot of
My mother gave me ~~many~~ advices.

             pieces of
He received three mails today.

3. Don't use a double negative.

           any
He doesn't have ~~no~~ time.   OR   *He has no time.*

4. Don't use *much* with an affirmative statement.

> Uncommon: There was much rain yesterday.
> Common: There was a lot of rain yesterday.

5. Don't use *a* or *an* before a plural noun.

> She has ~~a~~ blue eyes.

6. Use the plural form for plural count nouns.

> He has a lot of friend^s.

7. Omit *of* after *a lot* when the noun is omitted.

> My English teacher gives a lot of homework. My math teacher
>
> gives a lot ~~of~~ too.

8. Use *of* with a unit of measure.

> I ate three pieces *of* bread.

9. Don't use *of* after *many*, *much*, *a few*, or *a little* if a noun follows directly.

> She has many ~~of~~ friends.
>
> He put a little ~~of~~ milk in his coffee.

10. Only use *too/too much/too many* if there is a problem.

> He has a good job. He earns ~~too much~~ *a lot of* money.
>
> My grandfather is ~~too~~ *very* healthy.

11. Don't use *too much* before an adjective or adverb.

> I don't want to go outside today. It's too ~~much~~ hot.

12. Don't confuse *too* and *to*.

> If you eat ~~to~~ *too* much candy, you'll get sick.

Editing Quiz

Some of the shaded words and phrases have mistakes. Find the mistakes and correct them. If the shaded words are correct, write C.

My parents gave me a good advice: stay healthy. They told me to get
C   *(example)*

good nutrition and exercise every day. My parents follow their own advice,
(example)

and, as a result, they're too healthy. I try to follow their advices but
(1)   *(2)*

sometimes I can't. I'm very busy, and sometimes I don't have no time for
(3)

exercise. When I was in high school, I had a lot of free time, but now I

don't have a lot of. So for breakfast, I just have a cup coffee with a
(4)   *(5)*

little of sugar and two pieces of toasts.
(6)   *(7)*

I have a lot of friend at college, and we often go out to eat after class.
(8)

But they always want to go to a fast food places. I know the food is
(9)

too much greasy. When I suggest a healthier restaurant, they say it's to
(10)   *(11)*

expensive. When I get home from work at night, I just heat up a frozen

dinner. I know this is not healthy, but what can I do?

Lesson 10 Test/Review

PART 1   **Fill in the blanks with an appropriate measurement of quantity. Answers may vary.**

EXAMPLE   a ___*cup*___ of coffee

1. a _____ of water
2. a _____ of sugar
3. a _____ of milk
4. a _____ of furniture
5. a _____ of soup

6. a _____ of mail
7. a _____ of advice
8. a _____ of gasoline
9. a _____ of paper
10. a _____ of toothpaste

PART 2 **Read the following composition. Choose the correct quantity word or indefinite article.**

I had _____*some*_____ problems when I first came to the U.S. First, I didn't
(example: some / any / a little)

have _____ money. _____ friends of mine lent me _____
(1 much / a / some)   (2 A few / A little / A few of)   (3 some / a / any)

money, but I didn't feel good about borrowing it.

Second, I couldn't find _____ apartment. I went to see _____
(4 a / an / no)   (5 some / a little / an)

apartments, but I couldn't afford _____ of them. For _____
(6 an / any / none)   (7 a little / a few of / several)

months, I had to live with my uncle's family, but the situation wasn't good.

Third, I started to study English, but soon found _____ job and
(8 a / any / some)

didn't have _____ time to study. As a result, I was failing my course.
(9 no / much / a few)

However, little by little my life started to improve, and I don't need

_____ help from my friends and relatives anymore.
(10 no / some / much)

Expansion

Classroom
Activities

❶ Make a list of unhealthy things that you eat. Make a list of things that you need to eat for a healthy diet.

Unhealthy things I eat	Things I should eat

❷ These are some popular foods in the U.S. Put a check (✓) in the column that describes your experience of this food. Then find a partner and compare your list to your partner's list.

Food	I Like	I Don't Like	I Never Tried
pizza		✓	
hot dogs			
submarine sandwiches			
tacos			
hamburgers			
breakfast cereal			
peanut butter			
cheesecake			
tortilla chips			
potato chips			
popcorn			
chocolate chip cookies			
fried chicken			
pretzels			

❸ Cross out the phrase that doesn't fit and fill in the blanks to make a true statement about the U.S. or another country. Find a partner and compare your answers.

EXAMPLE People in _____Argentina_____ eat/~~don't eat~~ __a lot of__ meat.

a. People in _____ eat/don't eat _____ natural foods.

b. People in _____ drink/don't drink _____ tea.

c. People in _____ shop/don't shop for food every day.

d. People in _____ eat/don't eat in a movie theater.

e. People in _____ drink/don't drink _____ bottled water.

Talk
About It

❶ Look at the dialogue that takes place in a restaurant on pages 316–317. Do you think this man is eating a healthy breakfast? Why or why not?

❷ Americans often eat some of these foods for breakfast: cereal and milk, toast and butter or jelly, orange juice, eggs, bacon, coffee. Describe a typical breakfast for you.

3 Most American stores sell products in containers: bags, jars, cans, and so forth. How do stores in other countries sell products?

4 Do stores in other countries give customers bags for their groceries, or do customers have to bring their own bags to the store?

5 Some things are usually free in an American restaurant: salt, pepper, sugar, cream or milk for coffee, mustard, ketchup, napkins, water, ice, coffee refills, and sometimes bread. Are these things free in a restaurant in other countries?

6 The following saying is about food. Discuss the meaning. Do you have a similar saying in your native language?

You are what you eat.

Write
About It

1 Describe shopping for food in the U.S. or in another country. You may include information about the following:

- packaging
- open market vs. stores
- self-service vs. service from salespeople
- shopping carts
- fixed prices vs. negotiable prices
- freshness of food

2 Describe food and eating habits in your native country.

> ### Food in Mexico
>
> In my country, Mexico, we have our main meal in the
> middle of the day. We eat a lot of rice and beans. We
> don't use much bread, like Americans do. Instead, we
> eat tortillas with most of our meals . . .

 For more practice using grammar in context, please visit our Web site.

Grammar
Adjectives

Noun Modifiers

Adverbs

Context
Great Women

Helen Keller (1882–1968)

Helen Keller

1. Do you know of any special schools for handicapped people?

2. What kinds of facilities or services does this school have for handicapped people?

CD 2, TR 19

Read the following textbook article. Pay special attention to adjectives and adverbs.

Do you know of anyone with a disability who did **remarkable** things? Helen Keller was a truly **remarkable** woman.

Helen Keller was a **healthy** baby. But when she was 19 months old, she had a **sudden** fever. The fever disappeared, but she became **blind** and **deaf**. Because she couldn't hear, it was **difficult** for her to learn to speak. As she grew, she was **angry** and **frustrated** because she couldn't understand or communicate with people. She became **wild**, throwing things and kicking and biting.

When Helen was seven years old, a teacher, Anne Sullivan, came to live with Helen's family. First, Anne taught Helen how to talk with her fingers. Helen was **excited** when she realized that things had names. Then Anne taught Helen to read by the Braille system. Helen learned these skills **quickly**. However, learning to speak was harder. Anne continued to teach Helen **patiently**. Finally, when Helen was ten years old, she could speak **clearly** enough for people to understand her.

Helen was very **intelligent**. She went to an institute for the blind, where she did very **well** in her studies. Then she went to college,[1] where she graduated with honors when she was 24 years old. Helen traveled **extensively** with Anne. She worked **tirelessly**, traveling all over America, Europe, and Asia to raise money to build schools for **blind** people. Her **main** message was that **handicapped** people are like everybody else. They want to live life **fully** and **naturally**. Helen wanted all people to be treated **equally**.

While she was in college, Helen wrote her first of many books, *The Story of My Life*, in 1903.

Did You **Know?**

In Washington, D.C., there is a special college for deaf students—Gallaudet University.

[1] In the U.S., the words *college* and *university* usually have the same meaning.

11.1 Adjectives and Adverbs

EXAMPLES	EXPLANATION
Helen was a **healthy** baby. She seemed **intelligent**. She became **blind**. Anne Sullivan was a **wonderful** teacher.	Adjectives describe nouns. We can use adjectives before nouns or after the verbs *be, become, look, seem,* and other sense-perception verbs.
Anne taught Helen **patiently**. Helen learned **quickly**. People want to live life **fully**.	Adverbs of manner tell how or in what way we do things. We form most adverbs of manner by putting *-ly* at the end of an adjective. Adverbs of manner usually follow the verb phrase.

EXERCISE **1** **Decide if the underlined word is an adjective (*adj.*) or adverb (*adv.*).**

EXAMPLES   Helen was a $\overset{\textit{adj.}}{\underline{\text{healthy}}}$ baby.

When Helen couldn't communicate, she threw things $\overset{\textit{adv.}}{\underline{\text{angrily}}}$.

1. She seemed <u>wild</u>.

2. She was <u>blind</u> and <u>deaf</u> because of a <u>serious</u> illness.

3. She had a <u>good</u> teacher.

4. She learned to speak <u>clearly</u>.

5. Anne was a <u>patient</u> woman.

6. She worked <u>tirelessly</u> with Helen.

7. Helen learned <u>enthusiastically</u>.

8. Helen wanted to live a <u>full</u> life.

9. She was a <u>remarkable</u> woman.

10. We should respect all people <u>equally</u>.

Helen Keller and Anne Sullivan

11.2 Adjectives

EXAMPLES	EXPLANATION
Anne was a **patient** teacher. Helen was an **intelligent** person.	Adjectives describe nouns.
Anne was a **good** friend. I have many **good** friends.	Adjectives are always singular. *Wrong:* I have many *goods* friends.
Helen felt **frustrated** when she couldn't communicate. She was **excited** when she learned her first word. **Handicapped** people can live a full life.	Some *-ed* words are adjectives: *married, divorced, excited, frustrated, handicapped, worried, finished, tired, crowded.*
Helen had an **interesting** life. She was an **amazing** woman.	Some *-ing* words are adjectives: *interesting, boring, amazing, exciting.*
Helen was a **normal**, **healthy** baby. Anne was a **patient**, **intelligent** teacher.	Sometimes we put two adjectives before a noun. We can separate the two adjectives with a comma.
Some people have an easy childhood. Helen had a hard **one**. Do you like serious stories or funny **ones**?	After an adjective, we can substitute a singular noun with *one* and a plural noun with *ones* to avoid repeating the noun.
Anne was **a kind teacher**. Anne was kind.	Only use an article before an adjective if a noun follows. *Wrong:* Anne was *a kind.*

EXERCISE **2** **Fill in the blanks with an appropriate adjective. (Change *a* to *an* if the adjective begins with a vowel sound.) Answers may vary.**

EXAMPLES   When Helen couldn't communicate, she became _____wild_____.

Helen was a n interesting _____ person.

1. Helen was a _____ baby.

2. Before Helen learned to communicate, she felt

   very _____.

3. She had a _____ life.

4. She wanted _____ treatment for blind people.

5. Helen had a _____ teacher.

6. Helen was a very _____ woman.

7. The story about Helen Keller was _____.

8. _____ people can read with the Braille method.

EXERCISE **3**   Fill in the blanks with an appropriate adjective. (Change *a* to *an* if the adjective begins with a vowel sound.) Answers may vary.

EXAMPLES   This is a _____ big _____ class.

This is a n easy _____ class.

1. This classroom is _____.
2. The classrooms at this school are _____.
3. English is a _____ language.
4. This book is very _____.
5. We sometimes have _____ tests.
6. We read a _____ story about Helen Keller.
7. Did you learn any _____ words in the story?

EXERCISE **4**   **ABOUT YOU**   Ask a question of preference with the words given. Follow the example. Use *one* or *ones* to substitute for the noun. Another student will answer.

EXAMPLES   an easy exercise/hard

A: Do you prefer an easy exercise or a hard one?
B: I prefer a hard one.

funny movies/serious

A: Do you prefer funny movies or serious ones?
B: I prefer funny ones.

1. a big city/small
2. an old house/new
3. a cold climate/warm
4. a small car/big
5. a soft mattress/hard
6. green grapes/red
7. red apples/yellow
8. strict teachers/easy
9. noisy children/quiet
10. used textbooks/new

A Special Athlete

1. Do you know any disabled people who participate in sports?

2. Did you see the most recent Olympic games?

CD 2, TR 20

Read the following magazine article. Pay special attention to nouns that describe nouns.

Gina McWilliams is an inspiring person and great athlete.

As a child, she loved sports, but when she was 26 years old, she was in a **car accident** and lost part of her right leg. She still wanted to compete in sports. She tried many sports, including **waterskiing** and basketball, which she played in a **wheelchair**, before she decided on volleyball. At the 2008 Paralympic Games[2] in China, she and her team won the **silver medal**. When Gina's not practicing volleyball, she's busy raising her two children and working as a **sports director** for disabled adults and children.

[2]In the *Paralympic Games*, athletes with physical and visual disabilities compete.

11.3 Noun Modifiers

EXAMPLES	EXPLANATIONS
Gina is a **volleyball player**. Her team won a **silver medal**.	We can use a noun to describe another noun.
Gina sometimes uses a **wheelchair**. She can play **basketball**. She enjoys **waterskiing.**	Sometimes we write the two nouns as one word. The noun modifier and the noun become a compound word.
a. Gina played wheelchair **basketball**. b. Was she a **basketball** coach?	The first noun is more specific. The second noun is more general. In sentence (a), *wheelchair basketball* is a specific kind of basketball. In sentence (b), *basketball coach* is a specific kind of coach.
Does Gina have a **driver's** license? Did she have a **skiing** accident?	Sometimes the first noun ends with *'s* or *-ing*.
A chair with **wheels** is a **wheel**chair. A language that uses **signs** is **sign** language. A girl who is sixteen **years** old is a sixteen-**year**-old girl.	When two nouns come together, the first one is always singular.

Language Note:
There are many noun + noun combinations. Here are a few:

winter coat	driver's license	fingernail
cell phone	bachelor's degree	flashlight
wedding ring	master's degree	haircut
garbage can	shopping cart	daylight
summer vacation	washing machine	eyebrow
TV show	skiing accident	dishwasher
math course	running shoes	doorknob
art museum	reading glasses	drugstore
peanut butter	baking dish	earring

EXERCISE 5   Fill in the blanks. Make sure that the noun modifier is singular.

EXAMPLE   A store that sells groceries is a _____*grocery store*_____.

1. A store that sells books is a _____.

2. A store that has departments is a _____.

3. A department that sells shoes is a _____.

4. Language that communicates with signs is _____.

5. Glasses for eyes are _____.

6. A pot for flowers is a _____.

7. A garden of roses is a _____.

8. A bill of five dollars is a _____.

9. A child who is six years old is a _____.

10. A vacation that lasts two weeks is a _____.

11. A brush for teeth is a _____.

12. A man who is 6 feet tall is a _____.

EXERCISE **6** **Fill in the blanks by putting the words in parentheses ( ) in the correct order. Make any other necessary changes.**

Last night I saw a _____TV program_____ about the Paralympic Games.
(example: program/TV)

One of the athletes is Christina Ripp. Christina is in a

_____. But that didn't stop her from becoming a
(1 chair/wheels)

_____. She became interested in basketball when she
(2 player/basketball)

was just a _____. She played on her
(3 child/ten years old)

_____ at the University of Illinois. In 2005, she got her
(4 team/college)

_____ in _____. In 2008, she won a
(5 degree/bachelor's)   (6 community/health)

_____ at the Paralympic Games in China.
(7 medal/gold)

EXERCISE **7** **Fill in the blanks by putting the two nouns in the correct order. Make any other necessary changes.**

EXAMPLE A popular sport at the Paralympic Games is _____wheelchair basketball_____.
(basketball/wheelchair)

1. Christina Ripp has a _____.
(college/education)

2. Gina McWilliams had a _____.
(accident/car)

3. Gina is a _____.
(volleyball/player)

4. Helen Keller lost her _____ when she
(sight/eyes)

was a _____.
(19 months old /baby)

5. Helen Keller had a _____.
(degree/college)

EXERCISE `8` **ABOUT YOU** Ask and answer. Put the two nouns in the right order and make any other necessary changes. Ask another student the question.

EXAMPLE Do you have a (*license/driver's*)?

  A. Do you have a driver's license?
  B. No. I don't have a driver's license yet.

1. What's your favorite (*program/TV*)?
2. Do you have a (*phone/cell*)?
3. How many (*phone/calls*) do you make a day?
4. How many (*messages/text*) do you receive a day?
5. Are you wearing a (*ring/wedding*)?
6. What do you usually do during your (*summer/vacation*)?
7. Do you bring a (*bag/books*) to class?
8. Did you buy your (*text/books*) at the school (*books/store*)?

11.4 Comparing Adverbs of Manner and Adjectives

An adverb of manner tells *how* we do something. It describes the verb (action) of the sentence. An adjective describes a noun.

ADJECTIVES	ADVERBS	EXPLANATION
Anne was a **patient** teacher. Helen was a **quick** learner. She had a **clear** voice.	She taught **patiently**. She learned **quickly**. She spoke **clearly**.	We form most adverbs of manner by putting *-ly* at the end of an adjective.
This is a **fast** car. I have a **late** class. We had a **hard** test. I have an **early** appointment.	He drives **fast**. I arrived **late**. I studied **hard**. I need to wake up **early**.	Some adjectives and adverbs have the same form.
Helen was a **good** student.	She did **well** in school.	The adverb *well* is completely different from the adjective form *good*.

Observe word order with adverbs.

EXAMPLES	EXPLANATION
Helen learned sign language **quickly**. Helen **quickly** learned sign language.	An adverb of manner usually follows the verb phrase or it can come before the verb. It cannot come between the verb and the object. *Wrong*: Helen learned *quickly* sign language.
Helen learned **very** quickly. She did **very** well in college.	You can use *very* before an adverb of manner.

EXERCISE **9** **Check (✓) if the sentence is true or false.**

		True	False
EXAMPLE	Helen lost her hearing slowly.		✓
	1. Anne taught Helen patiently.		
	2. Helen learned quickly.		
	3. Helen never learned to speak clearly.		
	4. Helen didn't do well in college.		
	5. Helen wanted deaf people to be treated differently from hearing people.		

11.5 Spelling of -ly Adverbs

ADJECTIVE ENDING	EXAMPLE	ADVERB ENDING	ADVERB
y	easy lucky happy	Change y to i and add -ly.	eas**ily** luck**ily** happ**ily**
consonant + le	simple double comfortable	Drop the e and add -y.	simpl**y** doubl**y** comfortabl**y**
ll	full	Add -y.	full**y**
e	nice free brave	Just add -ly.	nice**ly** free**ly** brave**ly**

Language Note: There is one exception for the last rule: *true—truly*.

EXERCISE **10** **Write the adverb form of each adjective. Use correct spelling.**

1. bad _____

2. good _____

3. lazy _____

4. true _____

5. nice _____

6. full _____

7. responsible _____

8. polite _____

9. fast _____

10. constant _____

11. terrible _____

12. beautiful _____

EXERCISE 11 **Fill in the blanks with the adverb form of the underlined adjective.**

EXAMPLE He's a <u>careful</u> driver. He drives _____*carefully*_____.

1. She has a <u>beautiful</u> voice. She sings _____.
2. You are a <u>responsible</u> person. You always act _____.
3. You have <u>neat</u> handwriting. You write _____.
4. I'm not a <u>good</u> swimmer. I don't swim _____.
5. He is a <u>cheerful</u> person. He always smiles _____.
6. He is <u>fluent</u> in French. He speaks French _____.
7. You have a <u>polite</u> manner. You always talk to
   people _____.
8. Nurses are <u>hard</u> workers. They work _____.
9. She looks <u>sad</u>. She said goodbye _____.
10. You are a <u>patient</u> teacher. You explain the
    grammar _____.
11. My answers are <u>correct</u>. I filled in all the
    blanks _____.

EXERCISE 12 **ABOUT YOU** **Tell how you do these things.**

EXAMPLE write a composition
I write a composition carefully and slowly.

1. speak English
2. speak your native language
3. dance
4. walk
5. study
6. do your homework
7. drive
8. sing
9. type
10. work
11. dress for class
12. dress for a party

EXERCISE **13** **Read the story of Helen Keller's teacher, Anne Sullivan. Find the mistakes with adjectives, adverbs, and noun modifiers in the underlined words. Correct them. Not all underlined words have a mistake. If the underlined words are correct, write C.**

                                                       C

When Helen was a <u>small</u> child, she was <u>a blind</u> and <u>deaf</u>. She behaved
                   (example)   *(example)*   *(1)*

<u>wild</u>. When she was a seven-<u>years</u>-old child, her parents found a <u>wonderful</u>
(2)   *(3)*   *(4)*

teacher to work with her. The teacher's name was Anne Sullivan.

Anne was from a <u>poorly</u> immigrant family. She had a <u>terrible</u> life.
                    (5)   *(6)*

When she was a <u>child small</u>, she had a disease that left her almost blind.
                    (7)

When she was eight <u>years</u> old, her mother died. A few years later, her
                     (8)

father abandoned the family, and Anne went to live in an orphanage.

When she was 14 years old, she could not see <u>clear</u> and she could
                                        (9)

not read. But she got the opportunity to go to a school for the blind. So at

the age of 14, she started <u>school elementary</u>. She was a <u>student very bright</u>
                            (10)   *(11)*

and graduated from high school as the <u>top</u> student.
                                          (12)

She heard about a job to teach <u>a blind</u> girl, Helen Keller. Anne went to
                                   (13)

live with Helen's family. Anne worked <u>patient</u> with Helen, showing her that
                                    (14)

things had names. Within one month, Helen learned <u>signs language</u>. After
                                            (15)

that, Helen learned <u>quickly</u> and wanted to study in school. Anne attended
                       (16)

<u>classes college</u> with Helen, spelling out the lectures and reading to her after
(17)

class. Helen graduated from college with honors. Anne got <u>marry</u> in 1905,
                                              (18)

when Helen was 23. But it wasn't a <u>happy</u> marriage, and Anne separated
                                   (19)

from her husband. She continued to help Helen for the rest of her life.

But her <u>sight eyes</u> became worse and she became completely blind. She
          (20)

died in 1936. Helen lived until 1968.

EXERCISE 14 **Use the adjective in parentheses or change it to an adverb to fill in the blanks.**

CD 2, TR 21

I have two friends who are complete opposites. My friend Paula complains

<u>constantly</u> about everything. I always tell her that she is a _____
(example: constant)   (1 healthy)

person, and that is the most important thing in life. But she is never

_____. She says that everyone is _____. When she drives, she
(2 happy)   (3 impolite)

behaves _____ to other drivers. She says they're all _____, but I
(4 rude)   (5 crazy)

think Paula is the crazy one. She doesn't make changes _____. She
(6 easy)

had to move two months ago, and she hates her _____ apartment.
(7 new)

I think it's a _____ apartment, but she finds something wrong with
(8 nice)

everything.

I have another friend, Karla. Karla is handicapped, in a wheelchair,

but she has a _____ attitude about life. She's also an _____
(9 positive)   (10 active)

person. She swims _____. She's always learning new things. She's
(11 good)

studying French and can speak it _____ now. She learns _____
(12 fluent)   (13 quick)

and is _____ about everything. She goes to museums _____
(14 curious)   (15 frequent)

and knows a lot about art. She is a good role model for her friends.

Grandma Moses

Before You Read

1. Do you know of any old people who have a healthy, good life?

2. Who is the oldest member of your family? Is he or she in good health?

CD 2, TR 22

Read the following magazine article. Pay special attention to *very* and *too*.

They say you can't teach an old dog new tricks. But is this really true? Anna Mary Moses proved that even elderly people can start a new career or take up a new hobby.

Anna Mary Moses was born in 1860. She had a **very** hard life working as a farmer's wife in New York State. She was always interested in art, but she was **too** busy working on the farm and raising her five children to paint. In her 70s, she became **too** weak to do hard farm work. She liked to do embroidery, but as she grew older, she couldn't continue because of arthritis. It was easier for her to hold a paintbrush than a needle, so she started to paint. She painted pictures of farm life. A New York City art collector saw her paintings in a drugstore window and bought them. Today, some of her paintings are in major art museums.

embroidery

When she was 92, she wrote her autobiography. At the age of 100, she illustrated a book. She was still painting when she died at age 101. Better known as "Grandma Moses," she created 1,600 paintings.

Grandma Moses

11.6 Too vs. Very

EXAMPLES	EXPLANATION
Grandma Moses was **very** old when she wrote her autobiography. Her paintings became **very** popular.	*Very* shows a large degree. It doesn't indicate any problems.
She was **too** busy working on the farm to paint. She became **too** weak to do farm work.	*Too* shows that there is a problem. We often use an infinitive phrase after *too*.

EXERCISE 15 Fill in the blanks with *very* or *too*.

EXAMPLES Basketball players are ____very____ tall.

I'm ____too____ short to touch the ceiling.

1. In December, it's _____ cold to go swimming outside.

2. June is usually a _____ nice month.

3. Some elderly people are in _____ good health.

4. Some elderly people are _____ sick to take care of themselves.

5. It's _____ important to know English.

6. This textbook is _____ long to finish in three weeks.

7. The president has a _____ important job.

8. The president is _____ busy to answer all his letters.

9. Some Americans speak English _____ fast for me. I can't understand them.

10. I can speak my own language _____ well.

11. When you buy a used car, you should inspect it _____ carefully.

12. A turtle moves _____ slowly.

13. If you drive _____ slowly on the highway, you might get a ticket.

14. Gina McWilliams is a _____ good athlete.

15. When Grandma Moses had arthritis, embroidery became _____ difficult for her.

11.7 Too and Enough

	EXAMPLES	EXPLANATION
Too + Adjective/Adverb	In her 70s, Grandma Moses was **too weak** to do farm work. I'm working **too hard**. I need to relax.	Use *too* **before** adjectives and adverbs. **Be careful:** Don't use *too much* before adjectives and adverbs. *Wrong:* I'm working too *much* hard.
Adjective/Adverb + *Enough*	She was **talented enough** to get the attention of an art collector. She painted **skillfully enough** to get her pictures in art museums.	Enough means "as much as needed." Use *enough* **after** adjectives and adverbs.
Enough + Noun	When she was younger, she didn't have **enough time** to paint.	Use *enough* **before** nouns.

EXERCISE 16 Fill in the blanks with *too* or *enough* plus the word in parentheses ( ).

EXAMPLES Your son is four years old. He's _____ **too young** _____ to go to first grade.

(young)

My sister is 18 years old. She's _____ **old enough** _____ to get a driver's license.

(old)

1. I can't read Shakespeare in English. It's _____ for me.

(hard)

2. My brother is 21 years old. He's _____ to get married.

(old)

3. My grandfather is 90 years old and in bad health. My family takes care of him. He's _____ to take care of himself.

(sick)

4. I saved $5,000. I want to buy a used car. I think I have _____ _____.

(money)

5. I'd like to get a good job, but I don't have _____.

(experience)

6. She wants to move that piano, but she can't do it alone. She's not _____.

(strong)

7. The piano is _____ for one person to move.

(heavy)

8. I sit at my desk all day, and I don't get _____.

(exercise)

EXERCISE 17 Find the mistakes with the underlined words and correct them. Not all underlined words have a mistake. If the underlined words are correct, write *C.*

CD 2, TR 23

We just read a story about Grandma Moses. We learned that you are never too ~~much~~ old to learn something new.
<u>(example)</u>
I always thought I was <u>too old</u> to learn another language,
<u>(1)</u>
but now that I'm in the U.S. I have no choice. Most of
the students in class are young and learn very <u>quick</u>.
<u>(2)</u>
But I am 58 years old, and I'm not a <u>fast</u> learner at my age. I don't catch
<u>(3)</u>
on as quickly as my younger classmates. However, most of them have a
job, so they don't have <u>enough time</u> to study. Some of them have small
<u>(4)</u>
children, so they are very <u>busily</u> and don't always have <u>enough energy</u>
<u>(5)</u> <u>(6)</u>
to do their homework. I'm not working and my children are <u>enough old</u>
<u>(7)</u>
to take care of themselves. In fact, they're in college also. So I have
<u>enough time</u> to do all my homework. My kids are <u>proudly</u> of me for going
<u>(8)</u> <u>(9)</u>
to college at my age. My teacher always tells me I'm doing <u>too well</u> in her
<u>(10)</u>
class. After learning English, I'm planning to get a degree in history. I am
<u>too</u> interested in this subject. It was my favorite subject when I was in high
<u>(11)</u>
school. When I finish my degree, I'll be in my 60s. It will probably be
<u>too late</u> for me to find a job in this field, but I don't care. I just have a <u>very</u>
<u>(12)</u> <u>(13)</u>
great love of this subject. My kids think it will be <u>too much</u> hard for me
<u>(14)</u>
because history books are <u>hardly</u> to read. But I am <u>too</u> motivated, so I know
<u>(15)</u> <u>(16)</u>
I can do it. Besides, if Grandma Moses could learn to paint in her 70s and
write a book when she was 92, I can certainly study history at my age.
Grandma Moses is a very <u>well</u> role model. Who says you can't teach an
<u>(17)</u>
old dog <u>news</u> tricks?
<u>(18)</u>

Summary of Lesson 11

1. Adjectives and Adverbs:

ADJECTIVES	ADVERBS
She has a **beautiful** voice.	She sings **beautifully**.
She is **careful**.	She drives **carefully**.
She has a **late** class.	She arrived **late**.
She is a **good** driver.	She drives **well**.

2. Adjective Modifiers and Noun Modifiers:

ADJECTIVE MODIFIER	NOUN MODIFIER
a clean window	a store window
a new store	a shoe store
warm coats	winter coats
a new license	a driver's license

3. *Very/Too/Enough:*

He's **very** healthy.
He's **too** young to retire. He's only 55.
He's old **enough** to understand life.
He has **enough** money to take a vacation.

Editing Advice

1. Don't make adjectives plural.

Those are importants ideas.

2. Put the specific noun before the general noun.

truck driver
He is a ~~driver truck~~.

3. Some adjectives end in *-ed*. Don't omit the *-ed*.

ed
I'm finish with my project.

4. If the adjective ends in *-ed*, don't forget to include the verb *be*.

is
He married.

5. A noun modifier is always singular.

She is a letters carrier.

6. Put the adjective before the noun.

very important
He had a meeting ~~very important~~.

7. Don't use an article before an adjective if there is no noun.

Your house is ~~a~~ beautiful.

8. Don't confuse *too* and *very*. *Too* indicates a problem.

very
My father is ~~too~~ healthy.

9. Don't confuse *too much* and *too*. *Too much* is followed by a noun. *Too* is followed by an adjective or adverb.

It's too ~~much~~ hot today. Let's stay inside.

10. Put *enough* after the adjective.

old
He's enough ~~old~~ to drive.

11. Don't use *very* before a verb. *Very* is used only with adjectives and adverbs.

He ~~very~~ likes the U.S. very much. OR He really likes the U.S.

12. Put the adverb at the end of the verb phrase.

late
He ~~late~~ came home.

slowly
He opened ~~slowly~~ the door.

13. Use an adverb to describe a verb. Use an adjective to describe a noun.

ly
He drives careful.

That man is very nice~~ly~~.

well
You speak English very ~~good~~.

Editing Quiz

Some of the shaded words and phrases have mistakes. Find the mistakes and correct them. If the shaded words are correct, write C.

　　　　　　really　　　　　　　　　　　　　　　　　　*C*

I ~~very~~ admire my aunt Rose. She's very intelligent. She married and has
　(example)　　　　　　　　　　　　　*(example)*　　　　　　*(1)*

three grown children. When her children became enough old to take care
　　　(2)　　　　　　　　　　　　　　　　　　　*(3)*

of themselves, she decided to go back to college. She wants to study

programming computer. Some people say she's too much old to start a
(4)　　　　　　　　　　　　　　　　　　　*(5)*

new career, but she doesn't pay any attention. She loves computers.
(6)

She works part-time at a flowers shop. She thinks it's a job very interesting.
　　　　　　　　　　　　　(7)　　　　　　　　　*(8)*

She meets a lot of interestings people. She's a very nice to everyone, and
　　　　　　　　　　(9)　　　　　　　*(10)*

everyone loves her. Whenever I need advice, I can go to her. She listens

patiently and treats everyone kind.
(11)　　　　　　　　*(12)*

Rose came to the U.S. from Guatemala when she was 18. She had five

younger sisters and brothers. Her mother died when she was young,
　　　　　　　　　　　　　　　　　　　　　　　(13)

and she had to take care of her brothers and sisters. She took care of them

wonderfully. She didn't speak one word of English when she left Guatemala.
(14)

She learned quickly English, and now she speaks English very good.
　　　　(15)　　　　　　　　　　　　　　　　　　*(16)*

She's not only my aunt; she's a good friend.
　　　　　　　　　　　(17)

Lesson 11 Test/Review

PART 1 Fill in the blanks by putting the two words in the correct order. Make any other necessary changes. Some words are already in the correct order.

EXAMPLE Grandma Moses was a __n old woman__ when she started to paint.
(woman/old)

1. She painted _____.
(pictures/beautiful/very)

2. She was not _____ to learn something new.
(old/too)

3. When Helen Keller was a _____ she
(baby/nineteen/months/old)

became very sick.

4. Helen communicated with _____.
(language/signs)

5. Gina McWilliams was in a _____ when she was
(car/accident)

26 years old.

6. Her _____ won the _____.
(volleyball/team)   (medal/silver)

7. She sometimes uses a _____.
(chair/wheels)

8. She played volleyball _____ to be in the Paralympic
(well/enough)

Games.

PART 2 Sue and her brother, Don, are very different. Fill in the blanks with the correct form, adjective or adverb, of the word in parentheses ( ) to describe them.

EXAMPLE Sue is a __patient__ person. Don does everything __impatiently__.
(patient)   (impatient)

1. Sue has _____ handwriting. Don writes _____. I can't
(neat)   (sloppy)

even read what he wrote.

2. She talks _____. He talks _____.
(calm)   (fast)

3. She speaks English _____. He has a _____ time with English.
(fluent)   (hard)

4. She learns languages _____. Learning a new language is _____
(easy)   (difficult)

for Don.

5. She types _____. He makes a lot of mistakes. He needs someone
   (accurate)

   to check his work _____.
   (careful)

6. She has a very _____ voice. He speaks _____.
   (soft)   (loud)

7. She sings _____. He sings like a _____ chicken.
   (beautiful)   (sick)

8. She is always very _____. He sometimes behaves _____.
   (responsible)   (childish)

9. She saves her money _____. He buys things he doesn't need.
   (careful)

   He spends his money _____.
   (foolish)

10. She exercises _____. He's very _____ about exercising.
   (regular)   (lazy)

Expansion

Classroom
Activities

❶ **Circle the words that best describe your behaviors. Find a partner and compare your personality to your partner's personality. How many characteristics do you have in common?**

a.	I usually spend my money	carefully	foolishly
b.	I do my homework	willingly	unwillingly
c.	I write compositions	carefully	carelessly
d.	I usually walk	slowly	quickly
e.	I write	neatly	sloppily
f.	I talk	fast	calmly
g.	I write my language	well	poorly
h.	Before a test, I study	hard	a little
i.	I exercise	regularly	infrequently
j.	I play tennis	well	poorly
k.	I like to live	dangerously	carefully
l.	I make important decisions	quickly	slowly and methodically
m.	I learn languages	easily	with difficulty
n.	I learn math	easily	with difficulty
o.	I make judgments	logically	intuitively

❷ Name something.

EXAMPLE Name some things you do well.

I speak my native language well.
I swim well.

a. Name some things you do well.

b. Name some things you don't do well.

c. Name some things you do quickly.

d. Name some things you do slowly.

e. Name something you learned to do easily.

Talk About It

❶ In a small group or with the entire class, discuss the situation of older people in your native culture. Who takes care of them when they are too old or too sick to take care of themselves? How does your family take care of its older members?

❷ In a small group or with the entire class, discuss the situation of handicapped people in the U.S. or in another country. Are there special schools? Are there special facilities, such as parking, public washrooms, and elevators?

❸ Discuss the meaning of this quote by Grandma Moses:

"What a strange thing is memory, and hope. One looks backward, the other forward; one is of today, the other of tomorrow. Memory is history recorded in our brain. Memory is a painter. It paints pictures of the past and of the day."

❹ Aristotle said, "The sign of a great teacher is that the accomplishments of his students exceed his own." What do you think this means?

Write

About It

❶ Write about a famous woman you know about who accomplished something in spite of a handicap or age.

❷ Write about a woman whom you admire very much. You may write about a famous woman or any woman you know (family member, teacher, doctor, etc.).

My Grandmother

My grandmother is a person I admire very much. After her third child was born (my mother), my grandfather died and my grandmother had to raise her family all alone. She took a job as a housekeeper to support her children . . .

 For more practice using grammar in context, please visit our Web site.

The Willis Tower, Chicago

The Space Needle, Seattle

Lesson

12

Grammar
Comparatives

Superlatives

Context
U.S. Geography

The Empire State Building, New York

U.S. Facts

Before You Read

1. In your opinion, what is the most interesting city? Why is it interesting?

2. What cities or regions have the best climate?

CD 2, TR 24

Read the following information. Pay special attention to comparative and superlative forms.[1]

1. In area, the United States is the third **largest** country in the world (after Russia and Canada). In population, the U.S. is also the third **largest** country in the world (after China and India).

2. The **biggest** city in the U.S. in population is New York. It has about 8 million people.

3. The **tallest** building in the U.S. is the Willis Tower, in Chicago (442 meters or 1,450 feet tall). But it is not the **tallest** building in the world. That building is in Dubai (818 meters or 2,684 feet tall).

4. New York City has the **highest** cost of living in the U.S. But the cost of living in Tokyo is much **higher** than in New York.

5. Hispanics are the **fastest** growing minority in the U.S. In 2003, Hispanics passed African-Americans as the **largest** minority.

6. Rhode Island is the **smallest** state in area (1,145 square miles or 2,700 square kilometers).

7. Alaska is the **largest** state in area. Alaska is even **larger** than Colombia, South America.

8. The **least populated** state is Wyoming. It has slightly more than half a million people.

9. California is the **most populated** state. It has about 37 million people. There are **more** people in California than in Peru.

10. Valdez, Alaska, gets the **most** snow—about 326 inches per year.

11. Phoenix, Arizona, gets the **most** sunshine. Eighty-five percent of the days are sunny.

12. Mount McKinley is the **highest** mountain in the U.S. (20,320 feet or 6,193 meters). It is in Alaska.

13. There are five great lakes in the U.S. The **biggest** is Lake Superior. The others are Lake Huron, Lake Michigan, Lake Erie, and Lake Ontario.

14. The state that is the **farthest** north is Alaska. The state that is the **farthest** south is Hawaii.

Did You Know?

Before 1849, the population of California was very small. In 1849, gold was found in California and about 100,000 people rushed there to try to get rich.

[1]See Appendix K for a map of the U.S.

15. The **tallest** waterfall in the U.S. is in California. But Niagara Falls, in New York and Ontario, Canada, is **more famous**. It is one of the **most popular** tourist attractions. Twelve million tourists a year visit Niagara Falls. It has the **greatest** volume of water.
16. The **most recent** state to join the U.S. is Hawaii. It joined in 1959.
17. The **oldest** state is Delaware. It became a state in 1787.

Niagara Falls

12.1 Comparatives and Superlatives—An Overview

EXAMPLES	EXPLANATION
Los Angeles is **bigger** than Chicago. There are **more** people in California than in Peru.	We use the comparative form to compare two items.
New York City is the **biggest** city in the U.S. California is the **most populated** state in the U.S.	We use the superlative form to point out the number–one item in a group of three or more.

EXERCISE **1** **Circle the correct word to complete the statement.**

EXAMPLE Chicago is (*bigger* / *smaller*) than Los Angeles.

1. The tallest building in the world (*is* / *isn't*) in the U.S.

2. Alaska has a (*larger* / *smaller*) population than Wyoming.

3. The U.S. is (*bigger* / *smaller*) than Russia.

4. (*Alaska* / *California*) has the largest area.

5. The fastest-growing minority is (*Hispanics* / *African Americans*).

6. There are (*more* / *fewer*) Hispanics than African Americans in the U.S.

7. The most populated state is (*Alaska* / *California*).

8. The U.S. (*is* / *isn't*) the largest country in the world in area.

12.2 Comparative and Superlative Forms of Adjectives and Adverbs

	SIMPLE	COMPARATIVE	SUPERLATIVE
One-syllable adjectives and adverbs*	tall fast	taller faster	tallest fastest
Two-syllable adjectives that end in *y*	easy happy	easier happier	easiest happiest
Other two-syllable adjectives	frequent active	more frequent more active	most frequent most active
Some two-syllable adjectives have two forms.**	simple common	simpler more simple commoner more common	simplest most simple commonest most common
Adjectives with three or more syllables	important difficult	more important more difficult	most important most difficult
-ly adverbs	quickly brightly	more quickly more brightly	most quickly most brightly
Irregular adjectives and adverbs	good/well bad/badly far little a lot	better worse farther less more	best worst farthest least most

Language Notes:

*Exceptions to one-syllable adjectives:

| bored | more bored | the most bored |
| tired | more tired | the most tired |

**Other two-syllable adjectives that have two forms:
> *handsome, quiet, gentle, narrow, clever, friendly, tender, stupid*

Spelling Rules for Short Adjectives and Adverbs

RULE	SIMPLE	COMPARATIVE	SUPERLATIVE
Add -er and -est to short adjectives and adverbs.	tall fast	taller faster	tallest fastest
For adjectives that end in e, add -r and -st.	nice late	nicer later	nicest latest
For adjectives that end in y, change y to i and add -er and -est.	easy happy	easier happier	easiest happiest
For words ending in consonant-vowel-consonant, double the final consonant, then add -er and -est. **Exception:** Do not double final w. new—newer—newest	big sad	bigger sadder	biggest saddest

EXERCISE **2** **Give the comparative and superlative forms of the word.**

EXAMPLES   fat   <u>fatter</u>   <u>fattest</u>

important   <u>more important</u>   <u>most important</u>

1. interesting _____ _____
2. young _____ _____
3. beautiful _____ _____
4. good _____ _____
5. common _____ _____
6. thin _____ _____
7. carefully _____ _____
8. pretty _____ _____
9. bad _____ _____
10. famous _____ _____
11. lucky _____ _____
12. simple _____ _____
13. high _____ _____
14. delicious _____ _____
15. far _____ _____
16. foolishly _____ _____

12.3 Superlative Adjectives

EXAMPLES	EXPLANATION
New York is **the biggest** city in the U.S. California is **the most populated** state in the U.S. China has **the largest** population in the world.	We use the superlative form to point out the number-one item of a group of three or more. Use *the* before a superlative form. We often put a prepositional phrase at the end of a superlative sentence: in the world in my family in my class in my country
Niagara Falls is **one of the most popular** tourist attraction**s** in the U.S. The Willis Tower is **one of the tallest** building**s** in the world.	We often put "one of the" before a superlative form. Then we use a plural noun.

EXERCISE 3 **Fill in the blanks with the superlative form of the word in parentheses ( ). Include *the* before the superlative form.**

EXAMPLE   Alaska is ___the largest___ state in area.
                                    (large)

1. _____ lake in the U.S. is Lake Superior.
        (big)

2. _____ river in the U.S. is the Missouri River.
        (long)

3. _____ mountain in the U.S. is Mount McKinley.
        (high)

4. Niagara Falls is one of _____ tourist attractions.
                                    (popular)

5. San Francisco is one of _____ cities in the U.S.
                                    (expensive)

6. San Francisco is one of _____ American cities.
                                    (beautiful)

7. Harvard is one of _____ universities in the U.S.
                            (good)

8. The Willis Tower is _____ building in the U.S.
                            (tall)

9. The economy is one of _____ problems in the U.S.
                                (bad)

10. Boston is one of _____ cities in the U.S.
                            (old)

EXERCISE 4 **ABOUT YOU** Talk about the number-one person in your family for each of these adjectives.

EXAMPLES interesting
My aunt Rosa is the most interesting person in my family.

tall
My brother Carlos is the tallest person in my family.

1. intelligent
2. kind
3. handsome/beautiful
4. stubborn
5. lazy
6. tall

7. serious
8. nervous
9. strong
10. funny
11. responsible
12. neat

EXERCISE 5 Write a superlative sentence about each of the following items. You may include "one of the . . ." plus a plural noun.

EXAMPLE big problem today
The economy is one of the biggest problems in the U.S. today.

OR

Unemployment is the biggest problem in my country today.

1. exciting sport

2. interesting story in this book

3. bad tragedy in the world or in the U.S.

4. important invention of the last 100 years

5. interesting city in the world

6. big problem

7. bad job

8. good job

_____

9. hard teacher at this school

_____

10. popular movie star

_____

12.4 Word Order with Superlatives

EXAMPLES	EXPLANATION
What is *the biggest* lake in the U.S.? California is *the most populated* state.	A superlative adjective comes **before** a noun.
The Willis Tower is **the tallest building** in the U.S. OR **The tallest building** in the U.S. is the Willis Tower.	When the verb *be* connects a noun to a superlative adjective + noun, there are two possible word orders.
The Hispanic population **is growing** *the most quickly* in the U.S. The population of India **is increasing** *the most rapidly* in the world.	We put superlative adverbs **after** the verb (phrase).
It **rains** *the most* in Hawaii. It **snows** *the most* in Alaska.	We put *the most, the least, the best,* and *the worst* **after** a verb.
Phoenix gets *the most* sunshine. Alaska has *the least* sunshine in the winter.	We put *the most, the least, the fewest, the best,* and *the worst* **before** a noun.

EXERCISE **6**   **ABOUT YOU** Name the person in your family who is the superlative in each of the following activities. Put the superlative form after the verb phrase.

EXAMPLES   cook well
My mother cooks the best in the family.

eat a lot
My brother eats the most in my family.

1. talk a lot   **4.** speak English well   **7.** speak softly

2. drive well   **5.** stay up late   **8.** eat a lot

3. walk fast   **6.** get up early   **9.** dress badly

EXERCISE 7 **ABOUT YOU** Name the person in your family who is the superlative in each of the following activities. Put the superlative form before the noun.

EXAMPLE   watch a lot of TV
My brother watches the most TV. He watches TV four hours a day.

1. spend a lot of money
2. get little mail
3. drink a lot of coffee
4. spend a lot of time in the bathroom
5. spend a lot of time on the telephone
6. have a bad temper
7. make few mistakes in English

A Tale of Two Cities[2]

Before You Read

1. Compare this city to another city.
2. Do you have any friends or relatives in American cities? Do you visit them?

San Francisco

Chicago

[2]These statistics are from 2007.

◀)) **Look at the following chart. Then read the sentences that follow. Pay special attention to comparative forms.**

	San Francisco	Chicago
Population	800,000	2,900,000
Average cost of home	$765,000	$286,800
Unemployment	7%	5.7%
Cost of living (100 = national average)	177	128
Average family income	$68,023	$45,505
High school graduates	84.6% of population	71.8% of population
Average temperature in July	62 degrees	74 degrees
Average temperature in January	53 degrees	26 degrees
Rainfall (inches annually)	20.3	37.4
Number of clear days (no clouds) per year	160	84
Air pollution (amount of ozone in air; U.S. average = 100)	42	79
Robberies (per 100,000 people)	514	546

- Chicago has a **larger** population **than** San Francisco.
- A house in San Francisco is **more expensive than** a house in Chicago.
- Unemployment in San Francisco is **higher than** in Chicago.
- The average family income is **more** in San Francisco **than** in Chicago, but San Francisco has a **higher** cost of living.
- San Francisco has **fewer** high school graduates **than** Chicago.
- San Francisco has a **better** climate **than** Chicago. Chicago gets **more** rain **than** San Francisco. San Francisco is **sunnier than** Chicago.
- Chicago is **warmer** in the summer.
- Chicago is **colder** in the winter.
- Chicago has **more** air pollution **than** San Francisco.
- San Francisco has **less** crime than Chicago.

12.5 Comparisons

EXAMPLES	EXPLANATION
Chicago has a **larger** population **than** San Francisco. Houses in San Francisco are **more expensive than** houses in Chicago.	We use the comparative form to compare two items. We use *than* before the second item of comparison.
Chicago is **colder than** San Francisco in the winter, but it is **warmer** in the summer.	Omit *than* if the second item of comparison is not included.
San Francisco has **less** crime than Chicago. San Francisco has **fewer** people than Chicago.	The opposite of *more* is *less* or *fewer*.
The cost of living in San Francisco is **much higher than** in Chicago. Unemployment is **a little higher** in San Francisco.	*Much* or *a little* can come before a comparative form.
Formal: You know more about American cities than **I do.** **Informal:** You know more about American cities than **me.** **Formal:** I can speak English better than **he can.** **Informal:** I can speak English better than **him.**	When a pronoun follows *than*, the correct form is the subject pronoun (*he, she, I,* etc.). Usually an auxiliary verb follows (*is, do, did, can,* etc.). Informally, many Americans use the object pronoun (*him, her, me,* etc.) after *than*. An auxiliary verb does not follow.

EXERCISE **8** **Circle the correct words to complete the statement.**

EXAMPLE Chicago has ((more) / less) crime than San Francisco.

1. Chicago has a (*larger / smaller*) population than San Francisco.
2. Chicago is a (*safer / more dangerous*) place to live than San Francisco.
3. Houses in Chicago are (*more expensive / less expensive*) than houses in San Francisco.
4. Winter in Chicago is (*better / worse*) than winter in San Francisco.
5. Chicago has (*more / less*) rain than San Francisco.

EXERCISE **9**   **ABOUT YOU** **Compare yourself to another person, or compare two people you know using these adjectives.**

EXAMPLES tall
I'm taller than my father.

talkative
My mother is more talkative than my father.

1. tall	**5.** thin	**9.** successful
2. educated	**6.** quiet	**10.** strong
3. friendly	**7.** stubborn	**11.** nervous
4. lazy	**8.** patient	**12.** polite

EXERCISE **10** **Compare adults and children. Talk in general terms. You may discuss your answers.**

EXAMPLE responsible
Adults are more responsible than kids.

1. polite	**4.** playful	**7.** shy
2. strong	**5.** sweet	**8.** patient
3. imaginative	**6.** friendly	**9.** serious

EXERCISE **11** **Compare the city you live in now to another city you know.**

EXAMPLES big
Tokyo is bigger than Boston.

crowded
Tokyo is more crowded than Boston.

1. crowded	**4.** noisy	**7.** cold in winter
2. modern	**5.** beautiful	**8.** dirty
3. small	**6.** interesting	**9.** sunny

12.6 Word Order with Comparisons

EXAMPLES	EXPLANATION
Houses in San Francisco **are more expensive** than houses in Chicago. I want to move to a **warmer climate**.	Put comparative adjectives **after** the verb *be* or **before** a noun.
The Hispanic population **is growing more quickly** than the African-American population.	Put comparative adverbs **after** the verb (phrase).
It **rains more** in Chicago. It **snows more** in Chicago.	Put *more, less, better,* and *worse* **after** a verb.
San Francisco has **more sunshine** than Chicago. San Francisco has **less pollution**.	Put *more, less, fewer, better,* and *worse* **before** a noun.

EXERCISE 12 Compare yourself to another person, or compare two people you know using these verb phrases.

EXAMPLES work hard
My mom works harder than my dad.

talk a lot
My brother talks more than my sister.

1. talk fast
2. gossip a lot
3. worry a lot
4. speak English fluently
5. work hard
6. drive carefully
7. spend a lot on clothes
8. make decisions quickly

EXERCISE 13 Compare this city to another city you know. Use *better, worse, fewer, less,* or *more.*

EXAMPLES factories
Chicago has more factories than Ponce.

public transportation
Moscow has better public transportation than Los Angeles.

1. traffic
2. people
3. rain
4. crime
5. pollution
6. sunshine
7. factories
8. snow
9. apartment buildings
10. job opportunities
11. tall buildings
12. homeless people

EXERCISE **14**   **Make comparisons with the following words. Give your reasons. You may work with a partner or in a small group.**

EXAMPLE   men/women—have an easy life <u>In my opinion, men have an easier life than</u> <u>women. Women have to work two jobs—in the office and at home.</u>

1. men/women—have responsibilities _____

_____

2. American women/women in my native culture—have an easy life

_____

_____

3. married men/single men—are responsible _____

_____

4. American teenagers/teenagers in my native culture—have freedom

_____

_____

5. American teenagers/teenagers in my native culture—have

responsibilities _____

_____

6. American children/children in my native culture—have toys _____

_____

7. American children/children in my native culture—have a good

education _____

_____

8. American teachers/teachers in my native culture—get respect

_____

_____

EXERCISE **15**   **Fill in the blanks with the comparative or superlative form of the word in parentheses ( ). Include *than* or *the* where necessary.**

EXAMPLES   August is usually _____<u>hotter than</u>_____ May in Chicago.
               (hot)

January is usually _____<u>the coldest</u>_____ month of the year in Chicago.
               (cold)

1. Los Angeles is _____ San Francisco.
                    (warm)

2. Seattle is _____ city in Washington.
                (big)

3. The state of Hawaii is _____ south in the U.S.
(far)

4. Mexico City is _____ New York City.
(crowded)

5. New York City is _____ Los Angeles.
(crowded)

6. Mexico City is one of _____ cities in the world.
(crowded)

7. San Francisco is one of _____ cities in the U.S.
(beautiful)

8. _____ building in the world is not in the U.S.
(tall)

EXERCISE 16 **Two students in Seattle are talking. Fill in the blanks with appropriate words to make comparatives and superlatives.**

CD 2, TR 26

A: I'm planning to visit Chicago.

B: You're going to love it. It's a beautiful city. In fact, it's one of

___the most beautiful___ cities in the U.S.
(example)

A: It's the second largest city, isn't it?

B: Not anymore. Los Angeles is now _____ Chicago.
(1)

A: What should I see while I'm there?

B: You can visit the Willis Tower. It's _____ building in
(2)

the U.S. It has 110 stories. On a clear day, you can see for many miles.

A: Did you go to the top when you were there?

B: When I was there, the weather was bad. It was raining. I hope you

have _____ weather than I had. When are you going?
(3)

A: In August.

B: Ugh! August is the _____ month of the year. It's often 90
(4)

degrees or more. If you get hot, you can always go to the beach and cool off.

A: Is Chicago near an ocean?

B: No. It's near Lake Michigan.

A: Is it big like Lake Washington?

B: It's much _____ than Lake Washington. In fact, it's
(5)

one of the _____ lakes in the U.S.
(6)

(continued)

A: Is Chicago very rainy?

B: Not in the summer. It's sunny. In fact, it's much _____ (7) than Seattle.

A: What do you suggest that I see?

B: You should see the famous architecture downtown. The _____ (8) architects in the U.S. designed buildings in Chicago.

A: Do I need to take taxis everywhere, or does Chicago have a good public transportation system?

B: Taxis are so expensive! They're much _____ (9) than the buses and trains. You should use the public transportation. But remember that there's a lot of crime in Chicago, so it's not safe to travel alone at night. It's _____ (10) in the daytime.

A: Does Chicago have _____ (11) crime than Seattle?

B: Yes. But if you're careful, you'll be OK. I'm sure you'll enjoy it. It's an interesting place because it has people from all over the world. In fact, I think it's one of _____ (12) cities in the U.S.

Chicago skyline

Summary of Lesson 12

1. Adjectives

SHORT ADJECTIVES
Chicago is a **big** city.
Chicago is **bigger than** Boston.
New York is **the biggest** city in the U.S.

LONG ADJECTIVES
Houston is a **populated** city.
Chicago is **more populated than** Houston.
New York is **the most populated** city in the U.S.

2. Adverbs

SHORT ADVERBS
She walks **fast**.
She walks **faster than** her husband.
Her son walks **the fastest** in the family.

-LY ADVERBS
You speak English **fluently**.
You speak English **more fluently than** your brother.
Your sister speaks English **the most fluently** in your family.

3. Word Order

VERB (PHRASE) + COMPARATIVE ADVERB
She **speaks English more fluently** than her husband.
She **talks more** than her husband.

COMPARATIVE ADJECTIVE + NOUN
She has **more experience** than her husband.
She has a **better accent** than her sister.

Editing Advice

1. Don't use a comparison word when there is no comparison.

California is a ~~bigger~~ state.

2. Don't use *more* and *-er* together.

My new car is ~~more~~ better than my old one.

3. Use *than* before the second item in a comparison.

than
He is younger ~~that~~ his wife.

4. Use *the* before a superlative form.

> *the*
> China has ˄ biggest population in the world.

5. Use a plural noun after the phrase "one of the."

> *s*
> Jim is one of the tallest boy˄ in the class.

6. Use the correct word order.

> *drives faster*
> She ~~faster drives~~ than her husband.

> *more*
> I have ˄ responsibilities ~~more~~ than you.

> *person*
> My uncle is the ~~person~~ most interesting ˄ in my family.

7. Don't use *the* with a possessive form.

> My ~~the~~ best friend lives in London.

8. Use correct spelling.

> *happier*
> She is ~~happyer~~ than her friend.

Editing Quiz

Some of the shaded words and phrases have mistakes. Find the mistakes and correct them. If the shaded words are correct, write C.

I used to live in Mexico City. Now I live in St. Louis. These cities are

C *bigger*
very different. Mexico City is more biger than St. Louis. In fact, it's
(example) *(example)*

one of the biggest city in the world. It's certainly the most large city in
(1) *(2)*

Mexico. St. Louis has no mountains. Mexico City is surrounded by tall
(3)

mountains. I think Mexico City is prettyer that St. Louis. It has beautiful
(4)

parks. Mexico City is more interesting St. Louis. It has great museums.
(5)

But Mexico City has a few serious problems: it has more pollution than
(6)

St. Louis. My the oldest brother still lives there and he always complains
(7)

about the air quality. And I hate the subway. I think it's the more crowded
(8)

subway in the world.

No city is perfect. Each one has advantages and disadvantages. But my

heart is in Mexico City because my family and best friends live there.
(9)

Lesson 12 Test/Review

PART 1   **Find the mistakes with word order and correct them. Not every sentence has a mistake. If the sentence is correct, write C.**

EXAMPLES   You more know about the U.S. than I do.
Soccer is more interesting than football for me.   *C*

1. I have problems more than you.
2. I earlier woke up than you.
3. Paris is the city most beautiful in the world.
4. She speaks English more fluently than her brother.
5. You faster type than I do.
6. My father is the most intelligent person in the family.
7. Your car is expensive more than my car.
8. You sing more beautifully than I do.
9. I travel more than my friend does.
10. You have more money than I do.

PART 2   **Fill in the blanks with the comparative or the superlative of the word in parentheses ( ). Add *the* or *than* if necessary.**

EXAMPLES   New York City is ____**bigger than**____ Chicago.
                                            (*big*)

New York City is ____**the biggest**____ city in the U.S.
                                            (*big*)

1. Mount Everest is _____ mountain in the world.
                                            (*high*)

2. A D grade is _____ a C grade.
                                            (*bad*)

3. Johnson is one of _____ last names in the U.S.
    (common)

4. Tokyo is _____ Miami.
    (populated)

5. June 21 is _____ day of the year.
    (long)

6. The teacher speaks English _____ I do.
    (well)

7. Lake Superior is _____ lake in the U.S.
    (large)

8. Children learn a foreign language _____ adults.
    (quickly)

9. Do you think that Japanese cars are _____
    (good)

American cars?

10. A dog is _____ a cat.
    (friendly)

11. Do you think women drive _____ men?
    (carefully)

12. Who is _____ student in this class?
    (good)

13. The teacher speaks English _____ I do.
    (fluently)

14. A dog is intelligent, but a monkey is _____.
    (intelligent)

Expansion

Classroom
Activities

① **Form small groups of three to five students. Fill in the blanks to give information about yourself. Compare your list with the lists of other members of your group to make superlative statements.**

EXAMPLE   Susana has the most relatives in this city.

a. number of relatives I have in this city _____

b. my height _____

c. number of letters in my last name _____

d. number of sisters and brothers I have _____

e. number of hours I watch TV per week _____

f. number of hours I exercise per week _____

g. money I spent today _____

h. distance I travel to come to this school _____

i. cups of coffee I drank today _____

j. number of miles I usually drive or walk per day _____

k. number of movies I usually see per year _____

② Work with a partner from the same native culture, if possible. Compare American men and men from your native culture. Compare American women and women from your native culture. Report some of your ideas to the class.

③ Find a partner. Choose one of the following pairs and decide which of the two is better. Write five reasons why it is better. One person will make a statement saying that one is better than the other. The other person will follow with, "Yes, but . . ." and give another point of view.

EXAMPLE **A:** I think dogs are better pets than cats. They are more loyal.
B: Yes, but dogs need more attention.

- cats and dogs
- travel by train and travel by plane
- houses and condos
- spring and fall
- voice mail and answering machines
- leaving a spoken message or a text message

Talk
About It

① In your opinion, what is the biggest problem in the U.S. today?

② Talk about the advantages and disadvantages of living in a big city. Compare a big city to a small city or town.

③ In choosing where to live, what is the most important thing to consider?

Write

About It

1 **Write about the biggest problem in the world today. Why is this a problem? How can we solve the problem?**

2 **Choose one of the following topics to write a comparison:**

   a. Compare your present car with your previous car.

   b. Compare two cities you know well.

   c. Compare American women and women in your native culture.

   d. Compare American men and men in your native culture.

   e. Compare soccer and American football.

   f. Compare your life in the U.S. and your life in your native country.

   g. Compare a place where you lived before with the place where you live now.

Quito and Chicago

I am from Quito, Ecuador. I lived there for 21 years before I came to Chicago. There are many differences between Quito and Chicago. One difference is the climate. In Quito, the temperature is almost the same all year. The summers in Chicago are much hotter and the winters are much colder than in Quito. Another difference is the altitude. Chicago is at sea level and Quito is high in the mountains . . .

 For more practice using grammar in context, please visit our Web site.

Grammar
Auxiliary Verbs with
Too* and *Either

Auxiliary Verbs in
Tag Questions

Context
Dating and Marriage

Dating and Marriage

Before
You Read

1. How is dating different from marriage?

2. Do American married couples spend more or less time together than couples in your native culture?

CD 2, TR 27

Read the following magazine article. Pay special attention to auxiliary verbs and *too* and *either*.

Most married couples want to spend time together, but the busy American lifestyle often doesn't allow it.

Meg and Don are a typical American couple.

Before Meg and Don met, they were both lonely. Meg wanted to get married, and Don **did too**. Meg believed that marriage would mean a lot of togetherness, and Don **did too**. When they were dating, Don didn't get together with friends very often, and Meg **didn't either**. They spent all their free time together. They discovered they had a lot in common.

A year after they met, they decided to get married. As they planned their wedding, they discovered their first differences while making decisions about their wedding: Meg wanted a big wedding, but Don **didn't**. Meg wanted an outdoor wedding, but Don **didn't**. They solved their differences by having a big indoor wedding.

As a married couple, they are now facing the realities of busy schedules and different interests. Don works hard, and Meg **does too**. They often have to work overtime. Don likes to cook, and Meg **does too**, but they rarely have time to do it. They often bring home carry-out dinners or eat in fast-food restaurants. On weekends, Don likes to go fishing, but Meg **doesn't**. So Don takes fishing trips with his friends. Meg likes to go to movies, but Don **doesn't**. He prefers to stay home and watch TV when he comes home from work. Both of them are planning to take college courses soon, which will give them even less time together.

So how do they solve these differences and stay close as a married couple? Once a month, they invite friends over on a weekend to have dinner and watch a movie or a football game on TV. When Don goes on a fishing trip, Meg gets together with her best friend and they go to a movie. That way, Don enjoys himself, and Meg **does too**.

Even though the realities of marriage are different from the romance of dating, Meg and Don are finding ways to adjust to married life.

13.1 Auxiliary Verbs with *Too* and *Either*

The auxiliary verbs are *do*, *does*, *did*, the modals, and *be*. We use auxiliary verbs with *too* and *either* to show similarity and avoid repetition of the same verb phrase.

EXAMPLES	EXPLANATION
Don is busy, and Meg **is too**. Don likes to cook, and Meg **does too**. Don was lonely, and Meg **was too**. Don lived alone, and Meg **did too**.	For affirmative statements, use the auxiliary verb + *too*.
Don doesn't have much free time, and Meg **doesn't either**. Don didn't get together with friends very often, and **Meg didn't either**.	For negative statements, use the auxiliary verb + *either*.
Don: I like to cook. *Meg*: **Me too**. *Don*: I don't have much time. *Meg*: **Me neither**.	In informal speech, we often say *me too* and *me neither*.
American: Meg has a hard job, and Don **does too**. **British:** Meg has a hard job, and Don **has too**.	When *have* is the main verb, Americans usually use *do*, *does*, *did* as a substitute. The British often use *have*, *has*, or *had*.

EXERCISE 1 **Fill in the blanks with an auxiliary verb + *too* to show what Meg and Don have in common. Make sure that you use the same tense as the main verb.**

EXAMPLE   Don likes to cook, and Meg _____*does too*_____.

1. Don has a hard job, and Meg _____.

2. Don is a hard worker, and Meg _____.

3. Don will take some college courses next semester,

   and Meg _____.

4. Don was lonely before, and Meg _____.

5. Don worked last Saturday, and Meg _____.

EXERCISE 2 **Fill in the blanks with an auxiliary verb + *either* to show what Meg and Don have in common. Make sure you use the same tense as the main verb.**

EXAMPLE   Don doesn't like fast food, and Meg _____*doesn't either*_____.

1. Don didn't finish college, and Meg _____.

2. Don isn't interested in baseball, and Meg _____.

3. Don doesn't have much free time, and Meg _____.

4. Don can't find time to cook, and Meg _____.

5. Don doesn't have any brothers or sisters, and Meg _____.

13.2 Auxiliary Verbs with Opposite Statements

We can use auxiliary verbs to show contrast and avoid repetition of the same verb phrase.

EXAMPLES	EXPLANATION
Don likes to go fishing, **but** Meg **doesn't.** Don is happy watching TV, **but** Meg **isn't.** Don doesn't like to go to movies, **but** Meg **does.** Don didn't want to have a big wedding, **but** Meg **did.**	We can use *but* to connect opposite statements. We often put a comma before *but*.
Meg: I want a big wedding. **Don:** I **don't.** **Meg:** I'm not interested in sports. **Don:** I **am.**	In conversation, we don't need *but* when one person says the opposite of another.

EXERCISE **3** **Fill in the blanks with an auxiliary verb to show what Meg and Don don't have in common.**

EXAMPLES Don likes to go fishing, but Meg __*doesn't*__ .

1. Meg likes to go to movies, but Don _____.

2. Meg doesn't like to watch football on TV, but Don _____.

3. Meg reads when she has free time, but Don _____.

4. Don wanted to have a small wedding, but Meg _____.

5. Meg is interested in politics, but Don _____.

6. Meg isn't interested in cars, but Don _____.

7. Meg can play the piano, but Don _____.

EXERCISE **4** **Fill in the blanks to compare the U.S. and another country you know. Use *and . . . too* or *and . . . either* for similarities between the U.S. and the other country. Use *but* for differences. Use an auxiliary verb in all cases.**

EXAMPLE The U.S. is a big country, _____ *and Russia is too.* _____

OR

The U.S. is a big country, _____ *but Cuba isn't.* _____

1. The U.S. has more than 300 million people, _____

_____

2. The U.S. is in North America, _____

3. The U.S. has a president, _____

4. The U.S. doesn't have a prime minister, _____
_____

5. The U.S. fought in World War II, _____

6. The U.S. was a colony of England, _____

7. Americans like football, _____

8. Americans don't celebrate Labor Day in May, _____
_____

9. American public schools are closed on December 25, _____
_____

10. The U.S. has a presidential election every four years, _____
_____

EXERCISE **5**   **ABOUT YOU** Check (✓) *yes* or *no* to tell what is true for you. Exchange your book with another student. Make statements about you and the other student.

EXAMPLE   I don't speak Spanish, but Luis does.

	Yes	No
1. I speak Spanish.		
2. I'm interested in football.		
3. I'm interested in soccer.		
4. I have a car.		
5. I use the Internet every day.		
6. I can drive.		
7. I plan to move to another city.		
8. I'm going to buy a computer this year.		
9. I would like to visit Paris.		
10. I exercise every day.		
11. I'm studying math this semester.		
12. I studied English when I was in elementary school.		
13. I finished high school.		
14. I'm a vegetarian.		

EXERCISE 6 Fill in the blanks in the conversation below. Use an auxiliary verb and *too* or *either* when necessary.

CD 2, TR 28

A: I'm moving on Saturday. Maybe you and your brother can help me. Are you working on Saturday?

B: My brother is working on Saturday, but I **'m not** _____.
 (example)
I can help you.

A: I need a van. Do you have one?

B: I don't have one, but my brother _____. I'll ask him
 (1)
if we can use it. By the way, why are you moving?

A: There are a couple of reasons. I got married recently. I like the
apartment, but my wife _____. She says it's too small for
 (2)
two people.

B: How many rooms does your new apartment have?

A: The old apartment has two bedrooms, and the new one
_____. But the rooms are much bigger in the new one,
 (3)
and there are more closets. Also, we'd like to live near the lake.

B: I _____, but apartments there are very expensive.
 (4)

A: We found a nice apartment that isn't so expensive. Also, I'd like to own
a dog, but my present landlord doesn't permit pets.

B: Mine doesn't _____. What kind of dog do you plan
 (5)
to get?

A: I like big watchdogs. Maybe a German Shepherd or a Doberman.
I don't like small dogs, but my wife _____.
 (6)

B: I don't like small dogs either. They just make a lot of noise.

A: So now you know my reasons for moving. Can I count on you
for Saturday?

B: Of course you can.

13.3 Tag Questions

EXAMPLES	EXPLANATION
Married life is hard, **isn't it**? You don't like to go fishing, **do you**? Meg and Don work hard, **don't they**? Americans don't have much free time, **do they**?	A tag question is a short question that we put at the end of a statement. Use a tag question to ask if your statement is correct or if the listener agrees with you. The tag question uses an auxiliary verb in the same tense as the main verb.

Saturday with Meg and Don

Before
You Read

1. When families talk about "quality time," what do you think they mean?

2. What do you like to do in your free time?

CD 2, TR 29

Read the following conversation between Meg (M) and Don (D). Pay special attention to tag questions.

M: Would you like to go out to a movie tonight?

D: Not really.

M: Before we got married, you always wanted to go to movies, **didn't you**?

D: I suppose so. But I'm tired now. I'd rather stay home and watch TV or rent a movie.

M: You're always tired, **aren't you**?

D: Well, actually, yes. I work hard all week, and now I just want to relax.

M: When we got married, we planned to spend a lot of time together, **didn't we**?

D: I know. But married life is hard. Besides, we spend a lot of time together on weekends, **don't we**?

M: Yes, we do. We go shopping, we do the laundry, we visit your parents, we cut the grass, we clean the house. But we don't have any fun together anymore, **do we**?

(continued)

D: Fishing is fun for me. Next weekend I'm going fishing with my buddies. But you don't like fishing, **do you?**

M: Not really.

D: Before we got married, you said you'd try fishing with me, **didn't you?**

M: Yes, I did. But I was just trying to please you then. I realize I like to eat fish, but I don't like to catch them.

D: Well, somebody has to catch them if you want to eat them.

M: But we never eat them because we don't have time to cook. Now that it's Saturday, we're both too tired to cook. What are we going to do for dinner tonight?

D: We can get some carry-out from that new Chinese place nearby, **can't we?**

M: I suppose so.

D: You're not happy, **are you?**

M: That's not true! I love you, but I just want to spend more "quality time" with you.

D: I have an idea. Let's invite some friends over next weekend, and we can make our special fish recipe for them. That will be fun, **won't it?**

M: That's a great idea.

13.4 Auxiliary Verbs in Tag Questions

AFFIRMATIVE STATEMENTS	NEGATIVE TAG QUESTIONS	EXPLANATION
Don likes fishing,	**doesn't** he?	An affirmative statement has a negative tag question. Make a contraction with the auxiliary verb + *not* and then use a subject pronoun.
You're always tired,	**aren't** you?	
We can eat out,	**can't** we?	
We planned to spend time together,	**didn't** we?	
Meg is unhappy,	**isn't** she?	
NEGATIVE STATEMENTS	**AFFIRMATIVE TAG QUESTIONS**	**EXPLANATION**
You aren't happy,	**are you?**	A negative statement has an affirmative tag question. Use the auxiliary verb + a subject pronoun.
You don't like fishing,	**do you?**	
We never have fun together anymore,	**do we?**	

Special Cases with Tag Questions

EXAMPLES	EXPLANATION
There isn't a lot of free time, **is there**? There are a lot of things to do, **aren't there**?	If the sentence begins with *there is* or *there are*, use *there* in the tag.
This is a typical marriage, **isn't it**? That will be fun, **won't it**?	If the sentence begins with *this* or *that*, use *it* in the tag.
These are normal problems, **aren't they**? Those romantic days are over, **aren't they**?	If the sentence begins with *these* or *those*, use *they* in the tag.
Informal: I'm right, **aren't I**? **Formal:** I'm right, **am I not**?	*Am I not?* is a very formal tag. Informally, we usually say *aren't I?*

EXERCISE 7 Add a tag question. All the statements are affirmative and have an auxiliary verb.

EXAMPLE   This class is large, _____ *isn't it?* _____

1. You're a foreign student, _____
2. You can understand English, _____
3. We'll have a test soon, _____
4. We should study, _____
5. There's a library at this school, _____
6. You'd like to improve your English, _____
7. This is an easy lesson, _____
8. I'm asking too many questions, _____

EXERCISE 8 Add a tag question. All the statements are negative and have an auxiliary verb.

EXAMPLE   You can't speak Italian, _____ *can you?* _____

1. You aren't an American citizen, _____
2. The teacher can't speak your language, _____
3. We shouldn't talk in the library, _____
4. You weren't absent yesterday, _____
5. There aren't any Japanese students in this class, _____
6. This exercise isn't hard, _____

EXERCISE 9 Add a tag question. All the statements are affirmative. Substitute the main verb with an auxiliary verb in the tag question.

EXAMPLE   You have the textbook, _____don't you?_____

1. English has a lot of irregular verbs, _____
2. You want to speak English well, _____
3. You understood the explanation, _____
4. You have a cell phone, _____
5. They bought a laptop last week, _____
6. We had a test last week, _____

EXERCISE 10 Add a tag question. All the statements are negative.

EXAMPLE   We don't have class on Saturday, _____do we?_____

1. The teacher doesn't pronounce your name correctly, _____
2. Your brother didn't take the last test, _____
3. You didn't bring your dictionary today, _____
4. We don't always have homework, _____
5. I don't have your phone number, _____
6. Your mother doesn't speak English, _____

EXERCISE 11 This is a conversation between two acquaintances,[1] Bob (B) and Sam (S). Sam can't remember where he met Bob. Fill in the blanks with a tag question.

🔊
CD 2, TR 30

B: Hi, Sam.

S: Uh, hi . . .

B: You don't remember me, _____do you?_____
(example)

S: You look familiar, but I can't remember your name. We were in the

same chemistry class last semester, _____
_(1)_

B: No.

S: Then we probably met in math class, _____
_(2)_

B: Wrong again. I'm Meg Wilson's brother.

S: Now I remember you. Meg introduced us at a party last summer,

_____? And your name is Bob, _____
_(3)_   _(4)_

[1]An *acquaintance* is a person you don't know well.

B: That's right.

S: How are you, Bob? You graduated last year, _____
(5)

B: Yes. And I've got a good job now.

S: You majored in computers, _____
(6)

B: Yes. But I decided to go into real estate.

S: And how's your sister Meg? I never see her anymore. She moved back

to California, _____
(7)

B: No. She's still here. But she's married now, and she's very busy.

S: Who did she marry?

B: Don Tripton. You met him, _____
(8)

S: Yes, I think so. Say hello to Meg when you see her. It was great

seeing you again, Bob.

EXERCISE 12 **A mother (M) is talking to her daughter (D). Fill in the blanks with a tag question.**

M: You didn't get your scholarship, <u>did you?</u>
(example)

D: How did you know?

M: Well, you look very disappointed. You can apply again next

year, _____?
(1)

D: Yes. But what will I do this year?

M: There are government loans, _____?
(2)

D: Yes.

M: And you don't have to pay them back until you graduate, _____?
(3)

D: No.

M: And your professors will give you letters of recommendation,

_____?
(4)

D: I'm sure they will.

M: So don't worry. Just try to get a loan, and you can apply again next

year for a scholarship.

13.5 Answering a Tag Question

STATEMENT WITH TAG QUESTION	SHORT ANSWER	EXPLANATION
Meg and Don are married now, **aren't they?** They work hard, **don't they?**	**Yes,** they are. **Yes,** they do.	When we use a negative tag, we expect the answer to be *yes*.
They don't have much free time, **do they?** Meg doesn't like to go fishing, **does she?**	**No,** they don't. **No,** she doesn't.	When we use an affirmative tag, we expect the answer to be *no*.
Don: You aren't happy, **are you?** *Meg:* You like to go to movies, **don't you?**	*Meg:* **Yes,** I am. I love you. *Don:* **No,** I don't. I like to stay home and watch TV.	Answering *yes* to an affirmative tag shows disagreement. Answering *no* to a negative tag shows disagreement.

EXERCISE 13 **Complete the answer in the left column. Then check the meaning of the answer in the right column. You may work with a partner.**

A: You don't have a car, do you? **B:** Yes, _____I do._____ *(example)*	✔ Person B has a car. Person B doesn't have a car.
A: You aren't married, are you? **B:** No, _____ *(1)*	Person B is married. Person B isn't married.
A: You don't like this city, do you? **B:** No, _____ *(2)*	Person B likes this city. Person B doesn't like this city.
A: You don't have a watch, do you? **B:** Yes, _____ *(3)*	Person B has a watch. Person B doesn't have a watch.
A: You don't speak Russian, do you? **B:** No, _____ *(4)*	Person B speaks Russian. Person B doesn't speak Russian.
A: You can drive, can't you? **B:** No, _____ *(5)*	Person B can drive. Person B can't drive.
A: The U.S. is the biggest country in the world, isn't it? **B:** No, _____ *(6)*	Person B agrees with the statement. Person B doesn't agree with the statement.
A: You work on Saturday, don't you? **B:** Yes, _____ *(7)*	Person B works on Saturday. Person B doesn't work on Saturday.

EXERCISE 14 Read a statement to another student and add a tag question. The other student will tell you if this information is correct or not.

EXAMPLES   You speak Polish, _____*don't you?*_____
No, I don't. I speak Ukrainian.

You aren't from Poland, _____*are you?*_____
No, I'm not. I'm from Ukraine.

You came to the U.S. two years ago, _____*didn't you?*_____
Yes, I did.

1. You're not married, _____
2. You have a cell phone, _____
3. You didn't study English in elementary school, _____
4. You have the textbook, _____
5. You don't live alone, _____
6. You'll take another English course next semester, _____
7. You won't graduate this year, _____
8. You took the last test, _____
9. You have to work on Saturday, _____
10. The teacher doesn't speak your language, _____
11. You can drive, _____
12. This class isn't too hard for you, _____
13. There was a test last Friday, _____
14. You don't speak German, _____
15. I'm asking you a lot of personal questions, _____

EXERCISE 15 Fill in the blanks with a tag question and an answer that tells if the information is true or not.

A: You come from Russia, _____*don't you?*_____
(example)

B: _____. I come from Ukraine.
(1)

A: They speak Polish in Ukraine, _____
(2)

B: _____. They speak Ukrainian and Russian.
(3)

A: Ukraine isn't part of Russia, _____
(4)

B: _____. Ukraine and Russia are different. They were
(5)
both part of the former Soviet Union.

A: You come from a big city, _____
(6)

(continued)

B: _____. I come from Kiev. It's the capital of Ukraine.
      (7)
It's very big.

A: Your parents aren't here, _____
                                       (8)

B: _____. We came together two years ago. I live with them.
      (9)

A: You studied English in your country, _____
                                               (10)

B: _____. I studied only Russian and German. I never
      (11)
studied English there.

A: You're not going to go back to live in your country, _____
                                                          (12)

B: _____. I'm an immigrant here. I plan to become an
      (13)
American citizen.

EXERCISE 16   **This is a conversation between Meg (M) and her best friend, Lydia (L). Fill in the blanks with tag questions and answers.**

🔊

CD 2, TR 31

M: Hello?

L: Hi, Meg. This is Lydia.

M: Oh, hi, Lydia.

L: Can you talk? I hear the TV in the background. Don's home, _isn't he?_
                                                                 (example)

M: _____, he _____. He's watching TV, as usual.
      (1)   (2)

L: Are you busy?

M: I'm always busy, _____?
                   (3)

L: Well, _____, you _____.
           (4)   (5)

M: But I can make some time for you. What's up?

L: I have a new boyfriend. His name is Peter.

M: But you're dating Michael, _____?
                               (6)

L: _____. Not anymore. We broke up a month ago.
      (7)
The last time I talked to you was over a month ago, _____?
                                              (8)

M: Over a month ago? That's terrible. We used to talk every day.

L: Now that you're married, you don't have much free time anymore,

_____?
 (9)

M: _____, I _____. I almost never have time for myself anymore.
(10)　　　　　(11)
Or for my friends. Tell me about your new boyfriend.

L: We have so much in common. We both like sports, the same kind of music, the same kind of food. . . . If we get married, we'll have the rest of our lives to have fun together.

M: You're not thinking of getting married, _____?
(12)

L: _____. Not yet. I'm just dreaming.
(13)

M: Dating is so much fun, _____?
(14)

L: _____, it _____. But marriage isn't, _____?
(15)　　　　　(16)　　　　　　　　　　　(17)

M: "Fun" is not a word that describes marriage.

L: But you had a lot of fun with Don before you got married, _____?
(18)

M: _____, we _____. But things changed after the wedding.
(19)　　　　　(20)
Now all we do together is laundry, shopping, and cleaning.

L: That doesn't sound very interesting. But there are good things about being married, _____?
(21)

M: Of course. Don's my best friend. We help each other with all our problems.

L: Before you got married, I was your best friend, _____?
(22)
But now I almost never see you.

M: You're right, Lydia. I'll try harder to call you more often.

Summary of Lesson 13

1. Use auxiliary verbs to avoid repetition of the same verb phrase.

AFFIRMATIVE	AND	SHORTENED AFFIRMATIVE + *TOO*
Meg has a job,	and	Don does too.
Meg is busy,	and	Don is too.

NEGATIVE	AND	SHORTENED NEGATIVE + *EITHER*
Meg doesn't work on Saturdays,	and	Don doesn't either.
Meg can't find free time,	and	Don can't either.

AFFIRMATIVE	BUT	SHORTENED NEGATIVE
Meg finished college,	but	Don didn't.
Don likes fishing,	but	Meg doesn't.

NEGATIVE	BUT	SHORTENED AFFIRMATIVE
Don doesn't like movies,	but	Meg does.
Don didn't want a big wedding,	but	Meg did.

2. Use auxiliary verbs in tag questions.

AFFIRMATIVE	NEGATIVE TAG
You're busy now,	aren't you?
We have a hard life,	don't we?
There are a lot of things to do,	aren't there?

NEGATIVE	AFFIRMATIVE TAG
You don't like fishing,	do you?
I can't go fishing alone,	can I?
We never have time together,	do we?

Editing Advice

1. Don't omit the auxiliary from a shortened sentence with *too* or *either*.

   My brother has a new house, and I ^do^ too.

   John didn't take the test, and I ^didn't^ either.

2. Don't confuse *too* and *either*.

   Jack doesn't speak French, and his wife doesn't ~~too~~ ^either^.

3. If half your sentence is negative and half is affirmative, the connecting word is *but*, not *and*.

   He doesn't speak French, ~~and~~ ^but^ his wife does.

4. Be careful to answer a tag question correctly.

   New York isn't the capital of the U.S., is it? ~~Yes~~ ^No^, it isn't.

5. Use a pronoun (or *there*) in the tag question.

   That's your hat, isn't ~~that~~ ^it^?

   There's some milk in the refrigerator, isn't ~~it~~ ^there^?

6. Be careful to use the correct auxiliary verb and the correct tense.

   Her sister didn't go to the party, ~~does~~ ^did^ she?

   She won't go back to her country, ~~does~~ ^will^ she?

Editing Quiz

Don is calling Meg on her cell phone. Some of the shaded words and phrases have mistakes. Find the mistakes and correct them. If the shaded words are correct, write _C_.

D: Hi, Meg.

M: Hi, Don. What's up?

D: Some friends are coming over this afternoon to watch the football game.
I told you, _didn't I?_ You remember, ~~do you?~~
$\quad$ *C* $\qquad\qquad$ *don't you*
$\quad$ *(example)* $\qquad\qquad$ *(example)*

M: Of course I am.
$\quad\quad\;$ *(1)*

D: Can you pick up some things before you come home?

M: I think we have enough food at home. We have snacks, aren't we?
$\qquad\qquad\qquad\qquad\qquad\qquad\qquad\qquad\qquad\quad$ *(2)*

D: Yes, we do. But we don't have any cheese and crackers, don't we?
$\quad\;\;$ *(3)* $\qquad\qquad\qquad\qquad\qquad\qquad\qquad\qquad\qquad$ *(4)*

M: Yes, we don't. I'll get some. Who's coming tonight?
$\quad\;$ *(5)*

D: Sam called today. He's coming, but Nancy doesn't.
$\qquad\qquad\qquad\qquad\qquad\qquad\qquad\qquad$ *(6)*

M: Why not?

D: They can't find a babysitter for their daughter, Pam.

M: Tell them to bring their daughter. Pam's eight and Sofie does, too.
$\qquad\qquad\qquad\qquad\qquad\qquad\qquad\qquad\qquad\qquad$ *(7)*

$\quad\;\;$ I'm sure they can find something to do together.

D: But Sofie has a violin lesson this afternoon, doesn't she?
$\qquad\qquad\qquad\qquad\qquad\qquad\qquad\qquad\quad$ *(8)*

M: That's tomorrow, not today. I sure hope Sam's wife is coming. We can

$\quad\;\;$ watch a movie while you guys watch football. She doesn't like football,

$\quad\;\;$ and I too.
$\qquad$ *(9)*

D: How do you know? You never even watch football.

M: Don't you remember? I tried to watch football with you guys last time, and

$\quad\;\;$ Nancy was too, but we just saw a bunch of guys falling on top of each other.
$\qquad\qquad$ *(10)*

D: You can understand it if you try, can't you?
$\qquad\qquad\qquad\qquad\qquad\qquad\quad$ *(11)*

M: If I try. But the point is that I don't want to try.

Lesson 13 Test/Review

PART **1** This is a conversation between two students who are meeting for the first time. Fill in the blanks with an auxiliary verb to complete this conversation. Use *either* or *too* when necessary.

C: Hi. My name is Carlos. I'm a new student.

E: I _____am too_____. My name is Elena.
(example)

C: I come from Mexico.

E: Oh, really? I _____. I come from a small town in the
_(1)_
northern part of Mexico.

C: I come from Mexico City. I love big cities.

E: I _____. I prefer small towns.
_(2)_

C: How do you like living here in Los Angeles?

E: I don't like it much, but my sister _____. She has a
_(3)_
good job, but I _____. I miss my job back home.
_(4)_

C: I love it here, and my family _____. The climate is
_(5)_
similar to the climate of Mexico City.

E: What about the air quality? Mexico City doesn't have clean air, and
Los Angeles _____, so you probably feel right at home.
_(6)_

C: Ha! You're right about the air quality, but there are many nice things
about Los Angeles. Would you want to get a cup of coffee and continue
this conversation? I don't have any more classes today.

E: Yes, I _____, but I have to go home now. I enjoyed
_(7)_
our talk.

C: I _____. Maybe we can continue it some other time.
_(8)_
Well, see you in class tomorrow.

PART 2 In this conversation, a new student is trying to find out information about the school and class. Add a tag question.

A: There's a parking lot at the school, _____isn't there?_____
(example)

B: Yes. It's east of the building.

A: The teacher's American, _____
(1)

B: Yes, she is.

A: She doesn't give hard tests, _____
(2)

B: Not too easy, not too hard.

A: We'll have a day off for Christmas, _____
(3)

B: We'll have a whole week off.

A: We have to write compositions, _____
(4)

B: A few.

A: And we can't use a dictionary when we write a composition,

_____
(5)

B: Who told you that? Of course we can. You're very nervous about

school, _____
(6)

A: Yes, I am. It isn't easy to learn a new language, _____
(7)

B: No.

A: And I should ask questions about things I want to know,

_____
(8)

B: Yes, of course. You don't have any more questions, _____
(9)

A: No.

B: Well, I'll see you in the next class. Bye.

Expansion

Classroom
Activities

1 Complete each statement. Then find a partner and compare yourself to your partner by using an auxiliary verb.

EXAMPLES
A: I speak ___Chinese___.

B: I do too. OR I don't.

A: I don't speak ___Spanish___.

B: I don't either. OR I do.

   a. I speak _____.

   b. I don't speak _____.

   c. I can _____.

   d. I have _____.

   e. I don't have _____.

   f. I'm _____.

   g. I usually drink _____ every day.

   h. I'm going to _____ next week.

   i. I come from _____.

   j. I'm wearing _____ today.

   k. I bought _____ last week.

   l. I went _____ last week.

   m. I don't like _____.

   n. I brought _____ to the U.S.

   o. I don't like to eat _____.

   p. I can't _____ very well.

   q. I should _____ more.

❷ The teacher will read each statement. If the statement is true for you, stand up. Students will take turns making statements about any two classmates.

EXAMPLE   Teacher: Stand up if you drank coffee this morning.
           Student: I drank coffee this morning, and Tom did too.
                     Mario didn't drink coffee this morning, and Sofia didn't either.

Stand up if you . . .

- have more than five sisters and brothers
- walked to class today
- will graduate in the next two years
- are wearing running shoes
- have a photo of a family member in your pocket or bag
- want to review this lesson
- went to a movie last week
- can't swim
- plan to buy a car soon
- are tired now
- aren't married
- ate pizza today
- speak Polish
- don't like this game
- can understand American TV
- didn't take the last test

❸ Find a partner. Tell your partner some things that you think you know about him or her and about his or her native culture or country. Your partner will tell you if you are right or wrong.

EXAMPLES   The capital of your country is New Delhi, isn't it?
            Hindus don't eat beef, do they?
            You're studying engineering, aren't you?

❹ Tell the teacher what you think you know about the U.S. or Americans. You may work with a partner. The teacher will tell you if you're right or wrong.

EXAMPLES   Most Americans don't speak a foreign language, do they?
            Alaska is the largest state, isn't it?

❶ Do you think young people have realistic expectations of marriage?

❷ Some people say that opposites attract. Do you think that two people who are opposites in many ways can have a good marriage?

❸ What do you think are the ingredients of a good marriage?

Write

About It **Choose two sports, countries, people, or stores and write sentences comparing them.**

My Mother and My Father

My mother and my father have some things in common and some big differences too. My mother is the oldest of five children, and my father is too. So they both had a lot of responsibilities growing up. My father finished high school, but my mother didn't. My mother didn't have the opportunity. But they are both very intelligent . . .

For more practice using grammar in context, please visit our Web site.

Grammar
Verb Review

Context
Washington Interns

The Supreme Court, Washington, D.C.

Washington Interns

Before You Read

1. How can a college student get work experience?

2. What do most college students do during their summer break?

CD 2, TR 32

Read the information and e-mail that follows it. Pay special attention to verb tenses.

Some college students **want to find** interesting work and **gain** valuable experience over the summer. One way **is to work** as an intern in Washington, D.C. Interns **don't** get paid; the reward **comes** from the experience and knowledge they **gain**. Interns **learn** about the U.S. government and politics.

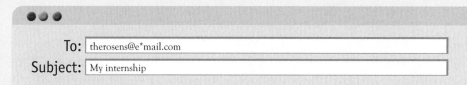

To: therosens@e*mail.com

Subject: My internship

Dear Mom and Dad,

I **can't** believe it! I**'m working** at the Supreme Court now. I**'m gaining** so much experience here. When I **go** to law school next year, I**'ll have** a much greater understanding of American law. And when I **apply** for a job, this internship **will look** really good on my résumé[1].

At first, I **felt** a little lost and lonely because I **didn't know** anyone. But that soon **changed**. Through my classes and job, I **meet** new and interesting people every day.

Besides my work, I**'m taking** classes at Georgetown University. My professors **are** great! I**'m learning** so much. My knowledge about American law **is increasing** greatly.

I **have** an interesting roommate, too. She**'s** from California. Her name **is** Nicole. She**'s working** at the Department of Education. She**'s planning** to become a teacher. We **have** a small but comfortable apartment. We **have to shop** and **make** our own meals. So besides learning about the Supreme Court, I**'m learning** how to cook. I**'m becoming** much more responsible. **Are** you surprised?

---

[1]A *résumé* is a document that lists job experience and education. A person looking for a job usually writes a résumé.

Whenever Nicole and I **have** free time, we **go** to see the interesting places in Washington. But we rarely **have** free time because of our jobs and our classes. We **might go** to the art museum this weekend if we **have** enough time.

There **is** one thing I **don't like**: I **have to wear** formal clothes every day. I **can't wear** jeans at my job. We **must look** very professional for work. I **didn't have** the right kind of clothes when I **arrived**, so I **went** shopping and **spent** about $500 on new clothes. I **hope** you **don't mind**. I **put** the charges on your credit card. As you **know**, I'm **not making** any money here. But **don't worry**. I promise I won't **spend** any more money on clothes.

When I **get** home, I'll **tell** you much more about my experience this summer. I **know** I **should write** more often, but I just **don't have** the time.

Love,
Lena

FAQs (Frequently Asked Questions) About Washington Internships

- How **does** a student **get** an internship?

  Students **should contact** their senators or representatives to apply for an internship.

- What kind of work **do** interns **do**?

  They **work** in research, **help** plan events, **manage** databases, and **write** for newsletters.

- Where **do** they **live**?

  They **live** in on-campus apartments at nearby universities.

- **Do** they **have to take** classes?

  Yes, they **do**. And they **must participate** in other activities.

- How busy **is** their schedule?

  It **is** very busy. Interns **learn** about education, politics, and government.

- **Will** they **receive** college credit for the internship?

  Yes. They **will receive** six hours of college credit.

14.1 Verbs

Simple Present Tense

EXAMPLES	USES
Washington **is** the capital of the U.S. Some students **want** summer jobs. Some interns in Washington **take** classes at Georgetown University.	Facts
Interns students **have** vacation in the summer. Many American students **wear** jeans to class.	Customs and habits
Interns **take** classes every day. When they **have** free time, they **go** to interesting places.	Regular activities
I **have** a great roommate now. I **like** my job now.	With nonaction verbs
When I **get** home, I'll tell you more.	In a future time clause
If you **become** an intern in Washington, you will get valuable experience.	In a future *if* clause
My roommate **is** from California. She **comes** from San Diego.	With place of origin

Present Continuous Tense

EXAMPLES	EXPLANATION
Lena **is writing** a letter to her parents now.	Actions that are happening now
Lena **is learning** how to cook. She **isn't making** any money this summer.	Actions that are happening in a present time period

Future Tense

EXAMPLES	EXPLANATION
They **are going to return** to college in the fall. Nicole **is going to become** a teacher.	Plans for the future (use *be going to*)
I **will** never **forget** this experience. This experience **is going to help** me in my future.	Predictions (use *will* or *be going to*)
I**'ll write** more later.	Promises (use *will*)

Simple Past Tense

EXAMPLES	EXPLANATION
I **went** shopping because I **needed** clothes. I **spent** $500 on clothes. I **used** your credit card.	Actions that happened at a specific time in the past

Be

EXAMPLES	EXPLANATION
Washington, D.C., **is** the capital of the U.S.	To classify or define the subject
Washington **is** interesting.	To describe the subject
The Supreme Court **is** in Washington.	To tell the location of the subject
Nicole **is** from San Diego.	With a place of origin
She **was born** in California.	With *born*
There **are** many government buildings in Washington.	With *there*

Modals

EXAMPLES	EXPLANATION
Lena **can** wear jeans to class. Lena **can** study at night.	Permission Ability
She **should** write to her parents more often. If you want more information about internships, you **should** write to your senator.	Advisability
She **must** look professional in her job. Interns **must** participate in activities.	Necessity
They **might** go to the art museum this weekend. Lena **may** visit Nicole in California next year.	Possibility

Infinitives

EXAMPLES	EXPLANATION
Lena wants **to have** an internship. It's important **to be** on time.	An infinitive doesn't show tense.

Imperatives

EXAMPLES	EXPLANATION
Write to me. **Don't worry** about me.	An imperative uses the base form. A negative imperative uses *don't* + base form.

EXERCISE **1** **Without looking at the reading on pages 398–399, fill in the blanks with the correct tense or form of the verb in parentheses ( ). Some answers may vary.**

I can't __believe__ it! I _____ at the Supreme Court now. I _____
    (example: believe)   *(1 work)*   *(2 gain)*

so much experience here. When I _____ to law school next year,
                            (3 go)

I _____ a much greater understanding of American law. And when
    (4 have)

I _____ for a job, this internship _____ really good on my résumé.
    (5 apply)   *(6 look)*

    At first, I _____ a little lost and lonely because I _____
             (7 feel)   *(8 not/know)*

anyone. But that soon _____. Through my classes and job,
            (9 change)

I _____ new and interesting people every day.
    (10 meet)

    Besides my work, I _____ classes at Georgetown University.
             (11 take)

My professors _____ great! I _____ so much. My knowledge
        (12 be)   *(13 learn)*

about American law _____ rapidly.
         (14 increase)

    I _____ an interesting roommate, too. She _____ from
      (15 have)   *(16 be)*

California. Her name is Nicole. She _____ at the Department of
               (17 work)

Education. She's planning to _____ a teacher. We _____ a small
          (18 become)   *(19 have)*

but comfortable apartment. We have to _____ and _____ our
             (20 shop)   *(21 make)*

own meals. So besides learning about the Supreme Court, I _____
                          (22 learn)

how to cook. I _____ much more responsible. Are you surprised?
      (23 become)

    Whenever Nicole and I _____ free time, we _____ to see
              (24 have)   *(25 go)*

the interesting places in Washington. But we rarely _____ free time
                      (26 have)

because of our jobs and our classes. We might _____ to the art
                  (27 go)

museum this weekend if we _____ enough time.
           (28 have)

    There is one thing I don't like: I have to wear formal clothes every day.

I can't _____ blue jeans at my job. We must _____ very
    (29 wear)   *(30 look)*

---

professional for our jobs. I _____ the right kind of clothes when I
(31 not/have)

_____, so I _____ shopping and _____ about $500 on
(32 arrive)   (33 go)   (34 spend)

new clothes. I hope you _____. I _____ the charges on your
(35 not/mind)   (36 put)

credit card. As you _____, I _____ any money here. But don't
(37 know)   (38 not/make)

_____. I promise I _____ any more money on clothes.
(39 worry)   (40 not/spend)

When I _____ home, I _____ you much more about my
(41 get)   (42 tell)

experience this summer. I _____ I should _____ more often,
(43 know)   (44 write)

but I just _____ the time.
(45 not/have)

Love,

Lena

14.2 Statements and Questions

Simple Present Tense

BASE FORM	-S FORM
Interns **wear** formal clothes.	Lena **lives** with a roommate.
They **don't wear** jeans.	She **doesn't live** alone.
Do they **wear** formal clothes to class?	**Does** she **live** in a dorm?
No, they **don't**.	No, she **doesn't**.
What **do** they **wear** to class?	Where **does** she **live**?
Why **don't** they **wear** jeans to work?	Why **doesn't** she **live** in a dorm?
How many students **wear** jeans?	Who **lives** in a dorm?

Present Continuous Tense

IS + VERB + ING	ARE + VERB + ING
Nicole **is planning** to become a teacher.	They **are taking** classes.
Lena **isn't planning** to become a teacher.	They **aren't taking** English classes.
Is she **planning** to teach in California?	**Are** they **taking** classes at Georgetown?
No, she **isn't**.	Yes, they **are**.
Where **is** she **planning** to teach?	What kind of classes **are** they **taking**?
Why **isn't** she **planning** to teach in California?	Why **aren't** they **taking** English classes?
Who **is planning** to teach in California?	How many students **are taking** classes?

Future Tense

WILL	BE GOING TO
They **will go** home at the end of the summer.	Lena **is going to buy** books.
They **won't go** on vacation.	She **isn't going to buy** more clothes.
Will they **go** back to college?	**Is** she **going to buy** a computer?
Yes, they **will**.	No, she **isn't**.
When **will** they **go** back to college?	What **is** she **going to buy**?
Why **won't** they **go** on vacation?	Why **isn't** she **going to buy** a computer?
Who **will go** back to college?	Who **is going to buy** a computer?

Simple Past Tense

REGULAR VERB	IRREGULAR VERB
She **used** her parents' credit card.	She **bought** new clothes.
She **didn't use** cash.	She **didn't buy** jeans.
Did she **use** their card a lot?	**Did** she **buy** formal clothes?
No, she **didn't**.	Yes, she **did**.
Why **did** she **use** their card?	Why **did** she **buy** formal clothes?
Why **didn't** she **use** cash?	Why **didn't** she **buy** jeans?
Who **used** the card?	Who **bought** formal clothes?

Be

PRESENT	PAST
They **are** in Washington, D.C.	Lena **was** lost at first.
They **aren't** at college.	She **wasn't** happy.
Are they in California?	**Was** she alone?
No, they **aren't**.	Yes, she **was**.
Why **are** they in Washington?	Why **was** she alone?
Why **aren't** they in California?	Why **wasn't** she happy?
Who **is** in California?	Who **was** alone?

Modals

CAN	SHOULD
She **can** wear jeans to class.	She **should** study every day.
She **can't** wear jeans to work.	She **shouldn't** go to parties every day.
Can she wear jeans at college?	**Should** she study history?
Yes, she **can**.	Yes, she **should**.
What **can** she wear?	What else **should** she study?
Why **can't** she wear jeans to work?	Why **shouldn't** she go to parties?
Who **can** wear jeans?	Who **should** study?

EXERCISE 2   Fill in the blanks with the negative form of the underlined verb.

EXAMPLE   Lena <u>is</u> in Washington this summer. She _____isn't_____ at home.

1. She's <u>getting</u> experience. She _____ money for her work.
2. She <u>bought</u> new clothes. She _____ jeans.
3. She <u>writes</u> a lot for her classes. She _____ a lot of letters.
4. She'll <u>finish</u> college next year. She _____ college this summer.
5. She's <u>going to return</u> to college in the fall. She _____ to Washington next summer.
6. She <u>can wear</u> jeans to class. She _____ jeans to work.
7. She <u>must look</u> professional at work. She _____ informal at work.

EXERCISE 3   Fill in the blanks with a question about interns, based on the responses that follow.

EXAMPLES   Do interns get money for their work? _____

No, they don't. They get experience, not money.

Will the internship end in September? _____

No, it won't. The internship will end in August.

1. _____

Yes, they do. They have to take classes.

2. _____

No, they don't live in dorms. They live in apartments.

3. _____

Yes, they are. They are very busy with classes, work, and activities.

4. _____

Yes, they will. They will receive six hours of college credit.

5. _____

No, she can't. Lena can't wear jeans to work.

6. _____

Yes, she is. She's learning how to cook.

7. _____

No, she didn't. She didn't know anyone when she arrived in Washington.

8. _____

Yes, she does. She works at the Supreme Court.

9. _____

Yes, she did. She bought some new clothes.

EXERCISE **4** **Write a question with the *wh-* words given. Use the same tense. An answer is not necessary.**

EXAMPLE Lena is calling her mother. Why _is she calling her mother?_

1. Lena will go home soon. When _____

   _____

2. Her mother doesn't remember the roommate's name. Why _____

   _____

3. Lena can't go home for a weekend. Why _____

   _____

4. Lena doesn't have much money. How much money _____

   _____

5. Lena is learning a lot this summer. What _____

   _____

6. She doesn't have time to write letters. Why _____

   _____

7. Lena went to Virginia last weekend. With whom _____

   _____

8. Nicole comes from a different state. Where _____

   _____ from?

9. Lena didn't cook before this summer. Why _____

   _____

10. Someone went to Virginia. Who _____

    _____

11. The internship will help Lena in the future. How _____

    _____

12. She is working at a branch of the government. At which branch

    _____

13. Lena felt lonely at first. Why _____

    _____

14. She can't wear jeans to work. Why _____

_____

15. She must take classes. How many classes _____

_____

16. She is going to get college credits for her internship. How many credits

_____

17. Lena should call her parents more often. How often _____

_____

EXERCISE **5** **Lena (L) is talking to her mother (M) on the phone. She is calling from Washington, D.C. Fill in the blanks with the correct form of the words in parentheses ( ).**

CD 2, TR 33

M: Hello?

L: Hi, Mom. This is Lena.

M: Hi, Lena. I __'m_____ happy to _____
            (example: be)   *(1 hear)*

your voice. You _____. You just send short text messages.
                        (2 never/call)

L: I'm sorry, Mom. I _____ much time.
                            (3 not/have)

M: Why _____ time?
              (4 you/not/have)

L: I have to work, go to classes, and participate in activities all day.

Last weekend we _____ to Virginia.
                          (5 go)

M: Who _____?
              (6 drive)

L: No one. We _____ the Metro. Public transportation is
                      (7 use)

really good here.

M: _____ enough to eat this summer? Who
          (8 you/get)

_____ for you?
      (9 cook)

L: I _____ to _____ this summer.
          (10 learn)   *(11 cook)*

_____ surprised?
      (12 be/you)

M: Yes, I am. When you were home, you never _____.
                                                          (13 cook)

You _____ it.
          (14 hate)

L: Not anymore. Nicole and I often _____ and
                                              (15 cook)

_____ our friends for dinner on the weekends.
      (16 invite)

(continued)

M: Who _____ Nicole?
(17 be)

L: I _____ you in my last e-mail. She's my roommate.
(18 tell)

_____?
(19 you/not/remember)

M: Yes, of course. Now I _____. How could I forget?
(20 remember)

L: She's the same age as I am—19. She _____ from
(21 come)

California.

M: How _____? _____ it?
(22 be/your job) (23 you/like)

L: It's great! I _____ so much this summer.
(24 learn)

M: _____ you in the future?
(25 this internship/help)

L: Yes, it will. It will be great on my résumé.

M: _____ enough money?
(26 you/have)

L: No, I don't. I _____ most of the money you
(27 spend)

_____ me when I got here.
(28 give)

M: You _____ my credit card. But don't spend money on
(29 can/use)

foolish things.

L: I won't.

M: I _____ you. _____ home for a
(30 miss) (31 you/can/come)

weekend? We _____ for your ticket.
(32 pay)

L: I can't, Mom. We _____ activities on weekends, too.
(33 have)

M: _____ again next week?
(34 you/call)

L: If I _____ time, I _____. But I
(35 have) (36 call)

_____ so little free time.
(37 have)

M: I'm sure you have enough time for a ten-minute phone call to your mother.

L: You're right. I _____ you again next week. Give my
(38 call)

love to Dad.

M: I will.

Editing Advice

1. Use the correct word order for questions.

   your brother work
   Where does ~~work your brother~~?

   can't you
   Why ~~you can't~~ find a job?

   is your brother
   How old ~~your brother is~~?

2. Don't forget to use *do*, *does*, or *did* in a question.

   does your father live
   Where ~~lives your father~~?

   did   *give*
   When the teacher ~~gave~~ a test?
        ^

3. Don't use *be* with a simple present-tense or past-tense verb.

   I ~~am~~ eat breakfast every morning.

   saw
   Yesterday, he ~~was see~~ a good movie.

4. Use the base form after *do*, *does*, and *did*.

   go
   I didn't ~~went~~ to the party.

   buy
   Did you ~~bought~~ a new car?

5. For the simple present tense, use the *-s* form when the subject is
   he, *she*, *it*, or a singular noun. Use the base form in all other cases.

   s
   Lisa never drink coffee in the morning.
             ^

   My friends usually visit~~s~~ me on Saturday.

6. Use the correct past form for irregular verbs.

   left
   We ~~leaved~~ the party early.

   fell
   He ~~felt~~ down on the ice.

7. Use the base form after *to*.

   drive
   I wanted to ~~drove~~ to New York.

   He likes to eat~~s~~ popcorn.

8. Use the base form after a modal.

study
She should ~~studies~~ more.

We must ~~to~~ obey the law.

I can't help~~ing~~ you now.

9. Connect two verbs with *to* (unless one is a modal).

to
I forgot ˰ do the homework.

to
She needs ˰ find a job.

10. Don't use the present continuous tense with nonaction verbs.

I ~~am~~ know~~ing~~ the answer now.

s
He ~~is~~ hear~~ing~~ the noise in the next room.

11. Don't use *be* before a simple future verb.

The doctor will ~~be~~ see you at 3 P.M.

12. Use the correct form of *be*.

were
They ~~was~~ late to the meeting.

are
You ~~is~~ always on time.

13. Use the correct negative form.

don't
They ~~not~~ know the answer.

don't
You ~~doesn't~~ need a pen.

14. Don't forget to include a form of *be* in a present continuous sentence.

is
She ˰ washing the dishes now.

am
I ˰ studying now.

15. Don't use the future tense in a time clause or an *if* clause. Use the simple present tense.

When I ~~will~~ graduate, I will get a job.

are
You will fail the course if you ~~will be~~ absent more than five times.

16. Do not use the *-ing* form for the simple present tense.

I drink~~ing~~ coffee every morning.

17. Do not forget the *-d* in *used to*.

I use ^d^ to live in Mexico.

18. Don't forget *to* after impersonal expressions like: *it's necessary, it's impossible, it's important.*

It's important ^to^ learn English.

Editing Quiz

Some of the shaded words and phrases have mistakes. Find the mistakes and correct them. If the shaded words are correct, write *C*.

A: ^C^ Does your family ~~lives~~ ^live^ in the U.S.?
(example)   *(example)*

B: Yes, but I doesn't live with them.
(1)

A: Why you don't live with them?
(2)

B: They live in Lexington. I use to live with them there, but I finded a job
(3)   *(4)*   *(5)*

here, so I was moved.
(6)

A: When you moved here?
(7)

B: Three years ago. I don't like to be so far from them, but I'm have no
(8)   *(9)*

choice. I didn't realized how much I would miss them. I lonely at
(10)   *(11)*

times, but my mom call me almost every day, so that helps.
(12)   *(13)*

A: I'm know how you feel. When I left home for the first time, it was very
(14)   *(15)*   *(16)*

hard for me.

B: Where your family lives?
(17)

A: They back in my country. They want visit me very much. When I
    (18)   (19)

will save enough money, I'm going to send them a plane ticket. I having
(20)   (21)   (22)

two jobs now, so soon I'll be have enough money for their trip.
                       (23)

A: How long they'll stay here?
              (24)

B: My mom can to stay for six months. She's retired. But my dad still working,
           (25)   (26)

so he can stay only for two weeks.
     (27)

A: How often do you talk to your parents?
              (28)

B: It's expensive talk by phone, so we usually send e-mail.
           (29)   (30)

A: How much costs a phone card?
           (31)

B: A phone card cost about $10, but we can only talk for about 30 minutes.
              (32)   (33)

A: Wow. That's expensive.

B: I prefer to saving my money for their trip.
       (34)

Lesson 14 Test/Review

PART 1 Fill in the blanks with the correct tense or form of the words in parentheses ( ).

I _____*come*_____ from India. I _____ to the
      (example: come)   (1 decide/move)

U.S. ten months ago. It was difficult _____ my friends
                                        (2 leave)

and family, but I _____ to the U.S. and have more
                   (3 want/come)

opportunities.

When I _____ in India, I was a draftsman. When
         (4 live)

I _____ to the U.S. in July, I _____
    (5 come)   (6 not/find)

a job at first because my English wasn't good enough. Last September,

I _____ a job in a restaurant. I don't like my job at all.
    (7 find)

I _____ (8 want/find) a better job soon. I know I _____ (9 get) a better job when I _____ (10 speak) English better.

I _____ (11 save) my money now. When I _____ (12 have) enough money, I _____ (13 begin/take) engineering courses at the university. My parents _____ (14 be) proud of me when I _____ (15 graduate).

Right now I _____ (16 take) ESL courses at a college near my house. I _____ (17 study) English in India, but it was different from American English. When I listen to Americans at my job or on TV, I _____ (18 can/not/understand) a lot of things they say. Sometimes when I _____ (19 speak) with Americans at my job, they _____ (20 not/understand) me. They sometimes _____ (21 laugh) at my pronunciation. They aren't bad people, but they _____ (22 not/understand) that it is hard _____ (23 learn) another language and live in another country.

I usually _____ (24 stay) by myself at work. I _____ (25 know) I _____ (26 should/practice) more, but I'm very shy.

When I _____ (27 be) in India, I _____ (28 live) in a big house with my parents, sisters and brothers, and grandparents.

Now I _____ (29 have) a small apartment and live alone.

Sometimes I _____ (30 be) lonely. I would like _____ (31 get) married someday, but first I want _____ (32 earn) some money and _____ (33 save) for my future.

PART 2 Write the negative form of the underlined words.

EXAMPLE   He moved to the U.S. He _____ *didn't move* _____ to England.

1. He studied English in India. He _____ German.

2. He wants to work as an engineer. He _____ in a restaurant.

3. He <u>is going to study</u> engineering. He _____ art.

4. He <u>is taking</u> courses at a community college now. He _____ courses at a university.

5. He'<u>s saving</u> his money to get married. He _____ his money to go back to his country.

6. His coworkers <u>know</u> that he is a foreigner. They _____ how difficult his life is.

7. He <u>should</u> practice English with Americans. He _____ be shy.

8. He <u>can understand</u> some TV programs. He _____ all TV programs.

PART **3** | **Read each statement. Then write a *yes/no* question about the words in parentheses ( ). Write a short answer using the words in parentheses ( ).**

EXAMPLE | He studied English in India. (American English) (no)
Did he study American English? No, he didn't.
_____

1. He'll study engineering. (accounting) (no)

_____

2. Americans don't understand him. (Indians) (yes)

_____

3. He's studying English now. (American English) (yes)

_____

4. He lives in a small apartment. (with his family) (no)

_____

5. He can understand British English well. (American English) (no)

_____

6. It is hard to learn another language. (live in another country) (yes)

_____

7. He wants to get married. (next year) (no)

_____

8. He lived with his parents in India. (with his grandparents) (yes)

_____

PART **4**   **Read each statement. Then write a _wh-_ question with the word in parentheses ( ). An answer is not necessary.**

EXAMPLE   He left India. (why)
<u>Why did he leave India?</u>

1. He is saving his money. (why)

   _____

2. He is going to get married. (when)

   _____

3. Some people laugh at him. (who)

   _____

4. He is lonely. (why)

   _____

5. His parents aren't in the U.S. (why)

   _____

6. He didn't find a job at first. (why)

   _____

7. He will graduate from the university. (when)

   _____

8. He came to the U.S. alone. (why)

   _____

9. His coworkers don't understand his accent. (why)

   _____

10. He lived in a big house. (when)

   _____

Expansion

Classroom Activities

1 Interview a student from another country. Use the words below to ask and answer questions. Practice the simple present, the present continuous, the future, and the simple past tenses.

EXAMPLES you/from Asia

A: Are you from Asia?

B: Yes, I am. OR No, I'm not.

where/you/from

A: Where are you from?

B: I'm from Pakistan.

a. when/you/leave your country

b. how/you/come to the U.S.

c. you/come/to the U.S. alone

d. where/you/born

e. what language(s)/you speak

f. you/return to your country next year

g. you/have a job now

h. you/have a job in your country

i. how many brothers and sisters/you/have

j. your country/big

k. your country/have a lot of problems

l. you/live in an apartment in your hometown

m. you/study English in your country

n. what/you/study this semester

o. what/you/study next semester

p. you/like this class

q. the teacher/speak your language

r. this class/hard for you

s. who/your teacher last semester

t. who/your teacher next semester

❷ Write sentences in each category, if you can. Write one for the simple present, one for the present continuous, one for the future, and one for the simple past tense.

	Simple Present	Present Continuous	Future	Simple Past
Job	I work in a factory.	I'm looking for a new job.	Next week I'm going to have an interview.	In my country, I was a taxi driver.
School				
Family				
Weather				
Apartment				

Talk
About It

❶ People often say you can't get a job without experience, and you can't get experience without a job. What do you think this means?

❷ How do you think an internship will help someone like Lena Rosen, the Washington, D.C., intern?

Write

About It **For one of the categories in Classroom Activity 2, write a paragraph.**

EXAMPLE

My Job

I work as a taxi driver. I work six days a week.

I started this job two years ago when I came to the

U.S. It's an interesting job. I speak to my passengers.

This way, I'm learning a lot of English . . .

For more practice using grammar in context, please visit our Web site.

Appendices

Appendix A

The Verb *GET*

Get has many meanings. Here is a list of the most common ones:

- get something = receive
  I got a letter from my father.

- get + (to) place = arrive
  I got home at six.
  What time do you get to school?

- get + object + infinitive = persuade
  She got him to wash the dishes.

- get + past participle = become

get acquainted	get worried	get hurt
get engaged	get lost	get bored
get married	get accustomed to	get confused
get divorced	get used to	get scared
get tired	get dressed	

  They got married in 1989.

- get + adjective = become

get hungry	get sleepy
get rich	get dark
get nervous	get angry
get well	get old
get upset	get fat

  It gets dark at 6:30.

- get an illness = catch
  While she was traveling, she got malaria.

- get a joke or an idea = understand
  Everybody except Tom laughed at the joke. He didn't get it.
  The boss explained the project to us, but I didn't get it.

- get ahead = advance
  He works very hard because he wants to get ahead in his job.

(continued)

- get along (well) (with someone) = have a good relationship
    She doesn't get along with her mother-in-law.
    Do you and your roommate get along well?

- get around to something = find the time to do something
    I wanted to write my brother a letter yesterday, but I didn't get around to it.

- get away = escape
    The police chased the thief, but he got away.

- get away with something = escape punishment
    He cheated on his taxes and got away with it.

- get back = return
    He got back from his vacation last Saturday.

- get back at someone = get revenge
    My brother wants to get back at me for stealing his girlfriend.

- get back to someone = communicate with someone at a later time
    The boss can't talk to you today. Can she get back to you tomorrow?

- get by = have just enough but nothing more
    On her salary, she's just getting by. She can't afford a car or a vacation.

- get in trouble = be caught and punished for doing something wrong
    They got in trouble for cheating on the test.

- get in(to) = enter a car
    She got in the car and drove away quickly.

- get out (of) = leave a car
    When the taxi arrived at the theater, everyone got out.

- get on = seat yourself on a bicycle, motorcycle, horse
    She got on the motorcycle and left.

- get on = enter a train, bus, airplane
    She got on the bus and took a seat in the back.

- get off = leave a bicycle, motorcycle, horse, train, bus, airplane
    They will get off the train at the next stop.

- get out of something = escape responsibility
    My boss wants me to help him on Saturday, but I'm going to try to get out of it.

- get over something = recover from an illness or disappointment
    She has the flu this week. I hope she gets over it soon.

- get rid of someone or something = free oneself of someone or something undesirable
    My apartment has roaches, and I can't get rid of them.

- get through (to someone) = communicate, often by telephone
    She tried to explain the harm of eating fast food to her son, but she couldn't get through
        to him.
    I tried to call my mother many times, but her line was busy. I couldn't get through.

- get through (with something) = finish
    I can meet you after I get through with my homework.

- get together = meet with another person
    I'd like to see you again. When can we get together?

- get up = arise from bed
    He woke up at 6:00, but he didn't get up until 6:30.

Appendix B

MAKE and DO

Some expressions use *make*. Others use *do*.

Make	Do
make a date/an appointment	do (the) homework
make a plan	do an exercise
make a decision	do the dishes
make a telephone call	do the cleaning, laundry, ironing, washing, etc.
make a reservation	do the shopping
make a meal (breakfast, lunch, dinner)	do one's best
make a mistake	do a favor
make an effort	do the right/wrong thing
make an improvement	do a job
make a promise	do business
make money	What do you do for a living? (asks about a job)
make noise	How do you do? (said when you
make the bed	meet someone for the first time)

Appendix C

Question Formation

1. Statements and Related Questions with a Main Verb

Wh- Word	Do/Does/Did (n't)	Subject	Verb	Complement
When	does	She she	watches watch	TV. TV?
Where	do	My parents your parents	live live?	in Peru.
Who(m)	does	Your sister she	likes like?	someone.
Why	did	They they	left leave	early. early?
How many books	did	She she	found find?	some books.
What kind of car	did	He he	bought buy?	a car.
Why	didn't	She she	didn't go go	home. home?
Why	doesn't	He he	doesn't like like	tomatoes. tomatoes?

Subject	Verb (base form or -s form or past form)	Complement
Someone Who	needs needs	help. help?
Someone's car Whose car	has has	problems. problems?
Someone Who	took took	my pen. my pen?
One teacher Which teacher	speaks speaks	Spanish. Spanish?
Some men Which men	have have	a car. a car?
Some boys How many boys	saw saw	the movie. the movie?
Something What	happened. happened?	

2. Statements and Related Questions with the Verb *Be*

Wh- Word	*Be*	Subject	*Be*	Complement
Where	is	She she?	is	in California.
Why	were	They they	were	hungry. hungry?
Why	isn't	He he	isn't	tired. tired?
When	was	He he	was	born in England. born?
		One student Who Which student	was was was	late. late? late?
		Some kids How many kids Which kids	were were were	afraid. afraid? afraid?

3. Statements and Related Questions with an Auxiliary (Aux) Verb and a Main Verb

Wh- Word	Aux	Subject	Aux	Main Verb	Complement
Where	is	She she	is	running. running?	
When	will	They they	will	go go	on a vacation. on a vacation?
What	should	He he	should	do do?	something.
How many pills	can	You you	can	take take?	a pill.
Why	can't	You you	can't	drive drive	a car. a car?
		Someone Who	should should	answer answer	the question. the question?

Alphabetical List of Irregular Past Forms

Base Form	Past Form	Base Form	Past Form
arise	arose	find	found
awake	awoke	fit	fit
be	was/were	flee	fled
bear	bore	fly	flew
beat	beat	forget	forgot
become	became	forgive	forgave
begin	began	freeze	froze
bend	bent	get	got
bet	bet	give	gave
bind	bound	go	went
bite	bit	grind	ground
bleed	bled	grow	grew
blow	blew	hang	hung[1]
break	broke	have	had
breed	bred	hear	heard
bring	brought	hide	hid
broadcast	broadcast	hit	hit
build	built	hold	held
burst	burst	hurt	hurt
buy	bought	keep	kept
cast	cast	kneel	knelt (or kneeled)
catch	caught	know	knew
choose	chose	lay	laid
cling	clung	lead	led
come	came	leave	left
cost	cost	lend	lent
creep	crept	let	let
cut	cut	lie	lay
deal	dealt	light	lit (or lighted)
dig	dug	lose	lost
do	did	make	made
draw	drew	mean	meant
drink	drank	meet	met
drive	drove	mistake	mistook
eat	ate	pay	paid
fall	fell	put	put
feed	fed	quit	quit
feel	felt	read	read
fight	fought	ride	rode

[1]*Hanged* is used as the past form to refer to punishment by death. *Hung* is used in other situations. She *hung* the picture on the wall.

Base Form	Past Form	Base Form	Past Form
ring	rang	stand	stood
rise	rose	steal	stole
run	ran	stick	stuck
say	said	sting	stung
see	saw	set	set
seek	sought	stink	stank
sell	sold	strike	struck
send	sent	strive	strove
forbid	forbade	swear	swore
shake	shook	sweep	swept
shed	shed	swim	swam
shine	shone (or shined)	swing	swung
shoot	shot	take	took
shrink	shrank	teach	taught
shut	shut	tear	tore
sing	sang	tell	told
sink	sank	think	thought
sit	sat	throw	threw
sleep	slept	understand	understood
slide	slid	upset	upset
slit	slit	wake	woke
speak	spoke	wear	wore
speed	sped	weave	wove
spend	spent	weep	wept
spin	spun	win	won
spit	spit (or spat)	wind	wound
split	split	withdraw	withdrew
spread	spread	wring	wrung
spring	sprang	write	wrote

Appendix E

Meanings of Modals and Related Words

- Ability, Possibility

  Can you drive a truck?
  You **can** get a ticket for speeding.

- Necessity, Obligation

  A driver **must** have a license. (legal obligation)
  I **have to** buy a new car. (personal obligation)

- Permission

  You **can** park at a meter.
  You **can't** park at a bus stop.

(continued)

- Possibility

   I **may** buy a new car soon.
   I **might** buy a Japanese car.

- Advice

   You **should** buy a new car. Your old car is in terrible condition.

- Permission Request

   May I borrow your car?
   Can I have the keys, please?
   Could I have the keys, please?

- Polite Request

   Would you teach me to drive?
   Could you show me your new car?

- Want

   What **would** you **like** to eat?
   I**'d like** a turkey sandwich.

Appendix F

Capitalization Rules

- The first word in a sentence: **M**y friends are helpful.

- The word "I": My sister and **I** took a trip together.

- Names of people: **J**ulia **R**oberts; **G**eorge **W**ashington

- Titles preceding names of people: **D**octor (**D**r.) **S**mith; **P**resident **L**incoln; **Q**ueen **E**lizabeth; **M**r. **R**ogers; **M**rs. **C**arter

- Geographic names: the **U**nited **S**tates; **L**ake **S**uperior; **C**alifornia; the **R**ocky **M**ountains; the **M**ississippi **R**iver

   NOTE: The word "the" in a geographic name is not capitalized.

- Street names: **P**ennsylvania **A**venue (**A**ve.); **W**all **S**treet (**S**t.); **A**bbey **R**oad (**R**d.)

- Names of organizations, companies, colleges, buildings, stores, hotels: the **R**epublican **P**arty; **H**einle **C**engage; **D**artmouth **C**ollege; the **U**niversity of **W**isconsin; the **W**hite **H**ouse; **B**loomingdale's; the **H**ilton **H**otel

- Nationalities and ethnic groups: **M**exicans; **C**anadians; **S**paniards; **A**mericans; **J**ews; **K**urds; **E**skimos

- Languages: **E**nglish; **S**panish; **P**olish; **V**ietnamese; **R**ussian

- Months: January; February
- Days: Sunday; Monday
- Holidays: Christmas; Independence Day
- Important words in a title: Grammar in Context; The Old Man and the Sea; Romeo and Juliet; The Sound of Music

  NOTE: Capitalize "the" as the first word of a title.

Appendix G

Metric Conversion Chart

Length

When You Know	Symbol	Multiply by	To Find	Symbol
inches	in	2.54	centimeters	cm
feet	ft	30.5	centimeters	cm
feet	ft	0.3	meters	m
yards	yd	0.91	meters	m
miles	mi	1.6	kilometers	km
Metric:				
centimeters	cm	0.39	inches	in
centimeters	cm	0.03	feet	ft
meters	m	3.28	feet	ft
meters	m	1.09	yards	yd
kilometers	km	0.62	miles	mi

Note:
12 inches = 1 foot
3 feet / 36 inches = 1 yard

Area

When You Know	Symbol	Multiply by	To Find	Symbol
square inches	in²	6.5	square centimeters	cm²
square feet	ft²	0.09	square meters	m²
square yards	yd²	0.8	square meters	m²
square miles	mi²	2.6	square kilometers	km²
Metric:				
square centimeters	cm²	0.16	square inches	in²
square meters	m²	10.76	square feet	ft²
square meters	m²	1.2	square yards	yd²
square kilometers	km²	0.39	square miles	mi²

Weight (Mass)

When You Know	Symbol	Multiply by	To Find	Symbol
ounces	oz	28.35	grams	g
pounds	lb	0.45	kilograms	kg
Metric:				
grams	g	0.04	ounces	oz
kilograms	kg	2.2	pounds	lb
Note:				
1 pound = 16 ounces				

Volume

When You Know	Symbol	Multiply by	To Find	Symbol
fluid ounces	fl oz	30.0	milliliters	mL
pints	pt	0.47	liters	L
quarts	qt	0.95	liters	L
gallons	gal	3.8	liters	L
Metric:				
milliliters	mL	0.03	fluid ounces	fl oz
liters	L	2.11	pints	pt
liters	L	1.05	quarts	qt
liters	L	0.26	gallons	gal

Temperature

When You Know	Symbol	Do this	To Find	Symbol
degrees Fahrenheit	°F	Subtract 32, then multiply by $\frac{5}{9}$	degrees Celsius	°C
Metric:				
degrees Celsius	°C	Multiply by $\frac{9}{5}$, then add 32	degrees Fahrenheit	°F

Sample Temperatures

Fahrenheit	Celsius
0	– 18
10	–12
20	–7
30	–1
40	4
50	10
60	16
70	21
80	27
90	32
100	38

Appendix H

Prepositions of Time

- **in** the morning: He takes a shower *in* the morning.
- **in** the afternoon: He takes a shower *in* the afternoon.
- **in** the evening: He takes a shower *in* the evening.
- **at** night: He takes a shower *at* night.

(continued)

- **in** the summer, fall, winter, spring: He takes classes *in* the summer.
- **on** that/this day: October 10 is my birthday. I became a citizen *on* that day.
- **on** the weekend: He studies *on* the weekend.
- **on** a specific day: His birthday is *on* March 5.
- **in** a month: His birthday is *in* March.
- **in** a year: He was born *in* 1978.
- **in** a century: People didn't use cars *in* the 19th century.
- **on** a day: I don't have class *on* Monday.
- **at** a specific time: My class begins *at* 12:30.
- **from** a time **to** another time: My class is *from* 12:30 *to* 3:30.
- **in** a number of hours, days, weeks, months, years: She will graduate *in* three weeks. (This means "after" three weeks.)
- **for** a number of hours, days, weeks, months, years: She was in Mexico *for* three weeks. (This means during the period of three weeks.)
- **by** a time: Please finish your test *by* six o'clock. (This means "no later than" six o'clock.)
- **until** a time: I lived with my parents *until* I came to the U.S. (This means "all the time before.")
- **during** the movie, class, meeting: He slept *during* the meeting.
- **about/around** six o'clock: The movie will begin *about* six o'clock. People will arrive *around* 5:45.
- **in** the past/future: *In* the past, she never exercised.
- **at** present: *At* present, the days are getting longer.
- **in** the beginning/end: *In* the beginning, she didn't understand the teacher at all.
- **at** the beginning/end of something: The semester begins *at* the beginning of September. My birthday is *at* the end of June.
- **before/after** a time: You should finish the job *before* Friday. The library will be closed *after* 6:00.
- **before/after** an action takes place: Turn off the lights *before* you leave. Wash the dishes *after* you finish dinner.

Appendix I

Glossary of Grammatical Terms

- **Adjective** An adjective gives a description of a noun.

    It's a *tall* tree.   He's an *old* man.   My neighbors are *nice*.

- **Adverb** An adverb describes the action of a sentence or an adjective or another adverb.

    She speaks English *fluently*.   I drive *carefully*.
    She speaks English *extremely* well.   She is *very* intelligent.

- **Adverb of Frequency** An adverb of frequency tells how often the action happens.

    I *never* drink coffee.   They *usually* take the bus.

- **Affirmative** means *yes*.

- **Apostrophe ’** We use the apostrophe for possession and contractions.

    My *sister's* friend is beautiful.   Today *isn't* Sunday.

- **Article** The definite article is *the*. The indefinite articles are *a* and *an*.

    I have *a* cat.   I ate *an* apple.   *The* teacher came late.

- **Auxiliary Verb** Some verbs have two parts: an auxiliary verb and a main verb.

    He *can't* study.   We *will* return.

- **Base Form** The base form, sometimes called the "simple" form, of the verb has no tense. It has no ending (*-s* or *-ed*): *be, go, eat, take, write*.

    I didn't *go* out.   We don't *know* you.   He can't *drive*.

- **Capital Letter** A B C D E F G . . .

- **Clause** A clause is a group of words that has a subject and a verb. Some sentences have only one clause.

    She speaks Spanish.

Some sentences have **a main clause** and a **dependent clause**.

MAIN CLAUSE	DEPENDENT CLAUSE (**reason clause**)
She found a good job	because she has computer skills.

MAIN CLAUSE	DEPENDENT CLAUSE (**time clause**)
She'll turn off the light	before she goes to bed.

MAIN CLAUSE	DEPENDENT CLAUSE (**if clause**)
I'll take you to the doctor	if you don't have your car on Saturday.

(continued)

- **Colon** :

- **Comma** ,

- **Comparative Form** A comparative form of an adjective or adverb is used to compare two things.

  My house is *bigger* than your house.
  Her husband drives *faster* than she does.

- **Complement** The complement of the sentence is the information after the verb. It completes the verb phrase.

  He works *hard*.   I slept *for five hours*.   They are *late*.

- **Consonant** The following letters are consonants: *b, c, d, f, g, h, j, k, l, m, n, p, q, r, s, t, v, w, x, y, z*.

  NOTE: y is sometimes considered a vowel, as in the world *syllable*.

- **Contraction** A contraction is made up of two words put together with an apostrophe.

  He's my brother.   *You're* late.   They *won't* talk to me.
  (*He's = he is*)   (*You're = you are*)   (*won't = will not*)

- **Count Noun** Count nouns are nouns that we can count. They have a singular and a plural form.

  1 pen – 3 pens   1 table – 4 tables

- **Dependent Clause** See **Clause**.

- **Direct Object** A direct object is a noun (phrase) or pronoun that receives the action of the verb.

  We saw *the movie*.   You have *a nice car*.   I love *you*.

- **Exclamation Mark** !

- **Frequency Words** Frequency words are *always, usually, generally, often, sometimes, rarely, seldom, hardly ever, never*.

  I *never* drink coffee.   We *always* do our homework.

- **Hyphen** –

- **Imperative** An imperative sentence gives a command or instructions. An imperative sentence omits the word *you*.

  Come here.   *Don't be* late.   Please *sit* down.

- **Infinitive** An infinitive is *to* + base form.

  I want *to leave*.   You need *to be* here on time.

- **Linking Verb** A linking verb is a verb that links the subject to the noun or adjective after it. Linking verbs include *be, seem, feel, smell, sound, look, appear, taste*.

  She *is* a doctor.   She *seems* very intelligent.   She *looks* tired.

- **Modal** The modal verbs are *can, could, shall, should, will, would, may, might, must.*

   They *should* leave.   I *must* go.

- **Negative** means no.

- **Nonaction Verb** A nonaction verb has no action. We do not use a continuous tense (*be* + verb *-ing*) with a nonaction verb. The nonaction verbs are: *believe, cost, care, have, hear, know, like, love, matter, mean, need, own, prefer, remember, see, seem, think, understand, want,* and sense-perception verbs.

   She *has* a laptop.   We *love* our mother.   You *look* great.

- **Noncount Noun** A noncount noun is a noun that we don't count. It has no plural form.

   She drank some *water.*   He prepared some *rice.*
   Do you need any *money?*   We had a lot of *homework.*

- **Noun** A noun is a person (*brother*), a place (*kitchen*), or a thing (*table*). Nouns can be either count (*1 table, 2 tables*) or noncount (*money, water*).

   My *brother* lives in California.   My *sisters* live in New York.
   I get *advice* from them.   I drink *coffee* every day.

- **Noun Modifier** A noun modifier makes a noun more specific.

   fire department   *Independence* Day   *can* opener

- **Noun Phrase** A noun phrase is a group of words that form the subject or object of the sentence.

   A very nice woman helped me at registration.
   I bought *a big box of cereal.*

- **Object** The object of the sentence follows the verb. It receives the action of the verb.

   He bought *a car.*   I saw *a movie.*   I met *your brother.*

- **Object Pronoun** Use object pronouns (*me, you, him, her, it, us, them*) after the verb or preposition.

   He likes *her.*   I saw the movie. Let's talk about *it.*

- **Parentheses** ( )

- **Paragraph** A paragraph is a group of sentences about one topic.

- **Participle, Present** The present participle is verb + *-ing.*

   She is *sleeping.*   They were *laughing.*

- **Period** .

- **Phrase** A group of words that go together.

   Last month my sister came to visit.
   There is a strange car *in front of my house.*

(continued)

- **Plural** Plural means more than one. A plural noun usually ends with *-s*.

  She has beautiful *eyes*.   My *feet* are big.

- **Possessive Form** Possessive forms show ownership or relationship.

  Mary's coat is in the closet.   *My* brother lives in Miami.

- **Preposition** A preposition is a short connecting word: *about, above, across, after, around, as, at, away, back, before, behind, below, by, down, for, from, in, into, like, of, off, on, out, over, to, under, up, with.*

  The book is *on* the table.   She studies *with* her friends.

- **Pronoun** A pronoun takes the place of a noun.

  I have a new car. I bought *it* last week.
  John likes Mary, but *she* doesn't like *him*.

- **Punctuation** Period . Comma , Colon : Semicolon ; Question Mark ? Exclamation Mark !

- **Question Mark** ?

- **Quotation Marks** " "

- **Regular Verb** A regular verb forms its past tense with *-ed*.

  He *worked* yesterday.   I *laughed* at the joke.

- **-s Form** A present tense verb that ends in *-s* or *-es*.

  He *lives* in New York.   She *watches* TV a lot.

- **Sense-Perception Verb** A sense-perception verb has no action. It describes a sense. The sense perception verbs are: *look, feel, taste, sound, smell.*

  She *feels* fine.   The coffee *smells* fresh.   The milk *tastes* sour.

- **Sentence** A sentence is a group of words that contains a subject[2] and a verb (at least) and gives a complete thought.

  SENTENCE: She came home.
  NOT A SENTENCE: When she came home

- **Simple Form of Verb** The simple form of the verb, also called the base form, has no tense; it never has an *-s*, *-ed*, or *-ing* ending.

  Did you *see* the movie?   I couldn't *find* your phone number.

- **Singular** Singular means one.

  She ate a *sandwich*.   I have one *television*.

- **Subject** The subject of the sentence tells who or what the sentence is about.

  My *sister* got married last April. *The wedding* was beautiful.

---

[2]In an imperative sentence, the subject *you* is omitted: *Sit down. Come here.*

- **Subject Pronouns** Use subject pronouns (*I, you, he, she, it, we, you, they*) before a verb.

  They speak Japanese.   *We* speak Spanish.

- **Superlative Form** A superlative form of an adjective or adverb shows the number one item in a group of three or more.

  January is the *coldest* month of the year.
  My brother speaks English the *best* in my family.

- **Syllable** A syllable is a part of a word that has only one vowel sound. (Some words have only one syllable.)

  change (one syllable)   after (af·ter = two syllables)
  look (one syllable)   responsible (re·spon·si·ble = four syllables)

- **Tag Question** A tag question is a short question at the end of a sentence. It is used in conversation.

  You speak Spanish, *don't you?*   He's not happy, *is he?*

- **Tense** A verb has tense. Tense shows when the action of the sentence happened.

  SIMPLE PRESENT: She usually *works* hard.
  FUTURE: She *will work* tomorrow.
  PRESENT CONTINUOUS: She *is working* now.
  SIMPLE PAST: She *worked* yesterday.

- **Verb** A verb is the action of the sentence.

  He *runs* fast.   I *speak* English.

  Some verbs have no action. They are linking verbs. They connect the subject to the rest of the sentence.

  He *is* tall.   She *looks* beautiful.   You *seem* tired.

- **Vowel** The following letters are vowels: *a, e, i, o, u.* Y is sometimes considered a vowel (for example, in the word *mystery*).

Appendix J

Verbs and Adjectives Followed by a Preposition

(be) accustomed to	forgive someone for	(be) proud of
(be) afraid of	(be) glad about	recover from
agree with	(be) good at	(be) related to
(be) angry about	(be) happy about	rely on/upon
(be) angry at/with	hear about	(be) responsible for
approve of	hear of	(be) sad about
argue about	hope for	(be) satisfied with
(be) ashamed of	(be) incapable of	(be) scared of
(be) aware of	insist on/upon	(be) sick of
believe in	(be) interested in	(be) sorry about
(be) bored with/by	(be) involved in	(be) sorry for
(be) capable of	(be) jealous of	speak about
care about/for	(be) known for	speak to/with
(be) compared to	(be) lazy about	succeed in
complain about	listen to	(be) sure of/about
(be) concerned about	look at	(be) surprised at
concentrate on	look for	take care of
consist of	look forward to	talk about
count on	(be) mad about	talk to/with
deal with	(be) mad at	thank someone for
decide on	(be) made from/of	(be) thankful to someone for
depend on/upon	(be) married to	think about/of
dream about/of	object to	(be) tired of
(be) engaged to	participate in	(be) upset about
(be) excited about	plan on	(be) upset with
(be) familiar with	pray to	(be) used to
(be) famous for	pray for	wait for
feel like	(be) prepared for	warn about
(be) fond of	prohibit someone from	(be) worried about
forget about	protect someone from	worry about

Appendix K

Map of the United States of America

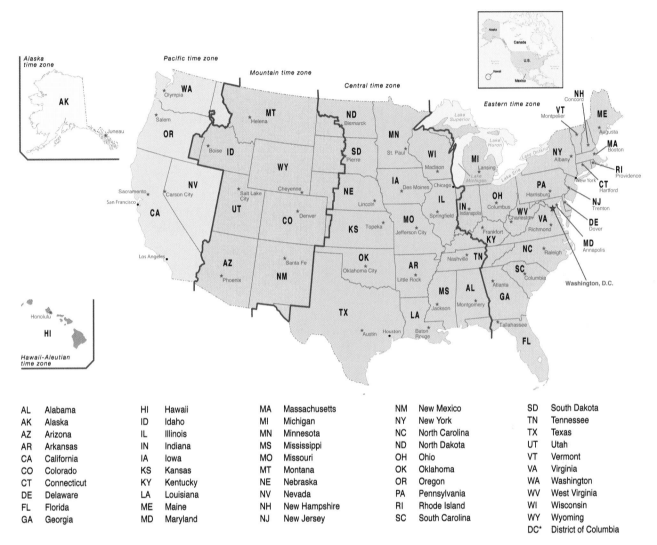

AL	Alabama	HI	Hawaii	MA	Massachusetts	NM	New Mexico	SD	South Dakota
AK	Alaska	ID	Idaho	MI	Michigan	NY	New York	TN	Tennessee
AZ	Arizona	IL	Illinois	MN	Minnesota	NC	North Carolina	TX	Texas
AR	Arkansas	IN	Indiana	MS	Mississippi	ND	North Dakota	UT	Utah
CA	California	IA	Iowa	MO	Missouri	OH	Ohio	VT	Vermont
CO	Colorado	KS	Kansas	MT	Montana	OK	Oklahoma	VA	Virginia
CT	Connecticut	KY	Kentucky	NE	Nebraska	OR	Oregon	WA	Washington
DE	Delaware	LA	Louisiana	NV	Nevada	PA	Pennsylvania	WV	West Virginia
FL	Florida	ME	Maine	NH	New Hampshire	RI	Rhode Island	WI	Wisconsin
GA	Georgia	MD	Maryland	NJ	New Jersey	SC	South Carolina	WY	Wyoming
								DC*	District of Columbia

*The District of Columbia is not a state. Washington, D.C., is the capital of the United States.
Note: Washington, D.C., and Washington state are not the same.

Index

Photo Credits